JEAN-MARC BUSTAMANTE

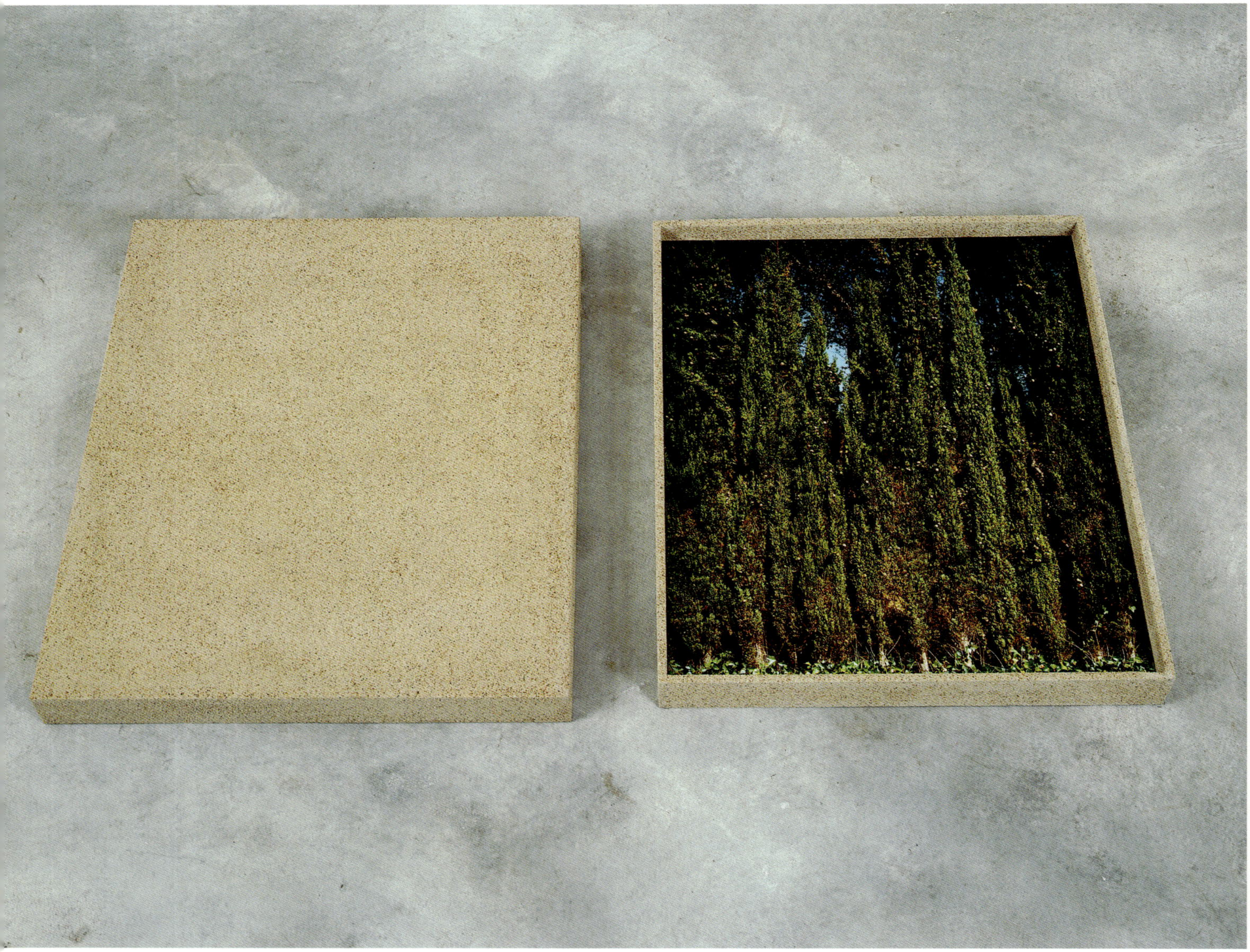

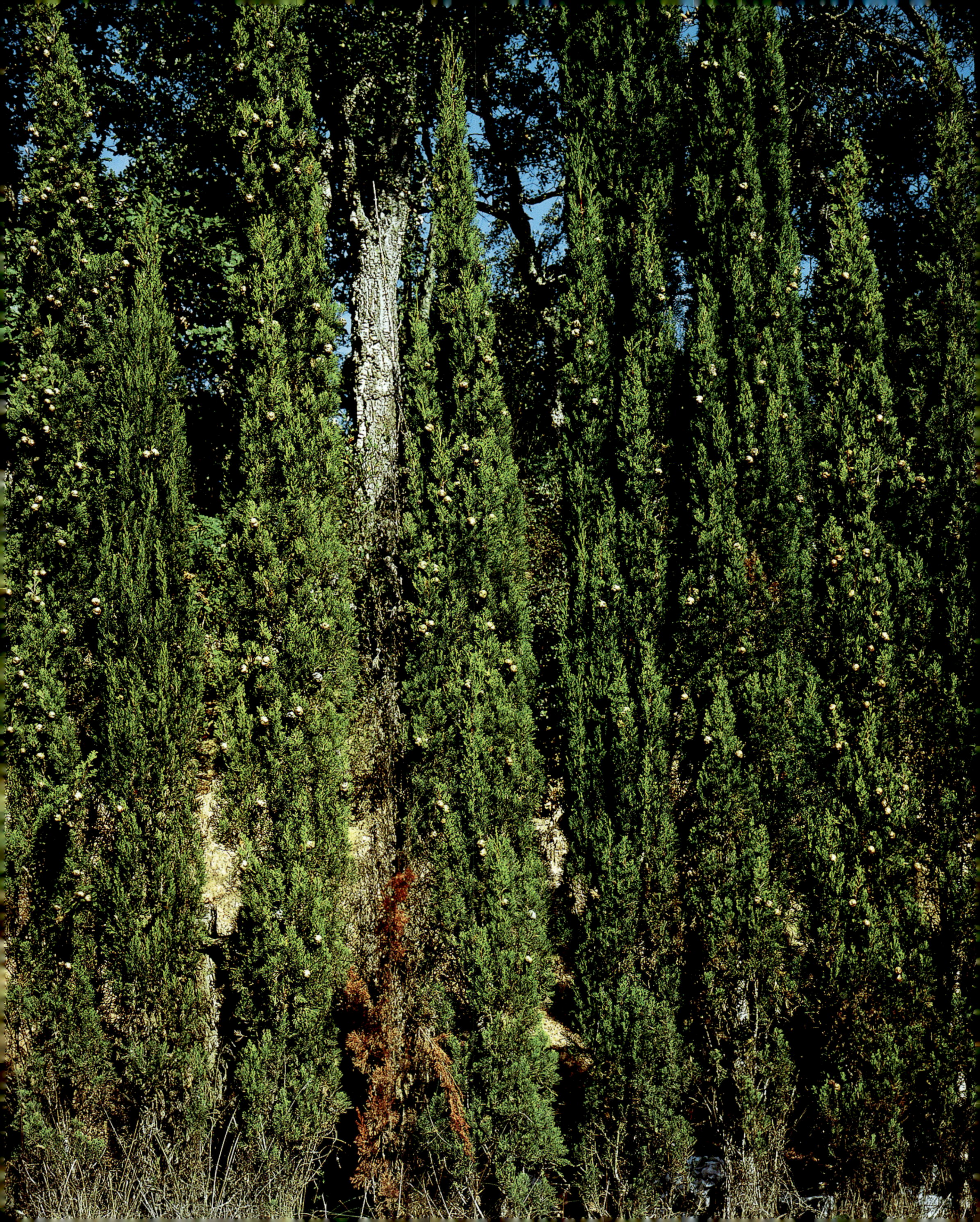

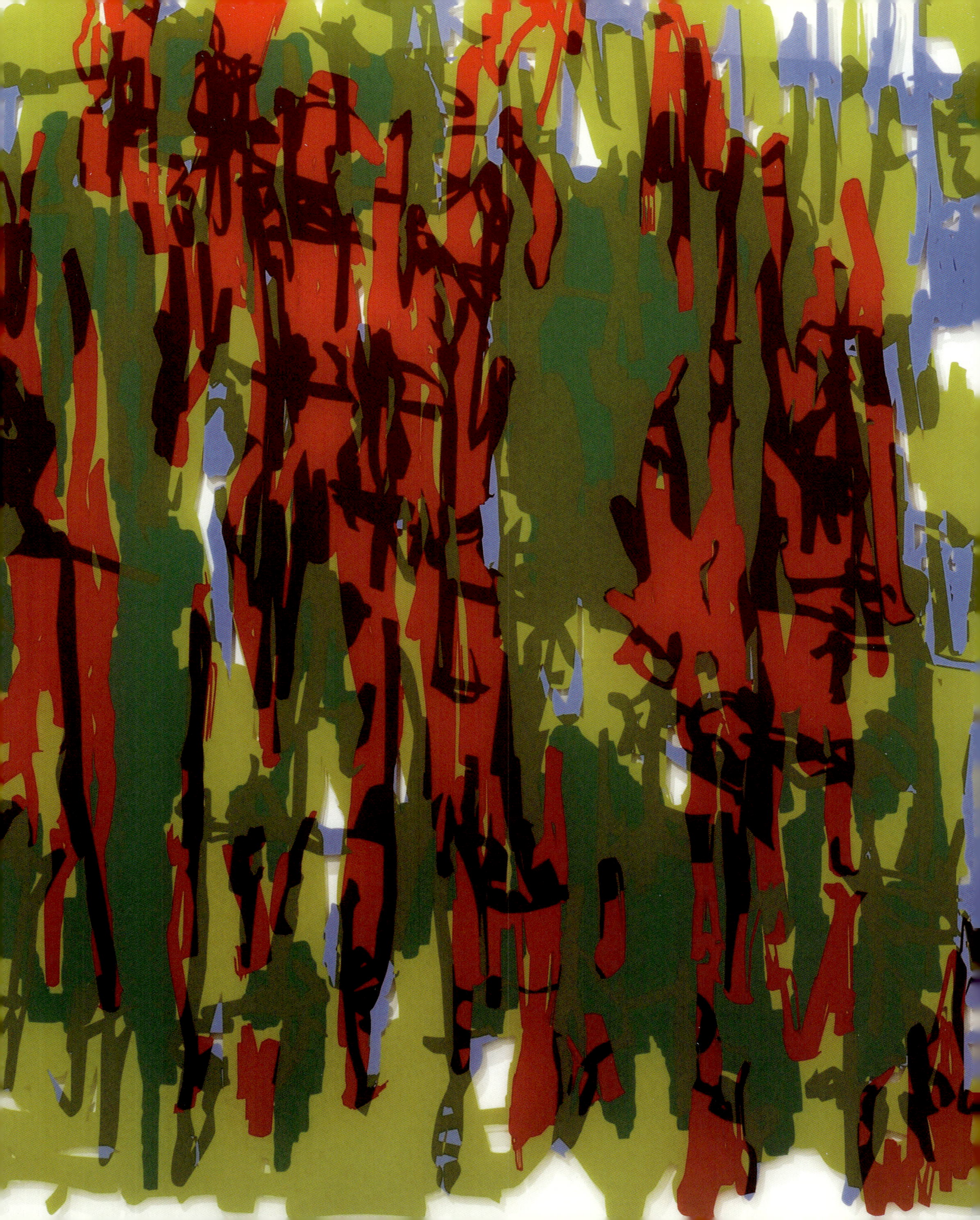

JEAN-MARC BUSTAMANTE
DEAD CALM

Published on the occasion of two complementary and overlapping exhibitions of the work of Jean-Marc Bustamante

JEAN-MARC BUSTAMANTE
DEAD CALM

The Fruitmarket Gallery, Edinburgh
4 February – 3 April 2011

The Fruitmarket Gallery is a publicly-funded art gallery of national and international significance, and is Scotland's leading contemporary art space. The Gallery aims to make contemporary art accessible without compromising art or under estimating audiences. Its programme of exhibitions of Scottish and international artists is world-class and always free.

Publishing is an intrinsic part of The Fruitmarket Gallery's creative programme, with books published to accompany each exhibition. Books are conceived as part of the exhibition-making process, with the book extending the reach and life of each exhibition and offering artists and curators a second space in which to present their work.

ISBN 978-0-947912-81-9

cover and p. 4: *Stationnaire II*, 1991 (detail)
C-print, cement boxes, 66 x 56 x 8 cm (each)

p. 5: *T.124.91*, 1991
C-print, 138 x 111 cm

p. 6: *Untitled*, 2010 (detail)
Ink on Plexiglas, 150 x 150 cm

JEAN-MARC BUSTAMANTE
DEAD CALM

Henry Moore Institute, Leeds
21 April – 26 June 2011

The Henry Moore Institute is an award-winning exhibitions venue, research centre, library and sculpture archive. Through exhibitions, conferences, lectures, research, fellowships and publications, the Institute generates scholarship and responds to the ever-changing nature of sculpture, addressing the engagement and understanding of sculpture across historical and contemporary registers. The Institute also curates the Leeds Museums & Galleries sculpture collection, including works on paper, and the archive of sculptors' papers which documents primarily British sculpture from c.1850 to the present.

The Henry Moore Foundation was founded by Moore in 1977 to encourage appreciation of the visual arts, especially sculpture. Its responsibilities are preserving Moore's legacy at his Hertfordshire home and in exhibitions worldwide; funding exhibitions and research at the Henry Moore Institute in Leeds; and awarding grants to arts organisations.

And the exhibition

TAKE SOMETHING HOT
AND COOL IT DOWN

Timothy Taylor Gallery, London
20 April – 28 May 2011

The Fruitmarket Gallery

Henry Moore Institute

The Henry Moore Foundation

Timothy Taylor Gallery

CONTENTS

/

Jean-Marc Bustamante's studio, Paris, 2010

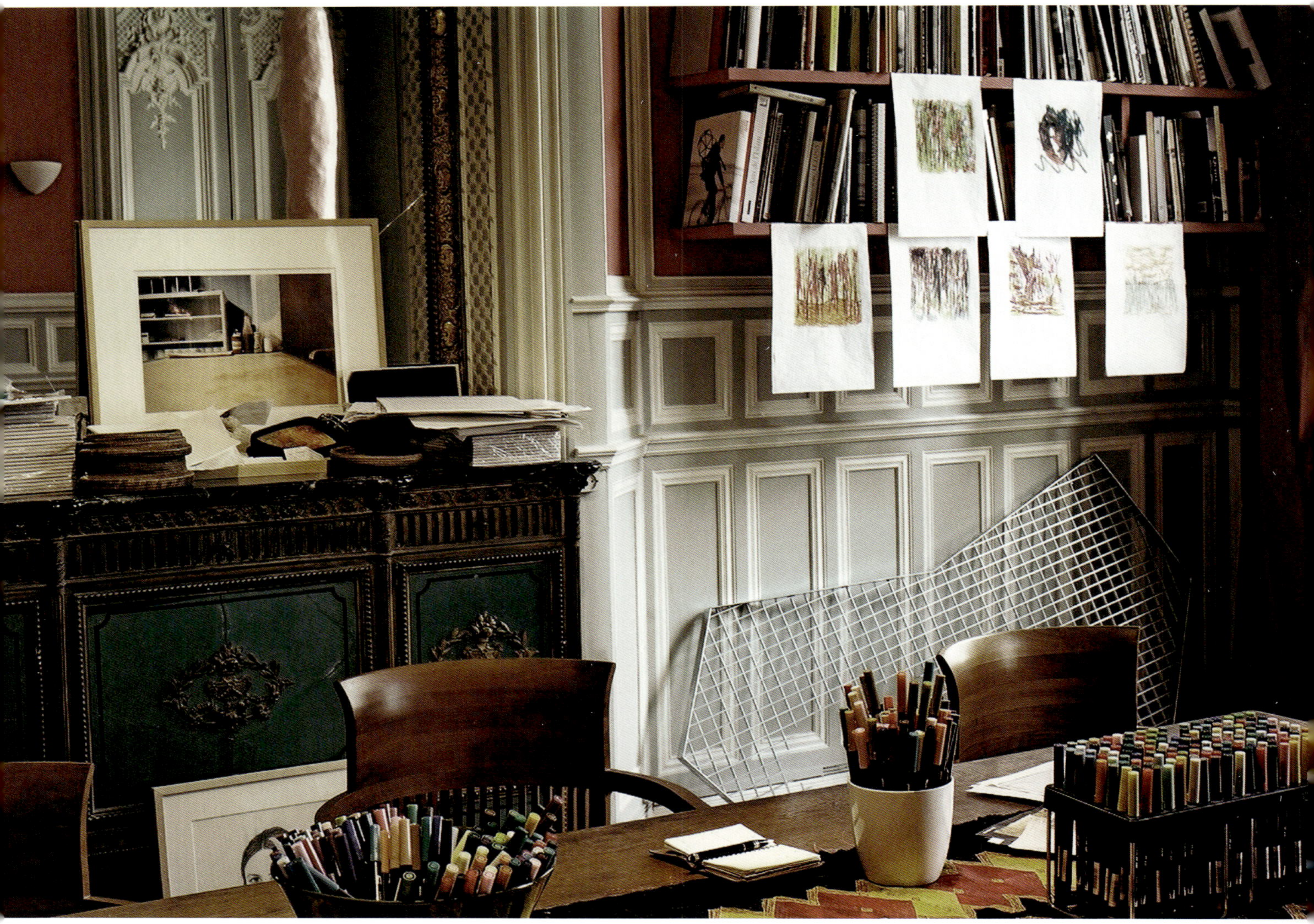

FOREWORD

/

FIONA BRADLEY
LISA LE FEUVRE

This book is published by The Fruitmarket Gallery and the Henry Moore Institute with the support of Timothy Taylor Gallery on the occasion of a major collaborative exhibition of the work of Jean-Marc Bustamante at The Fruitmarket Gallery in Edinburgh and the Henry Moore Institute in Leeds, and an exhibition of recent work at Timothy Taylor Gallery in London. The exhibition began with a conversation between Penelope Curtis (then Curator of the Henry Moore Institute, now Director of Tate Britain) and Bustamante about the complex intertwining of photography and sculpture in the artist's work. Together they made a selection of work for the galleries of the Henry Moore Institute, and invited The Fruitmarket Gallery to show this selection as part of a larger exhibition also incorporating Bustamante's painting. Many of the paintings in The Fruitmarket Gallery exhibition will also be presented at Timothy Taylor Gallery.

Jean-Marc Bustamante is one of France's senior artists and a major figure in the international art world. His clear, direct vision manifests itself in an almost bewildering array of materials and media – first photography, then sculpture, painting, architectural projects and installation. His work is unified and characterised by its calm intelligence and a kind of extraordinary ordinariness that helps us see its subject, the world around us, in a new way. Bustamante's art has not been seen enough in Britain, and we are delighted to bring it to new audiences in both England and Scotland.

This book brings together new and existing texts on every aspect of Bustamante's practice. Two, commissioned especially for this publication, frame the present project, and we thank Penelope Curtis and Emma Dexter for their insights into Bustamante's earlier and more recent work. Other texts have been reprinted from existing publications, several for the first time in English, and we thank the authors for giving us permission to reprint their words.

The publication and the exhibitions have benefited from the help and expertise of a good many people. We thank the lenders to the exhibitions, both public and private, who have generously agreed to part with their works for a substantial period of time. We thank The Henry Moore Foundation for supporting the exhibition at The Fruitmarket Gallery, and Timothy Taylor Gallery for supporting the publication as well as helping with every aspect of the exhibition preparation. Jean-Marc Bustamante runs an efficient studio, and we are extremely grateful to Luc Chopplet and Thierry Leviez who have been such a pleasure to work with.

Finally, of course, we thank Jean-Marc Bustamante. For his wonderful work, and for the energy and enthusiasm he has put into this project.

Fiona Bradley, Director, The Fruitmarket Gallery
Lisa Le Feuvre, Head of Sculpture Studies, Henry Moore Institute

INTRODUCTION

/

FIONA BRADLEY
EDINBURGH, 2010

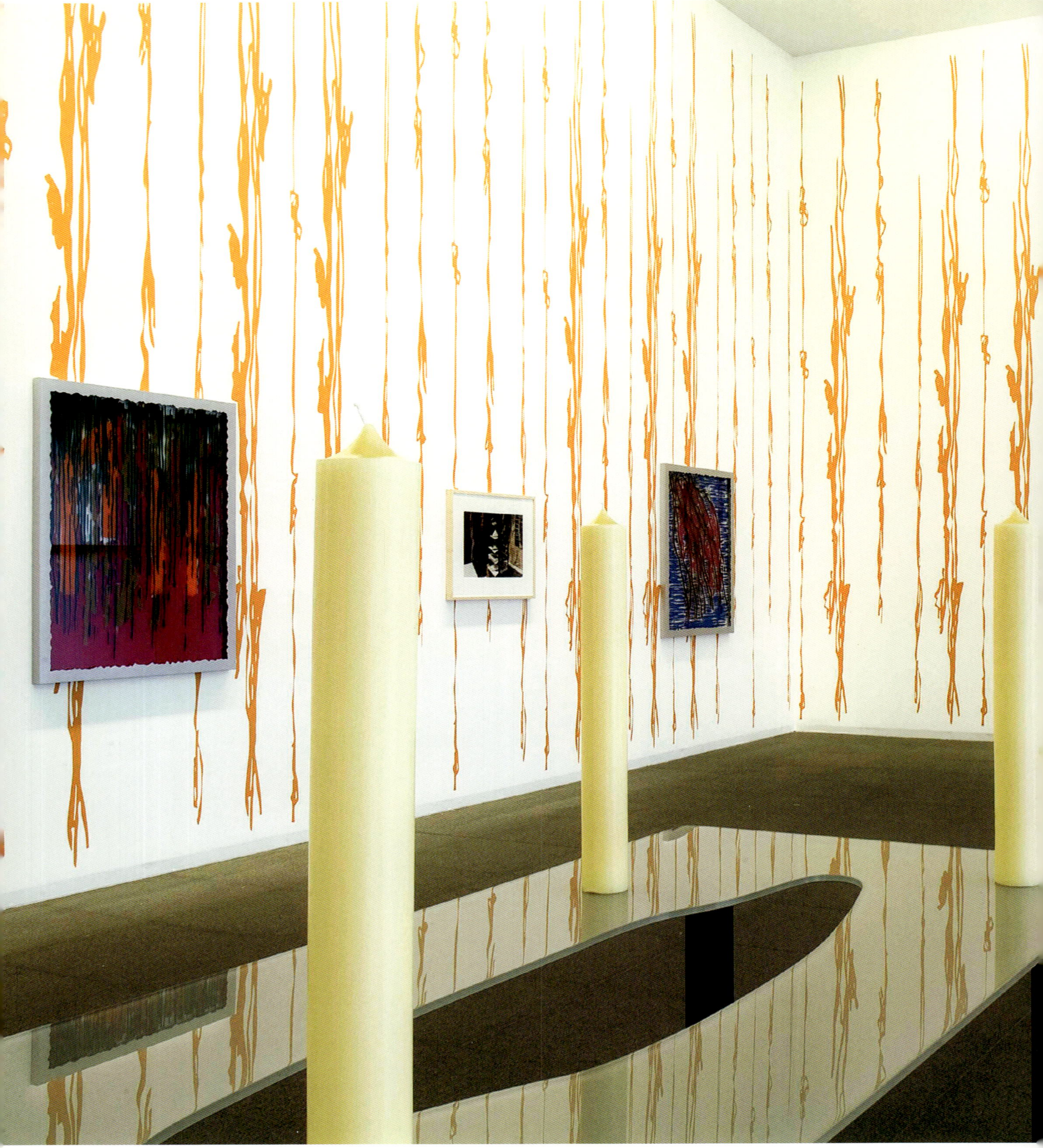

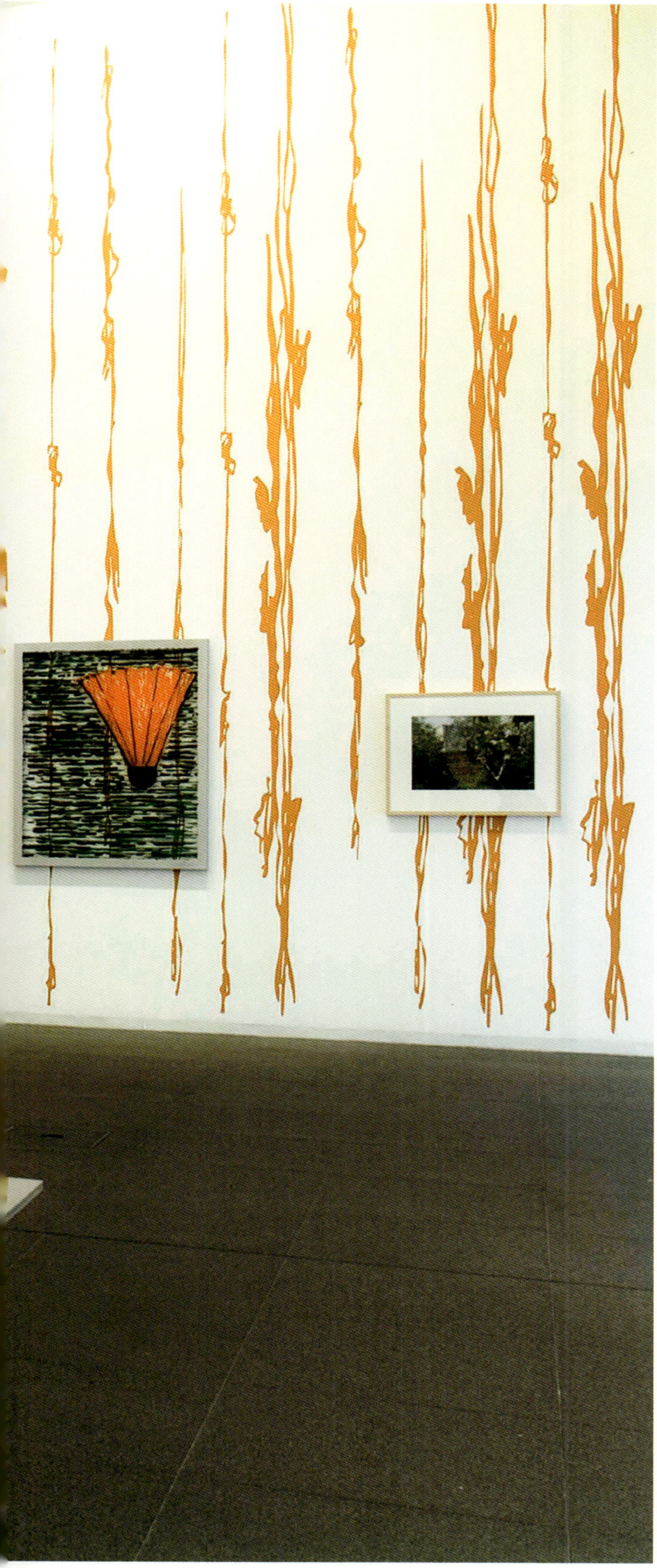

Le Grand Tour, Musée des Arts Contemporains,
Site du Grand-Hornu, 2008

'I like being situated in some kind of in-between.'
Jean-Marc Bustamante

Jean-Marc Bustamante was described in a text by Katy Siegel written for the book published to mark his representation of France at the 50th Venice Biennale as 'a photographer deeply engaged with sculpture, whose sculptures, like his photographs, are often closely tied to painting'. He himself has often characterised his work as being 'without qualities', yet his singularly various and variously singular practice has had, since his emergence onto the international art scene in the 1980s, a resolute and instantly recognisable formal and conceptual lucidity.

Bustamante first made his name with his *Tableaux* (*Pictures*), a series of large-scale photographs begun in 1978. Photographs classified as 'pictures', a designation more usually used in an art context for painting than photography, these images were of anonymous landscapes and nondescript urban places and were a first introduction to Bustamante's way of seeing, the quality of being without qualities, perhaps. Responding to speed with slowness, globalisation with attention to local detail, these photographs, famously described by Bustamante as 'slow snapshots', 'constituted an assertion of a specificity of photography, not fixing some rapid movement but rather a slow one like that of the earth' (his words again). Series and sequences have remained important, and his career has progressed in overlapping waves of *Tableaux*, *Paysages*, *Panoramas*, *Lumières*, *Stationnaires*, *Ouvertures*, *Intérieurs*,

Aquaramas, *Suspensions* or *Sites*. Each describes a particular way of making visual sense of the world, whether as a photograph, sculpture or painting, or something in suspended motion between all three.

Between 1983 and 1987, Bustamante worked as part of the collaborative partnership BAZILEBUSTAMANTE making hybrid objects which have been described as being 'somewhere between object and image'. Though the partnership was short-lived, it seems to have given Bustamante the courage both to bring his singular vision to bear on a wider range of media, and to nurture a plurality of style within his own individual practice. While photography has remained a constant, most notably in the long series of photographic encounters *Something is Missing* (*S.i.M.*) and *Amandes amères Bittere Almonds Bittere Mandeln*, the book of photographs from Buenos Aires, Miami and Tel Aviv Bustamante made for Documenta X, it has been by no means Bustamante's only, or even primary, way of engaging his vision. Photographs began to be made in relation to objects, or as painted surfaces, Bustamante playing with image and object in two dimensions and in three. Two highlights of his career have even enlisted architecture as their primary mode of expression: *Serena*, in 1995 (p. 57), for which he traced a sculpted line of pure colour through the Rietveld Pavilion at the Kröller-Müller Museum in Otterlo; and *La Maison close* of 2000 (p. 73), a small concrete house which sat in the urban landscape of Orléans like a hallucinated photograph.

Bustamante's is an additive aesthetic, with his work a close network of formal and representational cross-references. There are sculptures and paintings that look like elements recurring in his photographic work, and sculptures and paintings which use techniques particular to photography. Thus the holes in the ground of the *Bacs à sable*, the table tops of the *Ouvertures* and *Intérieurs*, the trees to which he returns. Likewise the painted photographs of the *Lumières*, small black-and-white photographs found in old architectural books, blown up and silk-screened onto Plexiglas; and the photographed paintings of the *Paysages*, their lines made through a mechanical rather than an indexical process.

Common to all Bustamante's work is, I think, a heightened awareness of the here and now. His work, though obviously made in the past and existing into the future, operates primarily in the present tense. He brings an element of the outside inside, and remakes it for the viewer – it is almost as if he is making it there and then, in your presence. His work exerts itself in space with a quietly hypnotic insistence, and it is this quality that makes it instantly recognisable as his, almost regardless of the actual form it takes. His willingness to embrace contradiction – the attention he pays to every detail of resolutely anonymous places throughout *Something is Missing*; the constant movement between three dimensions and back again in *Stationnaire II* – traps the viewer in the gap between one thing and another, forcing an intimate relationship with every object as and when encountered. He is interested and accomplished in the nuances of installation, and has referred to the moment at which a work is first installed and encountered by a viewer as its birth, the point at which it becomes what it is supposed to be. This gives his work a formal and perhaps also a political contemporaneity: though sitting outside recognisable trends in recent art, Bustamante's remains utterly relevant to the way art is made and mediated now.

The essays in this book look at Bustamante's career from its earliest beginnings to its most recent manifestations. First, Jean-Pierre Criqui makes an 'initial inventory' of Bustamante's work, tracing Bustamante's career from photographer's assistant to the triumph of *Amandes amères* at Documenta X in 1997 and discussing his practice both with reference to the new wave of large-scale photography made by artists in the 1980s and 1990s – Thomas Struth, Cindy Sherman, Jeff Wall, Andreas Gursky and work of a preceding generation – Lee Friedlander and Robert Smithson. Penelope Curtis moves on from Criqui, looking at the relationship of image to object in Bustamante's work in an essay which is a close and personal reading of the way Bustamante turns two dimensions into three, progressively giving images edges and form. Denys Zacharopoulos contributes a meditation on architecture in the context of Bustamante's *Serena*, and Marianne Le Pommeré writes on *La Maison close* with reference both to George Perec's *Les Choses* (*Things*) and Robert Musil's *Der Mann ohne Eigenschaften* (*The Man without Qualities*). Jacinto Lageira writes about Bustamante's *Suspensions*, an installation made initially for a Palestinian gallery in Jerusalem, in which Bustamante made minimalist sculptures into cages for living birds in a meditation on loneliness akin to his *Lumières* and Denis Gielen offers a geographical and historical account of the operation of Bustamante's photographs. Finally, Emma Dexter looks at Bustamante's most recent paintings, a body of work in which he proposes a new vision and a new way to paint. These texts, some commissioned for this publication and some reprinted from other publications and appearing here for the first time in English, provide an introduction to and an overview of Bustamante's practice, and an indication of why it remains so relevant to audiences and to other artists now. In the midst of the critical and analytical writing, there is Jean-Marc Bustamante's own voice, thinking through the difference between space and place with characteristic economy and eloquence of expression, making a plea for place over space in language absolutely reflective of his work: 'a place is indescribable. It is irreducible to any kind of representation. It has not only a physical reality but also a metaphysical reality particular to it. The relation of place to the world cannot be disassociated from the person who has conceived of it, or more properly inferred it, and the person who recognises it'.

BUSTAMANTE AS PHOTOGRAPHER (NOTES FOR AN UNFINISHED PORTRAIT)

/

JEAN-PIERRE CRIQUI
PARIS, 1999

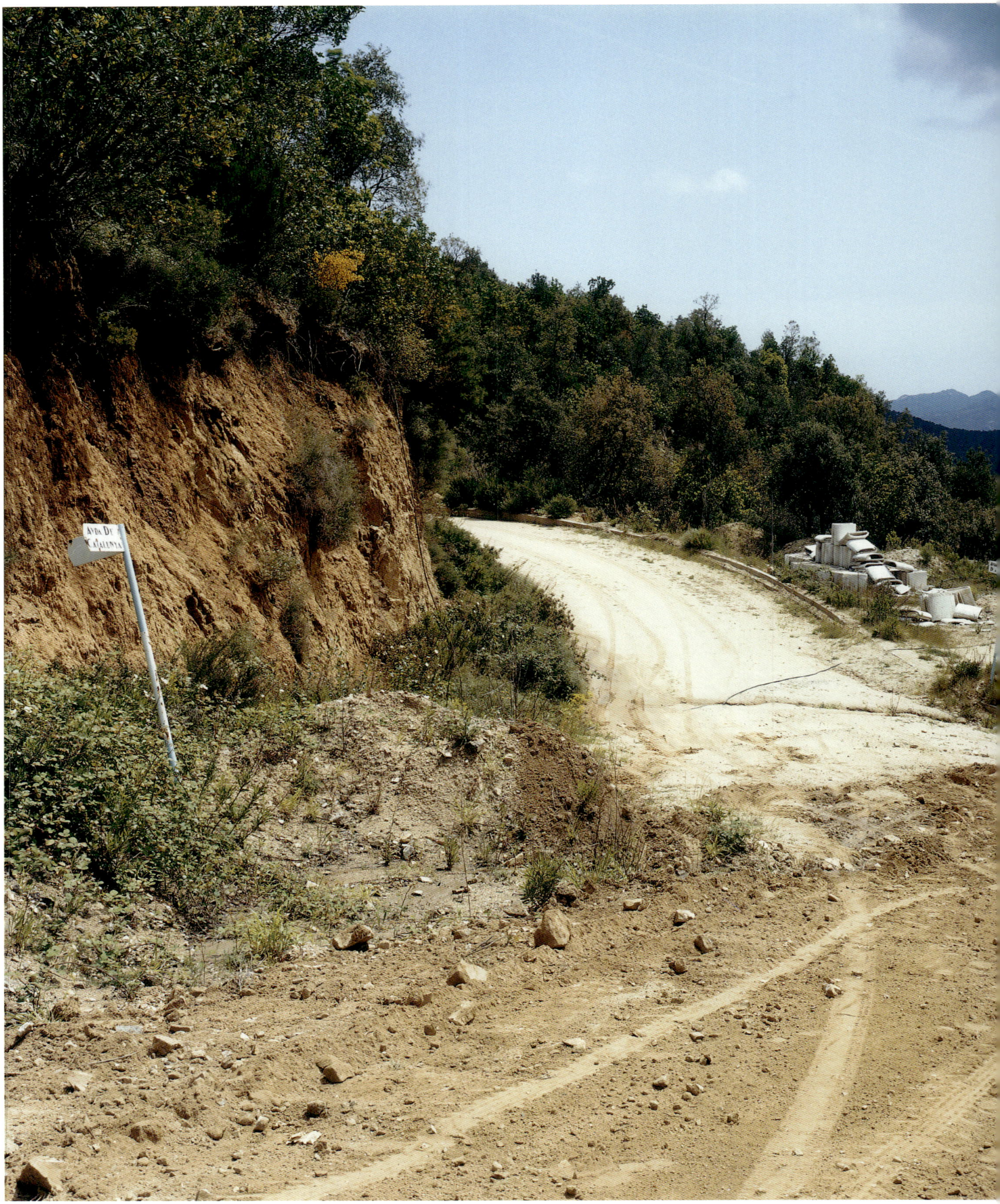
AVDA DE
CATALUNYA

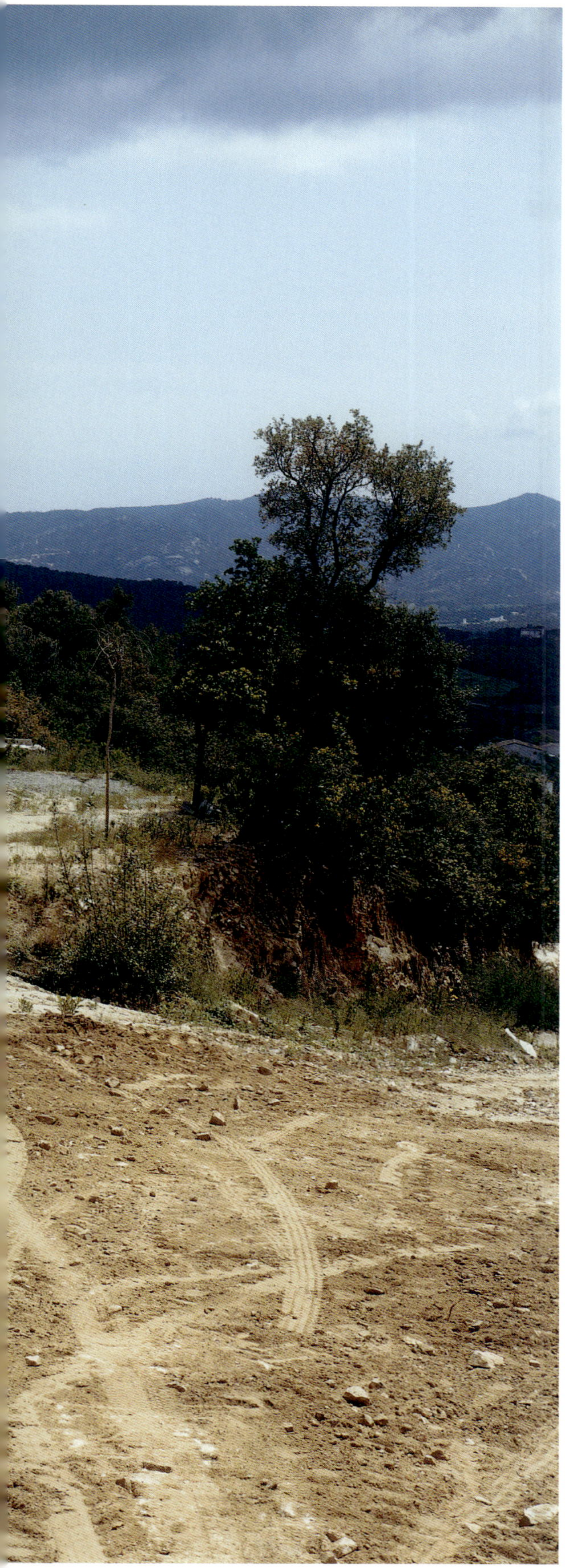

T.17.79, 1979
C-print, 103 x 130 cm

Twenty or so years of creating photographic works can produce the most unexpected results, including the extension of the work beyond the photographic field. Jean-Marc Bustamante definitely started out as a photographer, yet it seems crucial to mention right from the start that he has, for many years, been something other than only this. Anyone mentally tracking the course of his work and his exhibitions, or leafing through the books and catalogues devoted to him, comes upon various objects whose genre may not be that easy to define in no time. Yet it obviously tends towards sculpture and painting (these terms, here more than ever, being understood in a sense that is devoid of even the slightest essentialist connotation). Sometimes photography is added to these objects, or combinations of objects, so as to form what are often called 'installations' – a term whose current fortunes are now accompanied by a certain whiff of obsolescence. (The concept, which is extremely loose, still has very little evocative power, but I shall go along with it for the time being.) In other instances we shall see that even though the photograph is, strictly speaking, absent from the work, it still functions as source, principle and model. Things are becoming complicated. But all to the good, for there would be nothing more futile than suggesting – inadvertently or otherwise – that everything in the matter at hand is self-explanatory, and that each part of the whole fits neatly into the pigeonhole or category assigned to it. So this initial inventory of the 'photographic oeuvre' includes a dash of the arbitrary, which is also picked

T.26.80, 1980
C-print, 103 x 130 cm

up by the artist himself. It extracts from the work as a whole a semblance of coherence; it sets up a surface continuity behind which we can detect the habits of a historian or dealer (every medium has its place), or else the express calling of the institution prompting it. The fact remains that, within this partly entrenched camp, there actually emerges one or two surprises, and possibly one or two distortions in the laws of classification, which refer to a higher form of complexity and shed light on what the photograph here embodies: not membership, but agency.

It was in 1978, after attempts in this direction the year before, that Bustamante embarked on the open, non-systematic series of large-format colour photographs that would duly be called *Tableaux* (*Pictures*). (The then relatively unusual nature of this format no longer gives us pause for thought these days.) Cindy Sherman and Thomas Struth started out during this same period and, after a gap of several years, Jeff Wall had also taken up his artistic pursuits once again. Over and above their choice of photography as a medium, and making no mention of the various presentation methods employed to go along with it, such artists produced works with a quite different set of presuppositions, and a quite different logic. In group shows Bustamante has found himself associated with some of them – Struth and Wall in particular. But, to use the latter as an example – and for Wall the notion of 'picture' has a quite special sense – it is clear that his light-box images, so painstakingly devised and presented, based on a kind of preparation akin to cinematographic direction, and with a conspicuous eye on theatrical effect, tally with an aesthetic in which Bustamante's photographs barely participate. As far as Struth is concerned, it is conversely permissible to liken some of his cityscapes to the *Tableaux* (or the photographs that Bustamante would later put together in the project titled *Something is Missing* (*S.i.M.*)). Here again, however, the dissimilarities seem to far outmatch the affinities.

The world to which Bustamante belonged in the late 1970s was not really the contemporary art world. As a newcomer to Paris he worked there as a photographer's assistant – for William Klein, among others. Significantly enough, he moved away from the capital, which was nevertheless his choice of home, to make his first inroads as an independent artist. On many an occasion, travelling would act as a trigger for him. So, first and foremost, it would be as well to picture the following scene: Bustamante driving around the outskirts of Barcelona, with no fixed destination. In the back of the car, the cumbersome and impressive 8 x 10 box camera, which, needless to say, has to be fixed to a tripod for the simplest shot. Talking with Bustamante, I try to put my finger on what might have motivated him, but it is an impression of roaming, even maybe vagrancy, a mixture of drifting and readiness to work, which is uppermost in his memory. I imagine him with his mind in abeyance and drifting, spinning around something or other.

T.17.79 (1979) shows, in its foreground, an expanse of trodden earth littered with pebbles and criss-crossed by tyre marks. A narrow, dusty road comes to an end here, hemmed with trees, scrub and some building materials – breeze-blocks, stones – waiting for who knows what. On either side of the strip of earth, two small signs announce 'Avda de Catalunya'. In the distance are hills beneath a lowering sky. In contrast with the anything but grandiose character of this scene, the exactness of the visual data offered by this photograph is noteworthy. This kind of 'sharpness' makes the eye waver between afocality and the identification of discrete points, and the to-ing and fro-ing between these two factors presupposes a duration that greatly exceeds any mere assumption of awareness. Simply because of the absence of any spectacle and event, you have to look at the work for a long time. This is how I understand Bustamante's description of the *Tableaux* as 'kinds of slow snapshots'.[1] The image retains from the snapshot the crucial idea of not resorting to any kind of arrangement of what is being recorded; but, just as it requires of the photographer a sequence of operations whose execution can in no way be compared with merely

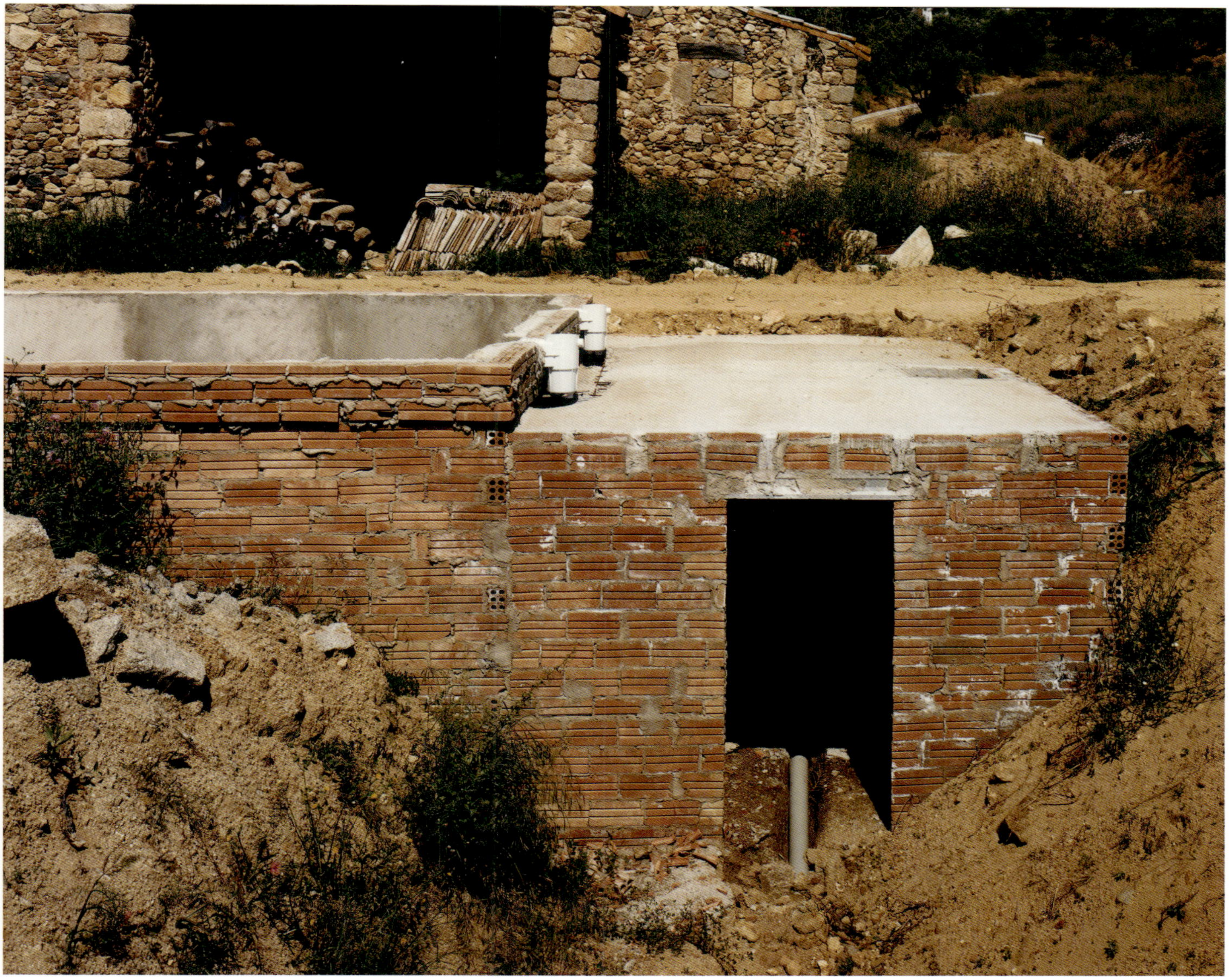

T.42.81, 1981
C-print, 103 x 130 cm

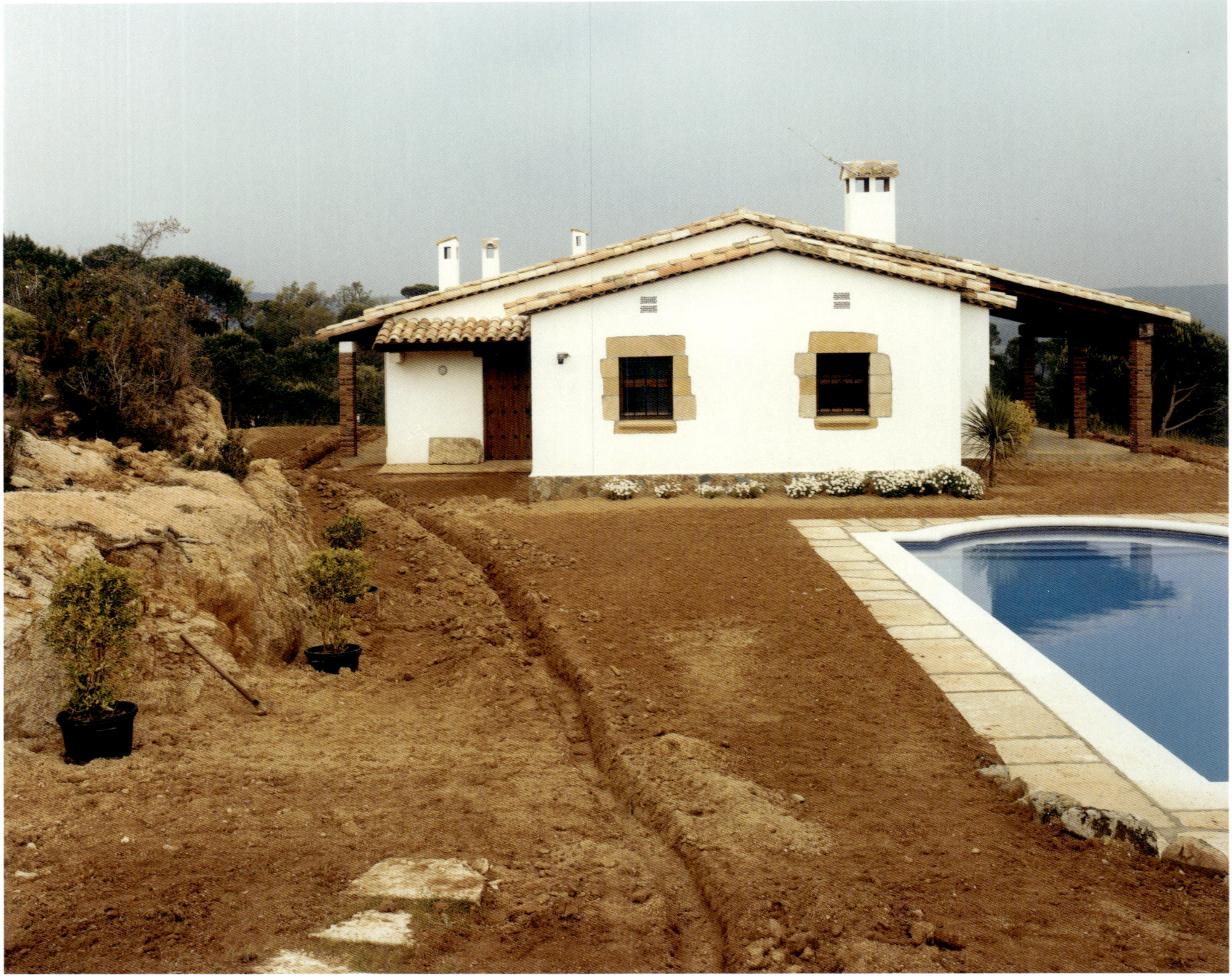

clicking one's fingers, it requires an extended attentiveness on the part of the onlooker, developed over time. The time that is frozen by this image does not, incidentally, have any common gauge with that of the snapshot (nothing has happened that can be snatched from the real in a fraction of a second). As if in parallel, it presupposes a similar extension of our perception. A quarter of an hour earlier or later, the light might well have altered, a cloud would definitely have moved, but the place would have remained basically identical.

In the catalogue published in 1994 to accompany a travelling show of a selection of *Tableaux*, *T.17.79* was the first reproduction in the book.[2] You turn the page and an arresting contrast is created with the second photograph, a contrast that is swiftly perceived in terms of complementarity, as *T.43.81* (1981) is organised around a metal enclosure that splits the image in two (in the front, a lick of pale gravel like part of a bullring; behind, moved far back beyond this wall which only lets parts of their bodies show, a woman or girl with two children, and a greyish mass of unsightly buildings). Together these two photographs form a sort of diptych in which the entire repertory of motifs explored by the series is summed up. Areas of wasteland, peripheral zones, constructions unfinished or in the process of being built, roads engulfed and faded, dead ends: everywhere the signs of man, who nevertheless remains aloof, withdrawn, and only rarely appears, blending in with a set that he is forever redesigning. A faint sense of disaster wafts up from this paradoxical combination of invasion and abandonment.

Interest in these thankless suburban landscapes, and these vague outskirts where city and industry can be glimpsed beneath the smallest blade of grass, is part and parcel of the history of modernism.[3] From the early 1870s onwards it regularly fuelled the work of the best artists. In 1872 Alfred Sisley painted the Argenteuil toll bridge in the background of a large scene depicting the surrounding semi-countryside (two years later, and on several different occasions, Monet would depict the same subject); in 1873, Pissarro painted a waterside factory at Saint-Ouen-l'Aumône. Twentieth-century art would extend this interest in many ways, be it Italian Neo-Realist cinema or, closer still to Bustamante in terms of both time and medium, contemporary American photographers such as Lee Friedlander, Robert Adams and Lewis Baltz. Friedlander is a photographer Bustamante has admired ever since his years as an apprentice, and it seems to me that it is possible to detect here and there in Bustamante's work, one or two oblique tributes to his illustrious elder – in particular to Friedlander's work on the theme of the monument.[4] For example, in *T.27.80* (1980) Bustamante shows a headless statue rising up from a jumble of plants and rocks. A virtually identical counterpart appears many years later in an image of a commemorative bust lost in a small wooded area, part of the *Something is Missing* series of the late 1990s. As far as Adams and Baltz are concerned, Bustamante's photos are reminiscent of their investigations into the variously destructive effects of human activity on the land.[5]

However, the predominant theme of the *Tableaux* is not particularly sociological or topographical (there is not much point in looking for anything remotely resembling a caption in their titles which are whittled down to a laconic numbering), but hangs rather on the fact that these images offer us the equivalents of a certain mental condition in the photographer. Poised on the threshold of his work, Bustamante records the signs of beginning and construction, a hybrid of constructive impetus and indefinite suspense, in which the landscape echoes the state of mind informing its choice. As much moments of awareness as moments of the world, the *Tableaux* are thus eminently reflective. In them, nonetheless, projection holds sway over reminiscence, and shields them from that 'Albertinian perspective' which Roland Barthes referred to with regard to photography, in a slip that has passed more or less unnoticed.[6] For what is involved here, first and foremost, is elaboration, and not disappearance.

Like the vast majority of people who look at them, I, therefore, recognise nothing in these views, bar the odd

T.25.79, 1979
C-print, 103 x 130 cm

iconic motif and one or two recurrent compositional features, which leads me to presuppose a specific arrangement on the part of their creator. If their creator roundly suggests to me a kind of similarity to his own attempt at self-definition, I must then, in return, invent myself as viewer of his works. (Bustamante often alludes to the type of relationship he would like to see introduced by his work – a non-directive relationship, based on a form of fertile indeterminacy that he calls 'between the two [*entre-deux*]', and which puts the onlooker in the position of becoming 'equally responsible for the work'.) One thing is quite clear: there is plenty to see in these photographs, and pride of place should be given, above all, to the eye and the way it looks, in contemplation. The title of the series also acts as a hint in this respect. Faced with the luxuriousness of the different types of materials, the density of details, the chromatic consistency – greens, ochres, browns – and the surface cohesion shown by, among others, *T.26.80* (1980), *T.45.82* (1982) and *T.55.82* (1982), it is quite acceptable to allow yourself be gradually absorbed by the image, and let it rise slowly up through you like a pure object of vision. Otherwise, what should I make of an image of, say, an unidentified nook of pine forest, or a thoroughly commonplace house stranded on bare rubble? The power of such works resides, to a considerable degree, in the way they reduce their referents in order to attract our eye in an experience that can be called pictorial. But apart from the fact that Bustamante's photography is well removed from what is traditionally called 'pictorialism' (it is as 'straight' as you can get – no prior preparation of the shot, no fiddling with the negative, no computerised touching-up), this recourse to the painterly model is a constant source of fascination, which can be seen if we take the artist's visual work as a whole.

In 1983, Bustamante joined forces with another artist, Bernard Bazile, collaborating under the name BAZILEBUSTAMANTE until 1987. The manufactured object, the advertising image, the pictograph and the logo all lay at the root of their works, which might, for example, combine a limited-edition rug based on a Sonia Delaunay drawing, the cut-out outline of a table and two chairs reduced to their essential signifiers, and two neon tubes – all laid flat on the floor to make *Le Tapis* (*The Rug*, 1984). There were contributions from Diderot's *Encyclopedia* and supermarket shelves alike – treasures to be recycled and appropriated. This development was hardly foreseeable on the basis of the *Tableaux*, and an analytical history of the art of the 1980s will possibly enable us, one day, to gauge its full extent. Whatever the case may be, when the pair split up, Bustamante was no longer just a photographer. From then on his work took on a new complexity, based in particular on an interplay between photography and 'plastic' or 'visual' propositions (the terminological hesitancy – the words 'object', 'installation' and 'sculpture' being by turns relevant and inadequate – clearly points to a problem when it comes to describing the undertaking that concerns us here). In Bustamante's first post-BAZILEBUSTAMANTE one-man show (at Galerie Ghislaine Hussenot, Paris, 1988), the works on view included *T.37.80* (1980), a picture of a little spick and span house, resembling a model or a toy, and pointing the way towards the markedly 'objectal' nature of the pieces surrounding it. The colour, outline and mirror-like expanse of *Le verre bleu* (1987; p. 42) which it has an even closer connection with, reintroduced the swimming pool that could be partly glimpsed in *T.42.81* (1981). Here we are touching on one of the most intriguing aspects of the use Bustamante has made of photography and, in particular, his own photographs. Certain works conceived in the years that followed this resumption of one-man activity actually seem to have emerged from the world of the *Tableaux* as if, by looking anew at what he had examined at length through the lens, the artist derived from it a kind of vocabulary of materials and figures: brick, cement, sand, red-painted metal. Similarly, though, as with the *Sites*, we see various ways of delimiting a space.

The apparent strategy may not be as conscious as this and Bustamante's objects may not be such a deliberate part

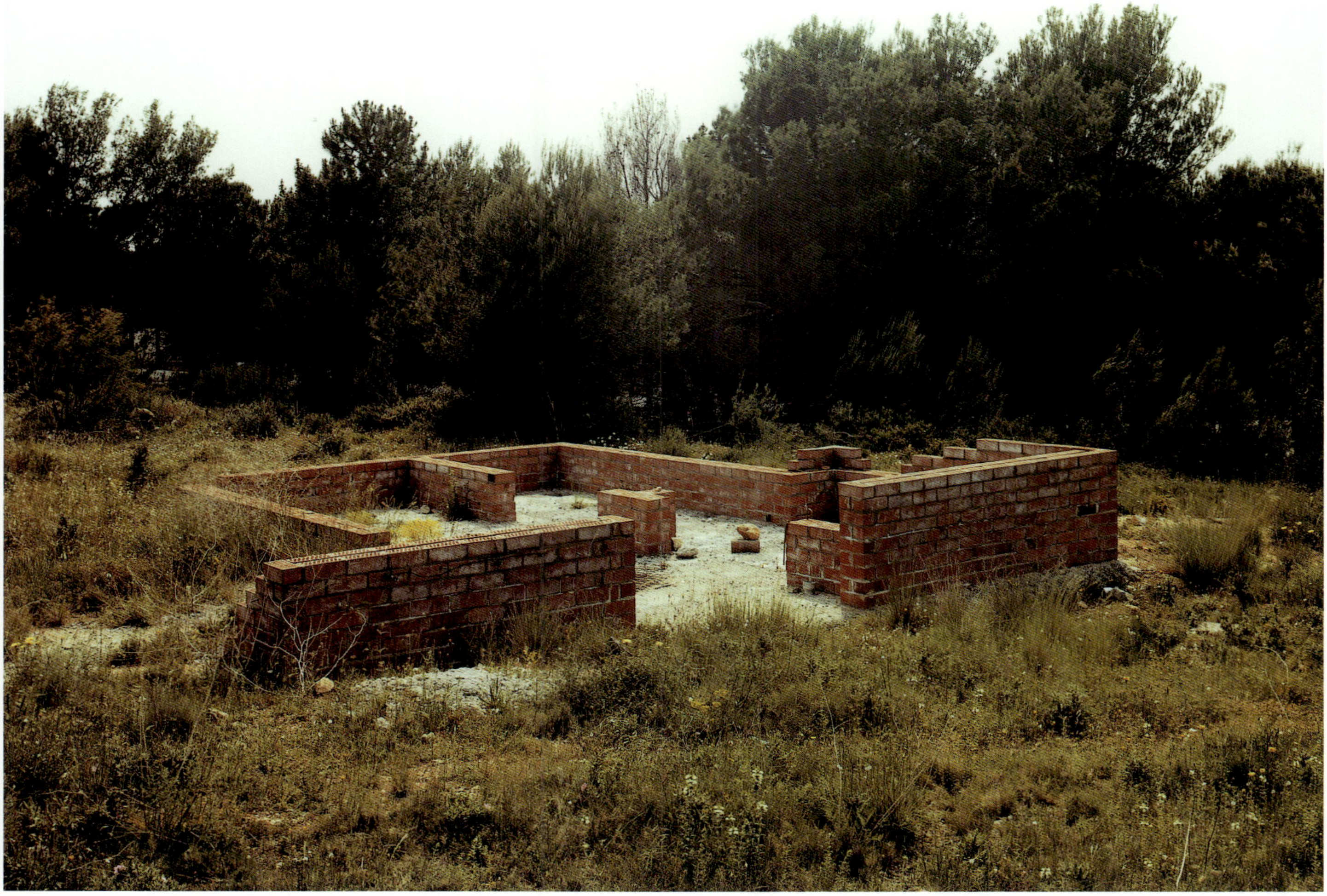

T.1.78, 1978
C-print, 103 x 130 cm

of the unusual visual culture in which he was steeped – and which he had fashioned for himself – at the time when he produced the *Tableaux*. This doesn't greatly alter my argument, however, which attempts to detect the role of a 'photographic way of seeing' in the way in which a visual work is put together. By this I mean the ability to extract an unassuming element from the continuum of the real, so as to lend it, by translation, a new kind of autonomy. This is the operation peculiar to the readymade which, as has been amply demonstrated by Rosalind Krauss, is not conceivable without the existence of photography.[7] In a recent article about Andreas Gursky, Michel Gauthier has put forward the idea that, in a perfect return to sender, the readymade could also find a way of potentially occupying the photograph, the latter then acting, far from any objective and documentary transparency, like a 'converter'.[8] A photographic assumption of a 'seeing-as' relative to art from time immemorial, the final conclusion of which might perhaps reside in a simple act of viewing – a strictly private act, occurring within the onlooker, and with no material reinstatement of any sort.[9] In a similar vein, Robert Smithson comes specifically to mind, telling the tale of a pilgrimage to his childhood haunts (a suburb, let it be noted) and using that occasion to celebrate improbable 'monuments', the nature of which does indeed seem to pertain, through and through, to a form of mechanical reproduction:

> 'The bus passed over the first monument. I pulled the buzzer-cord and got off at the corner of Union Avenue and River Drive. The monument was a bridge over the Passaic River that connected Bergen County with Passaic County. Noon-day sunshine cinema-ized the site, turning the bridge and the river into an over-exposed *picture*. Photographing it with my Instamatic 400 was like photographing a photograph. The sun became a monstrous light-bulb that projected a detached series of 'stills' through my Instamatic into my eye. When I walked on the bridge, it was as though I was walking on an enormous photograph that was made of wood and steel, and underneath the river existed as an enormous movie film that showed nothing but a continuous blank.'[10]

The fact that photography is a sort of capture or catchment, and thus comparable with the readymade, is the lesson drawn by Bustamante when he turns away from the camera to work with an already existing object. The first limitation, in this instance, is not to be content with a repetition of Duchamp's gesture by becoming a new kind of removal man, by merely shifting a thing into the museum or gallery. We have seen one or two examples in the *Tableaux* of the way Bustamante produces certain pieces by three-dimensionally developing different motifs (the image acting, as it were, like a filter between an element of the world and its borrowed use by the artist). On other occasions, what is involved is *exhibition*, with all that that implies by way of adding and adjustment: *Le Vêtement* (*Clothing*, 1988) shows a precious fabric within an open metal volume, the dimensions of which seem to be painstakingly deduced from the coat it contains, pinned there like a shimmering insect. *Serena*, created in 1995 in the gardens of the Kröller-Müller Museum (p. 57), temporarily takes possession of an object that is much more impressive, and has very different connotations: the pavilion designed by Gerrit Rietveld in 1955, first built in Arnhem, then rebuilt in Otterlo in 1965. Bustamante was invited to occupy this building traditionally earmarked for sculpture, and chose to exhibit the exhibition venue itself, which he traversed with a green coil-like line, so that the visitor followed the route, discovering at the same time the detail of the architecture. Through the introduction of this visual disruption, which is as minimal as it is effective, *Serena* put Rietveld's structure in quotation marks, and appropriated it while simultaneously offering it up to a new way of looking.

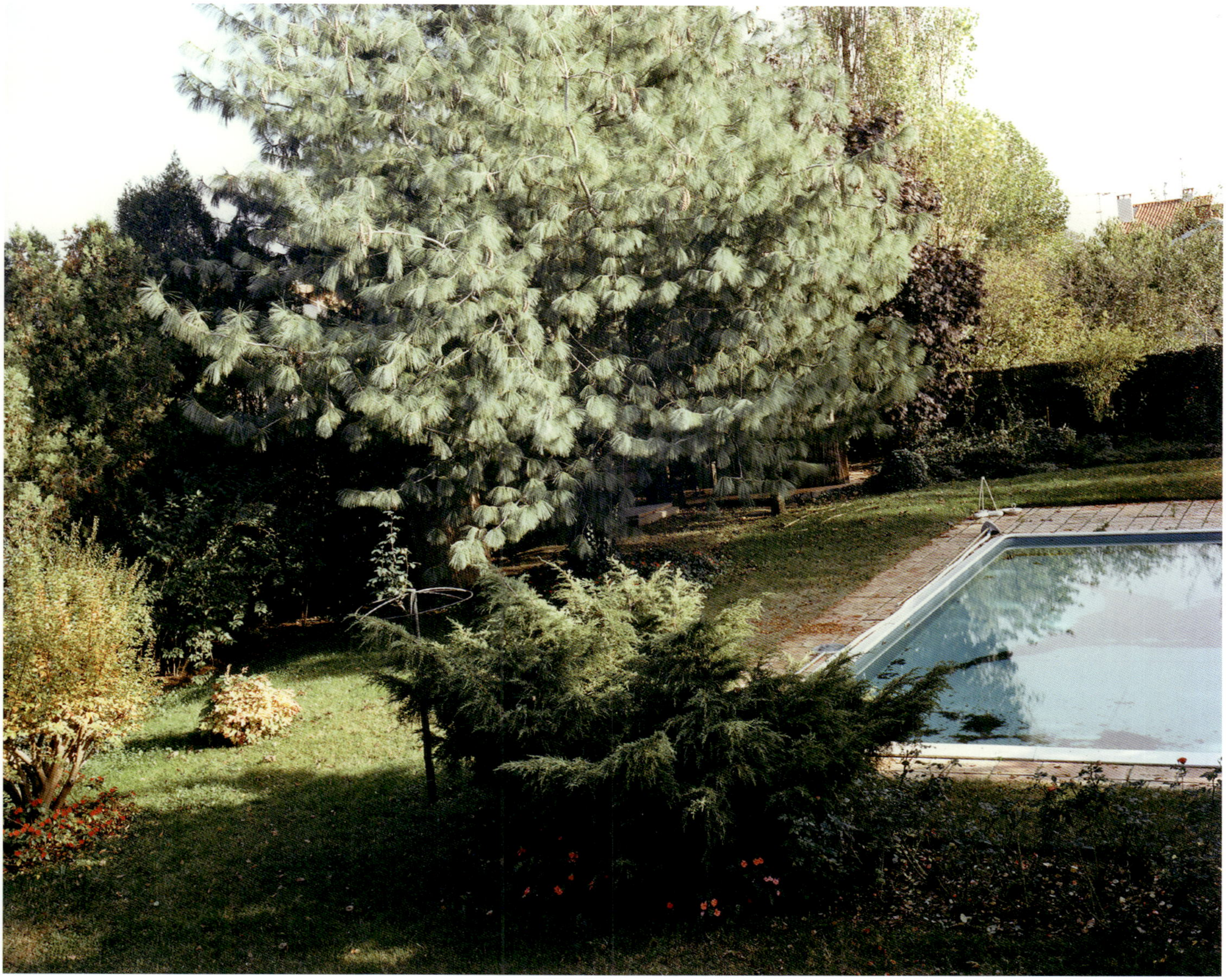

T.45.82, 1982
C-print, 103 x 130 cm

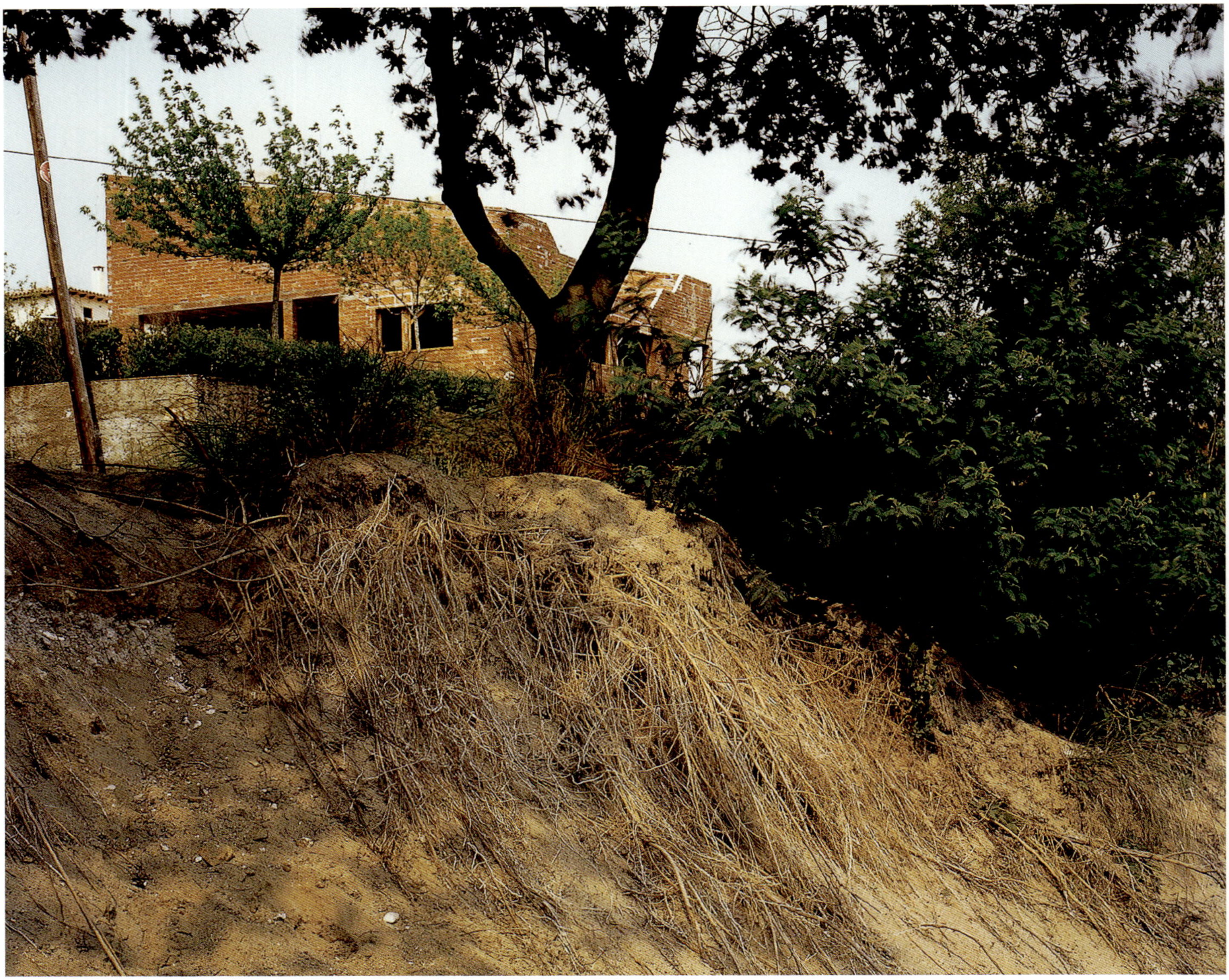

The *Lumières* transfer the concepts of appropriation and transformation to photography itself. The sources for these works, first devised back in 1987, are actually snapshots dating mainly from the 1930s to the 1950s, and discovered by Bustamante in art and architectural books and magazines.[11] These *photos trouvéels* (an invented combination of *photos trouvées* and *photos réelles*: found and real photos) are re-photographed and silk-screened onto large-format Plexiglas sheets, which are fixed to the wall with metal fasteners that keep them an inch or two away from it. Depending on the lighting, a *Lumière* thus enables the wall accommodating it to duplicate more or less completely, by projection, what it itself duplicates – the work appears like a transitory, intermediate thing, a kind of passage, an insubstantial screen through which passes a flow of images separated from their origin. The transparency of the surface, combined with the density of the printing ink, contributes to a maximum contrast of values, from the most absolute clarity to a deep black, which here and there conjures up a veritable 'shadow painting', a *skiagraphia* (the fact that this technique was paired, in the imagination of the ancient Greeks, with the attempt to preserve the memory of a dear departed one, or a beloved momentarily out of reach, is perhaps not unconnected with the diffuse melancholy that emanates from the *Lumières*[12]).

There is a history of the shadow in twentieth-century art, dealing with the way it is produced as well as with the way it is captured. It should come as no surprise that it mixes together the development of the readymade and photography. In a note written in 1913 or thereabouts, Duchamp observed: 'After the bride ... / make a picture of shadows cast / by objects 1st on a plane. / 2nd on its surface of such (or such) curvature / 3rd on several transparent surfaces.'[13] In 1918, *Tu m'*, his last picture, displayed shadows cast by readymades, and a photo dated that same year, *Shadows of a Readymade*, taken in his New York studio, tackles the same subject (although we cannot tell whether the author is Duchamp, Man Ray, or some other anonymous person). Then, among others, came Robert Rauschenberg and his *White Paintings* produced from 1951 – monochromes whose primary purpose was to capture the shadows of people passing in front of them, in particular of people taking part in *Theatre Piece No. 1*, a multimedia event presented by John Cage in 1952 at Black Mountain College. Then came Andy Warhol, Christian Boltanski and Sigmar Polke ....[14] The unusualness of the *Lumières* certainly lies in fact that they rouse this theatre of the fugitive from the very interior of the photograph, while at the same time coming across like objects of an uncertain and quite novel genre. In this respect, it is worth noting that the *Panoramas* of 1998–99 may not be included in a descriptive catalogue of Bustamante's photographic oeuvre – which would seem, at first glance, to be self-explanatory, given the degree to which their appearance likens them to painting – but they still borrow the same production process as the *Lumières*: that is, silk-screenprinting of a considerably enlarged source-image on Plexiglas. However, the point of departure is a drawing by the artist, not a photograph.

The seductive quality of the *Lumières* – a mixture of obsolescence, abandonment, melancholy and uncanniness – is curious. An extended arm has just lit (or is about to extinguish?) a lamp, which points towards the precarious and sporadic kind of existence that is both represented and exemplified by the whole series (this ambiguity is a feature of nature, as when a *Lumière* is removed from the wall, which has acted as its vital complement, it also loses some of its effect). The series is like an ill-defined collection of images – memories from books, reported events, snippets of dreams, places glimpsed and then forgotten – which emerge on these weird surfaces but which have no direct comparison with other contemporary work involving photographic appropriation (Sherrie Levine, Richard Prince, and their various followers and imitators). Quite a few children, classrooms, places that induce innate boredom, and black-and-white imagery typical of what has already been seen by other eyes: the 'subject of the visible'

S.i.M.8.97D, 1997
C-print, 60 x 40 cm

opposite: *S.i.M.12.97*, 1997
C-print, 60 x 40 cm

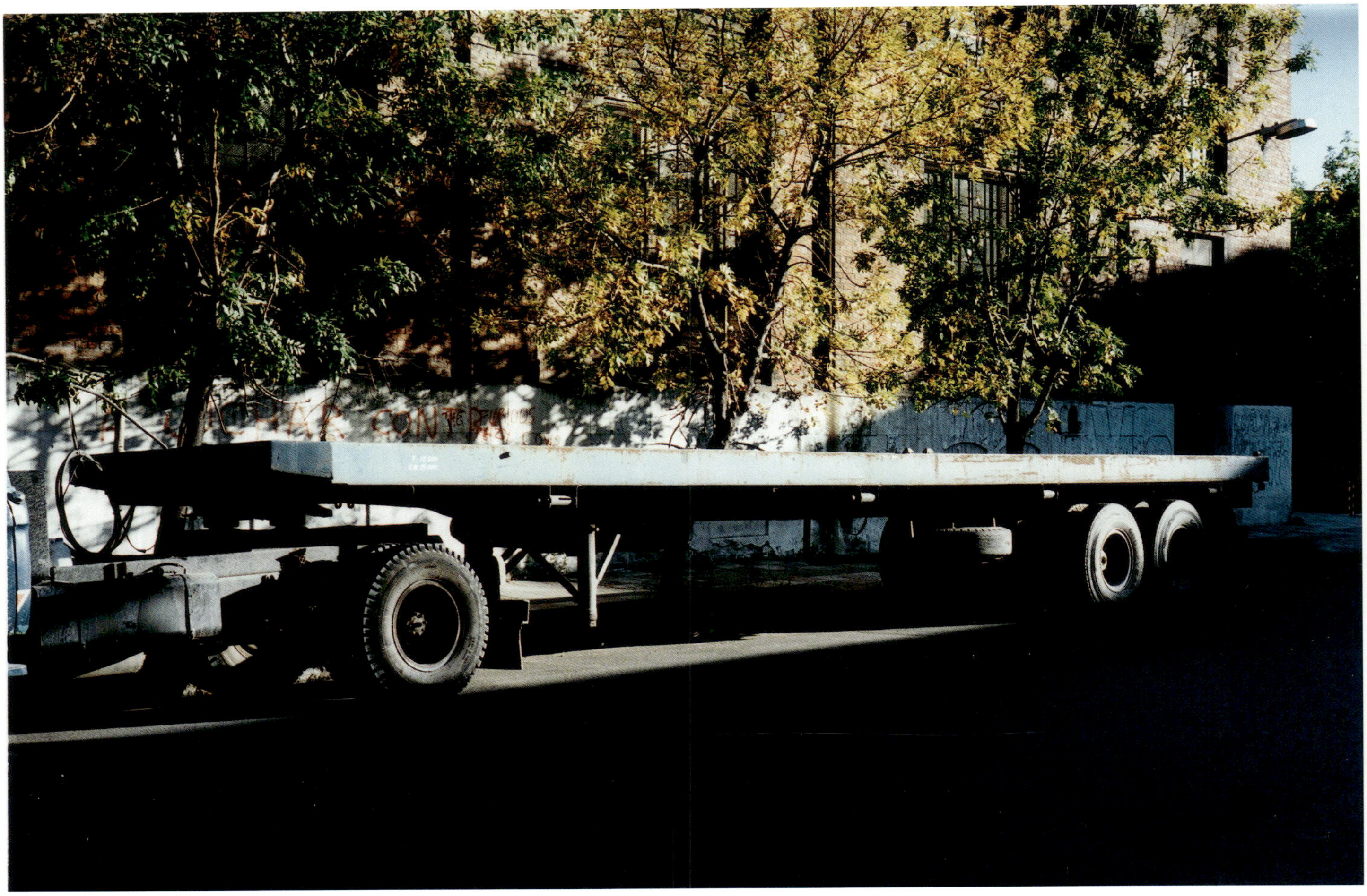

tinged by a remnant of childhood, the photograph as it 'opens up to us this fictional spot whereby we are not the judges of what we see, but eventually possible actors in this bygone past of the image.'[15] (This now comes back to me, something that then struck me forcibly, although I was unable to explain altogether why: during the Bustamante exhibition at the Van Abbemuseum in Eindhoven in 1992, one room – the first or last room on the circuit, depending on the visitor's choice – remained in darkness. Inside, on the rear wall of this space, devoid of all objects apart from a smallish sound projector set on a tripod at the other end of the room, you could view Michelangelo Antonioni's *La Notte* (*The Night*, 1961). Here, apparently, there was neither hijacking nor appropriation – no desire on the part of the artist to make this work his own in any way whatsoever , but rather a simple presentation, that took today's regular cinema-goer back to the kind of intimate screenings related to family and school, of a film whose very date, especially for those of Bustamante's generation, is an evocation of childhood. This presentation involved a specifically spatial, not to say sculptural experience, in which the viewer – whether moving about, standing on a particular spot or sitting on the floor – was forced to change the ritual of ordinary viewing, before deciding

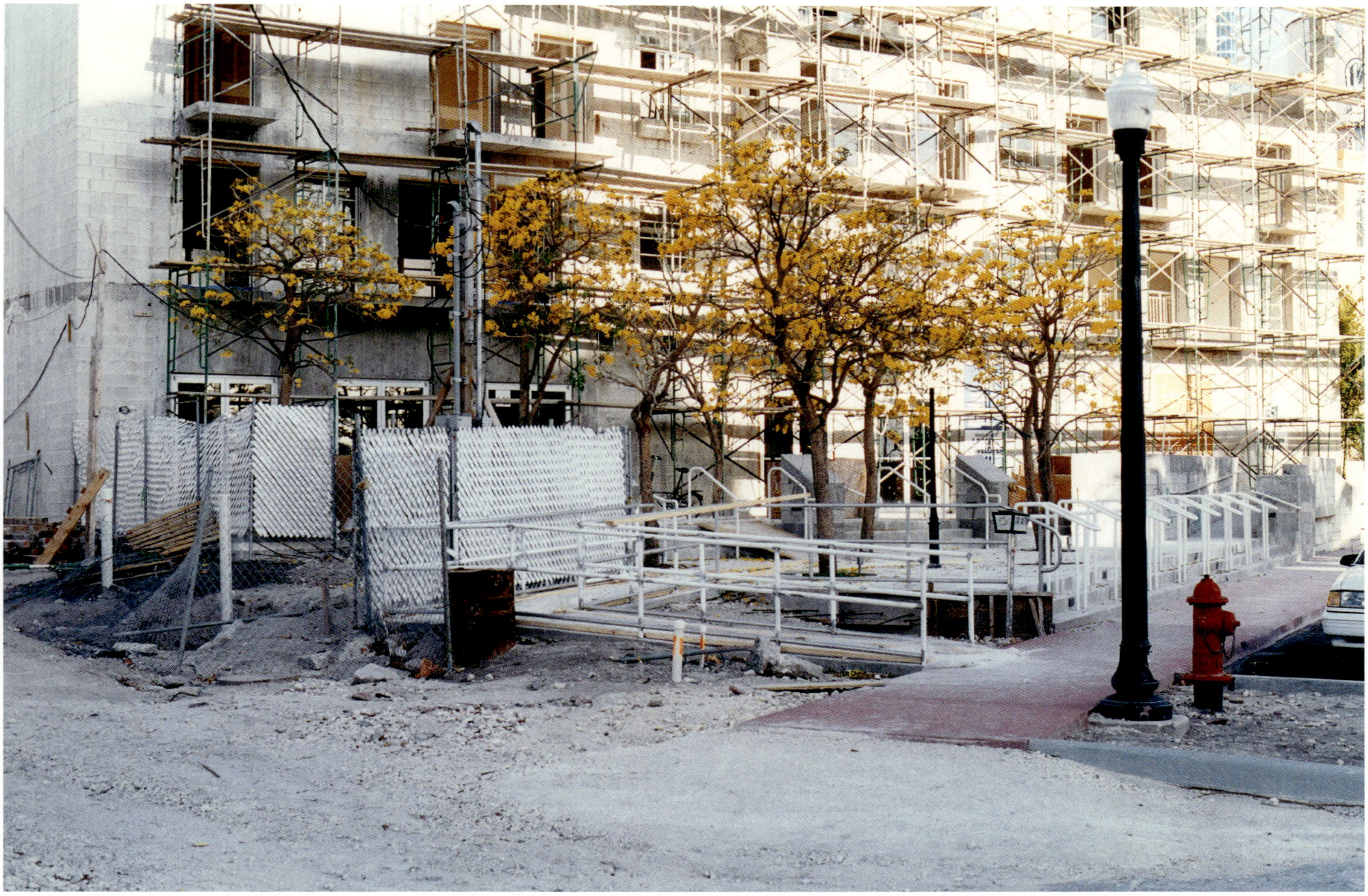

on the attention he would pay to these images, where plenty of things seemed to serve as pcints of reference with regard to what had been seen, or what was about to be seen, in the other museum rooms. This was a particular way of dealing with time, light, silence and architecture, and even certain sequences, such as the gambling scene with the evening's guests. Stripped of any overtly premeditated associations, these machinations were left for all to appreciate.)

On several occasions, by removing photography from a contrived independence, Bustamante combined it with eclectic elements in one and the same work. Latterly, new *Lumières* have been shown alongside metal cages designed by the artist to hold live birds. But it is with the two *Stationnaires* produced in 1991 that this practice of combining elements really got under way; this approach was related neither to montage nor assemblage, stemming rather from the *ambiente* of which Lucio Fontana and certain Arte Povera artists were fond. *Stationnaire I*, intended to occupy a huge room all by itself, is composed of sixteen identical modules made of cement and brass, set at variable angles in different areas of the floor, accompanied by six Cibachromes showing close-ups of cypress trees and a Japanese paper panel, affixed to the

T.37.80, 1980
C-print, 103 x 130 cm

wall and all at the same size of 150 x 120 cm. Here, again, without being expressly used, we get a strong sense of the pictorial model, but *in absentia* and combined with a three-dimensional treatment of space – between 'specific objects' and scattered pieces – which blurs any attempt to attach a generic label to it. What is more, the *Cyprès* (pp. 5, 48–49) – which are part of the *Tableaux* series and are the photographic works that are the closest to abstract painting that Bustamante has produced – form a group that can be independently exhibited, either together or separately. *Stationnaire II* (1991; p. 4), for its part, puts the image at the very hub of the ensemble, with each of its cement boxes, shown either open or closed, containing a Cibachrome (again, a *Cyprès*). An identical concern with dovetailing the photographic and the sculptural object comes across clearly in the three *Ouvertures*, the earliest of which dates from 1993 (p. 45). Here, table and picture are brought together to cooperate in a physical lowering of the photograph. On these large, slightly raised surfaces that Bustamante has created (each one of them is extended on the right-hand side by a kind of opening) lie suburban views: an access road, a lane that forks, a bend. An older piece, *Intérieur I* (1988; p. 47), already had something akin to a table in it – although it did not include a photograph. A lovely reproduction installation image of it shows the work displayed in the Haus Lange, Krefeld, opposite one of the large bay windows that Ludwig Mies van der Rohe had the brilliant idea of incorporating in his design.[16] One can see outside, the terrace, trees, a lawn and a house in the background. All that remains to be done is to slip the landscape over the sculpture.

'People feel at home everywhere, in their own country as much as elsewhere – or as much as nowhere,' Siegfried Kracauer observed in 1925 in an essay where the current taste for travel was already thoroughly analysed.[17] *Something is Missing*, first presented to the public in a book, *Amandes amères*, produced for Documenta X in 1997,[18] is based on this availability of the contemporary subject – happy or anxious, you can never really know. It is a kind of anti-logbook in pictures, a reflex camera clutched all the way through various unidentified wanderings in South America, the United States, Israel, Spain and maybe elsewhere too (although he seems to put his camera away as soon as he is back in France). I have listed these parts of the world because Bustamante happens to mention them, or because certain details in his photographs – advertising hoardings, number plates – help to identify them, but the viewer is offered no information about the places visited. The real motif here, in the dual sense of 'pretext' and 'figurative theme', is displacement or movement, much more than what might be distinctive about such and such a spot on the globe. (Kracauer put it thus: 'Goethe's Italian journey had to do with the country his soul was seeking; today's soul – or what we call the soul – is looking for the change of place that the journey offers it. The aim of the modern journey is not its avowed destination, but quite simply a new place.'[19]) Henceforth, what is outside the frame loses all its importance and each image becomes a free element, an irremediably *disinterested* surface, based on a principle that is set forth as follows: 'The photograph just places everything before us, and neither explains nor deduces anything. Because everything is spread out beneath our eyes, there is nothing to explain. For what is hidden, for example, is of no interest to us.'[20]

Something is Missing, which, in my view, must be regarded as a single work that is being gradually constructed before us, is offered to the eye as so many isolated blocks that, at the time of writing, may include up to twelve photographs. These blocks do not convey a narrative, and they do not indicate any reading direction (at his exhibition at Tate Gallery in the winter of 1998–99, the artist hung one of the elements in the largest block upside down, as if to make a point in this respect). When they contain only a single image, they are archipelagos – or islands – whether our eye scans or examines them, whether we linger in front of them or whether we are content to walk on past them (like those 'moved' figures, caught in motion, often shown in installation images), all they possibly do is suggest this:

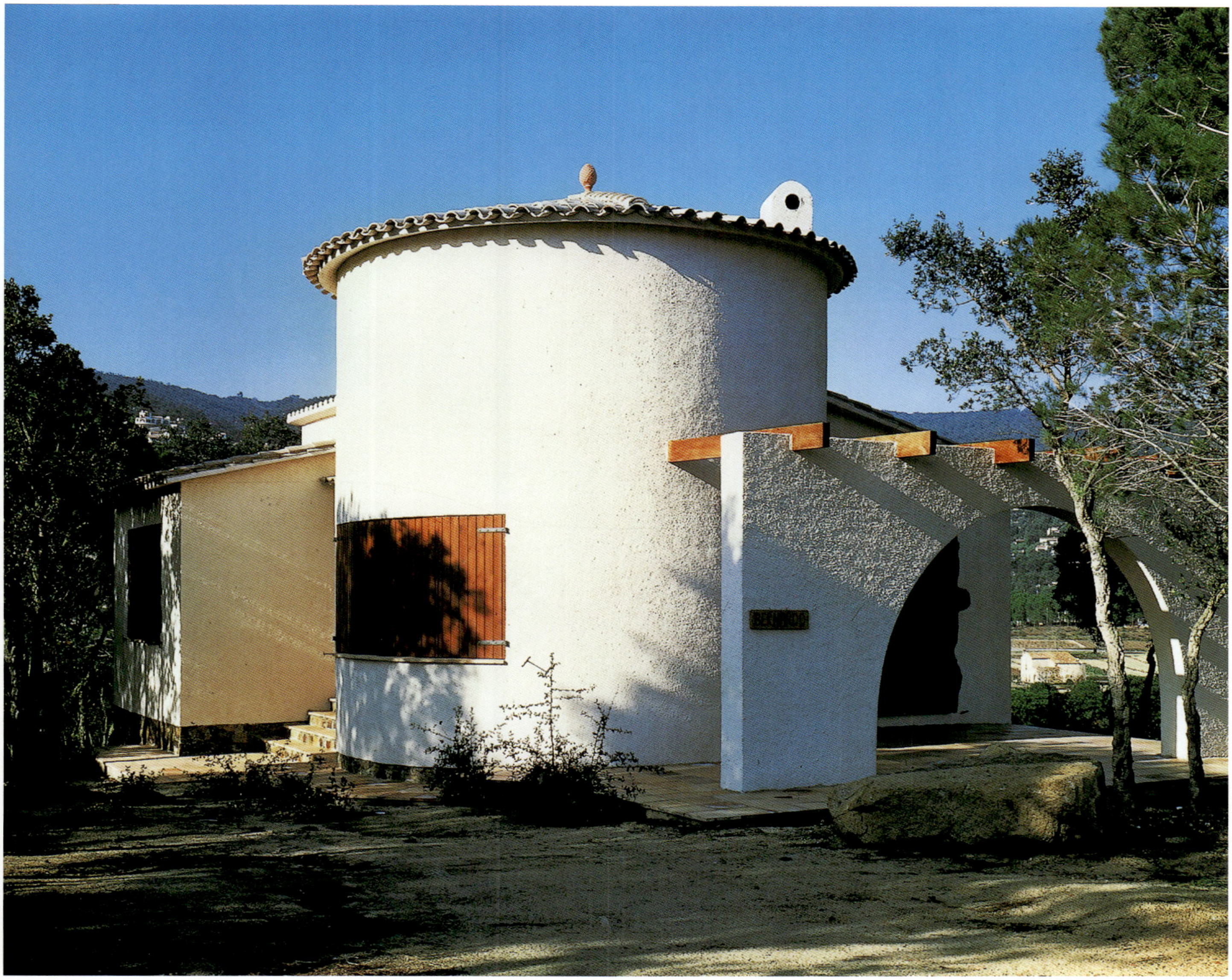

T.55.82, 1982
C-print, 103 x 130 cm

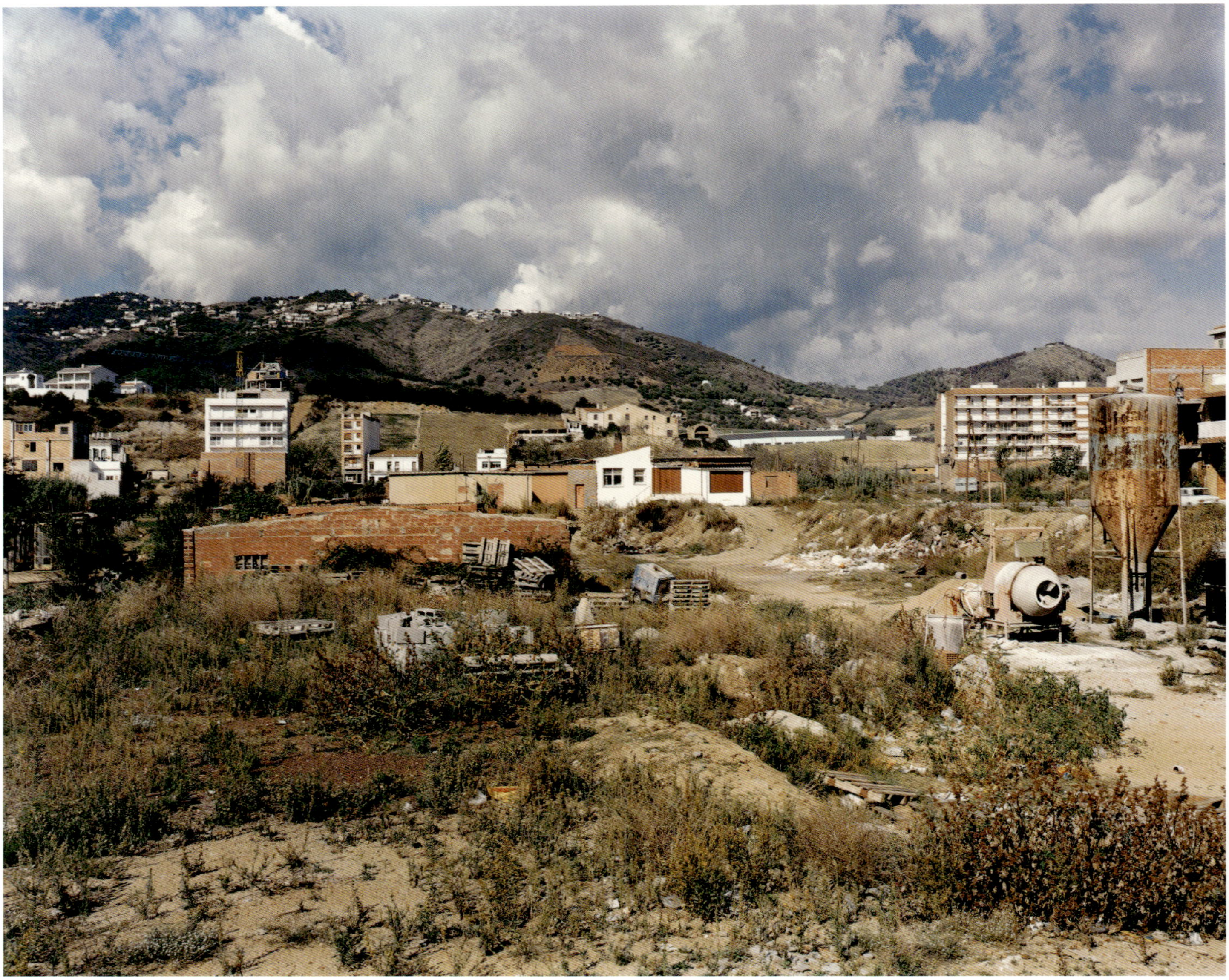

'Count up the almonds,
count what was bitter and kept you waking,
count me in too.'[21]

Translated from the French 'Bustamante photographe (Notes pour un portrait inachevé)', Jean-Marc Bustamante: Oeuvres Photographiques 1978–1999, *Centre National de la Photographie, Paris, 1999. Translated by Simon Pleasance and Fronza Woods.*

NOTES

1. 'Fragments of an interview: Jean-Marc Bustamante, Jan Debbaut and Yves Gevaert', *Jean-Marc Bustamante*, Van Abbemuseum, Eindhoven, 1993, p. 12.
2. *Jean-Marc Bustamante: Tableaux 1978–1982*, Musée départemental d'art contemporain de Rochechouart, Rochechouart, FRAC Languedoc Roussillon and Kunsthalle Bern, Bern, 1994, p. 19 and p. 21.
3. See T. J. Clark, *The Painting of Modern Life. Paris in the Art of Manet and His Followers*, Knopf, New York, 1984 and in particular chapter 3, 'The Environs of Paris'.
4. Lee Friedlander, *The American Monument*, The Eakins Press Foundation, New York, 1976.
5. Adams and Baltz both featured in the major exhibition held in 1975, where the works of Bernd and Hilla Becher, in particular, were also shown. Exhibition catalogue: William Jenkins, *New Topographics: Photographs of a Man-Altered Landscape*, International Museum of Photography, at George Eastman House, Rochester, New York, 1975.
6. In *Camera Lucida* (Editions du Seuil, Paris, 1980), Roland Barthes is swept away along the Proustian path of memory, recollection and recall, and on two occasions (p. 126 and p. 138) uses the term 'Albertinian perspective' (*perspective albertinienne*) – and not, as it should be, Albertian (*albertienne*) – to describe the spatial arrangement also known as *costruzione legittima*, referring to the figure of the famous fugitive Albertine Simonet from *In Search of Lost Time* or *Remembrance of Things Past* instead of Leon Battista Alberti, the great humanist of the Italian Renaissance.
7. Rosalind Krauss, 'Marcel Duchamp ou le champ imaginaire', 1980, *Le Photographique* (trans. M. Bloch and J. Kempf), Macula, Paris, 1990, pp. 71–88.
8. Michel Gauthier, 'Vues imprenables sur readymades. La photographie selon Andreas Gursky', in *Les Cahiers du Musée national d'art moderne*, no. 67, Spring 1999, pp. 64–87. Esp. p. 84: 'Just as, in the case of the *Bottle Rack*, it is not a matter of understanding the object exhibited but of appreciating the operation that made this object what it henceforth is in its exhibition situation, so in the case of Gursky's photographs it is not a matter of understanding and deciphering the content of the image, but of grasping the meaning of photographic indeterminacy: the conversion into a work.'
9. On the notion of 'seeing-as', borrowed from Wittgenstein's *Philosophical Investigations*, see Richard Wollheim, *Art and its Objects*, Cambridge University Press, 1980; esp. the chapter 'Seeing-as, seeing-in, and pictorial representation', pp. 187–205.
10. Robert Smithson, Jack Flam (ed.), 'A Tour of the Monuments of Passaic, New Jersey', 1967, in *The Collected Writings*, University of California Press, Berkeley and Los Angeles, 1996, p. 70.
11. References to some of these publications appear at the end of Bustamante's, *Lumières 1987–1993*, Centre d'art Imprimé, Paris, 1994, unpaginated. Conceived, within the space of printed material, as the equivalent of an exhibition of the *Lumières*, this book reproduces the *Lumières* as silk screen prints on acetate, retaining both their original printing technique and their transparency.
12. 'The *skiagraphia* is strictly speaking a substitute work: the girl of Corinth has a portrait painted of her boyfriend to keep an image of him when he is away from her, and as J.-P. Vernant's study of the *kolossos* shows, primitive painting retains very strong ties to magic. It is a matter, quite literally, of a "shadow painting" or a "ghost painting", and this value is definitely decisive in its use as funerary painting.' (Agnès Rouveret, *Histoire et imaginaire de la peinture ancienne*, École Française de Rome, 1989, p. 20).
13. Marcel Duchamp, 'Ombres portées', in *Duchamp du signe*, writings compiled and introduced by M. Sanouillet with the help of E. Peterson, Flammarion, Paris, 1975, p. 103.
14. For an overview of this recent history of the shadow, and even more so for the various manifestations in the art of previous centuries, see Victor L. Stoichita, *A Short History of the Shadow*, Reaktion Books, London, 1997.
15. Jean-Louis Schefer, 'Sujet du visible' (1986), in *Images mobiles*, P.O.L., Paris, 1999, p. 109.
16. *Jean-Marc Bustamante*, exhibition catalogue, Haus Lange Museum, Krefeld, 1990, p. 5.
17. Siegfried Kracauer, 'Le Voyage et la Danse' (1925), in *Le Voyage et la Danse*, selected and introduced by Philippe Despoix (trans. S. Cornille), Presses Universitaires de Vincennes, Paris, 1996, p. 4. On the themes of the journey and the city stroll, see also another collection of writings by Kracauer: *Rues de Berlin et d'ailleurs* (1964) (trans. J.-F. Boutout), Le Promeneur, Paris, 1995.
18. Jean-Marc Bustamante, *Amandes amères Bitter Almonds Bittere Mandeln*, Phaidon Press, London, 1997.
19. Kracauer, 'Le Voyage et la Danse', op. cit., p. 23.
20. Paragraph 126 of part one of Wittgenstein's *Philosophical Investigations*, amended by replacing 'philosophy' with 'the photograph'.
21. 'Zähle die Mandeln/zähle, was bitter war und dich wachhielt,/zähl mich dazu' are the opening lines of an untitled poem by Paul Celan in his collection, *Mohn und Gedächtnis*, 1952.

THE SCULPTURAL TURN

/

PENELOPE CURTIS
MAZÈRES, 2010

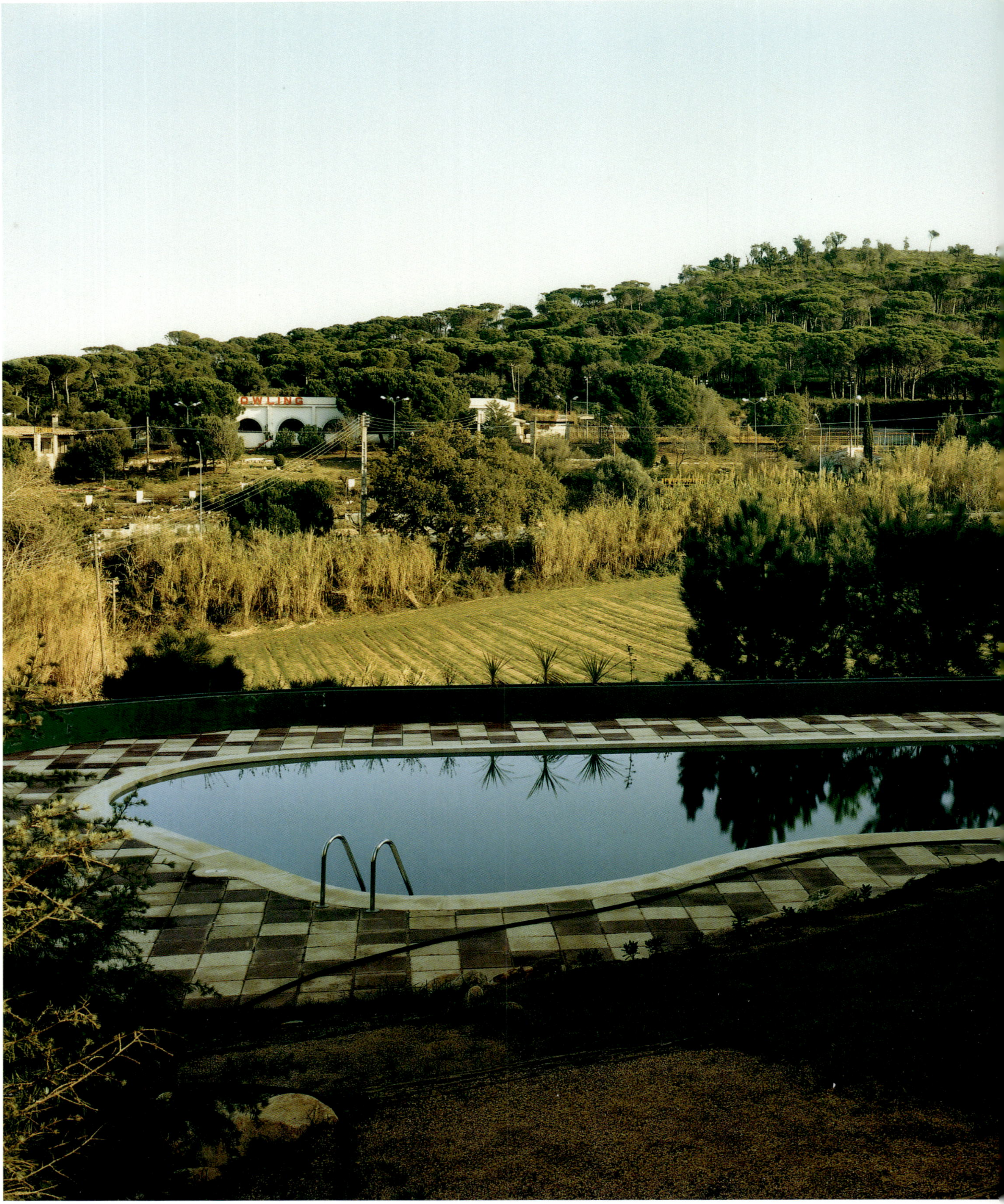
OWLING

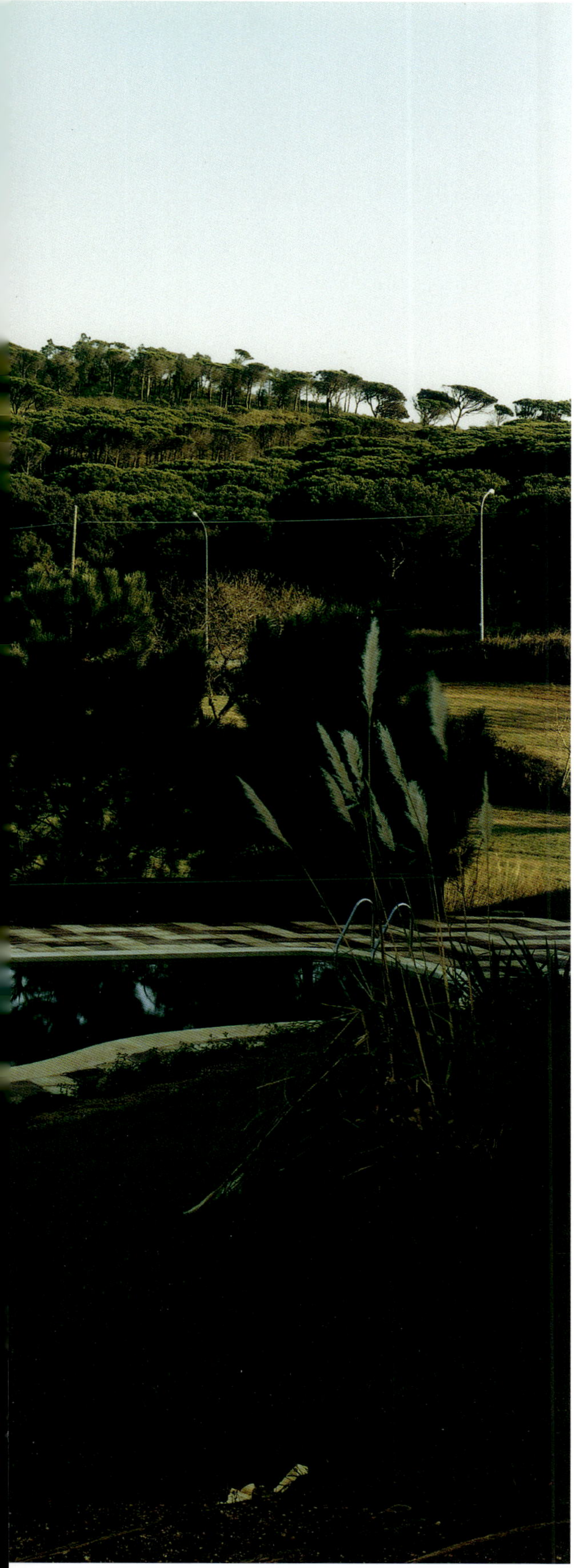

T.50.82, 1982
C-print, 103 x 130 cm

I always liked to see the work of Jean-Marc Bustamante – whatever it might be – and I never knew why. In seeking him out in the hope of making an exhibition I began to realise that what I found to be the superficially baffling quality of his work was also its deeper reality. This is what I shall try to explain.

The selection we (Jean-Marc and I) have made for the exhibition this publication accompanies is a very small selection of his work as a whole, but it embodies quite precisely the quality that I have found intriguing, and that speaks of the relationship of image to object. This relationship is a thread that runs through much of the work as a whole, and represents its problem-seeking nature.

In the beginning Bustamante was a photographer, a photographer who shifted gradually from a commercial milieu to that of fine art.[1] The photographs that he took thirty years ago are still a mainstay of his exhibitions, and provide a platform on which to construct an understanding of his art.[2]

An extensive series of photographs goes under the title of *Something is Missing* (*S.i.M.*). Sometimes I think of another title for Bustamante's work, a title like *Nothing is Happening*. The quietude of his imagery can be almost aggressive – aggressive in the sense that it penetrates the way in which we see, in which the stuff around us gathers the force of a motif.

In the dry Mediterranean countryside, dense shrub and poorly-managed woodland stand by the deserted road

Le verre bleu, 1987
Painted glass, 3 x 260 x 340 cm

opposite: *Bac à sable II*, 1990
Cement, steel, 28 x 185 x 231 cm

in *T.17.79* (1979; pp. 20–21). Leaves are still in the breathless air. The sun is overhead; the shadows are short, if visible at all. Nothing is happening; there is no timetable, there is no narrative, other than what is in front of our eyes.

Before our eyes is something that has no ostensible history; this stuff seems, like the vegetation on common ground, to have no reason for being there, to be part of no larger design. Its photographer fixes its particular nature, allowing its ubiquity to impart a sense of seriality and a sense of purpose.

On occasion the stillness of these marginal spaces has been pierced by construction work – a pool has been excavated, a fence erected, a villa begun. Their image is collected before, or after, they have come to life. For the present they inhabit a similar space to that of the woodland, a no man's land outside time. Though their space is similarly on the edge of conventional limits, they are differently constructed. For while the woodland is, apparently, endless, the constructions are all most clearly defined. Here already, we have something of what makes Bustamante want to give his images edges, or to turn them into objects. (The large format of the early photographs – their presentation as *Tableaux* (*Pictures*) – demonstrates, from the outset, his interest in giving them not just status, but also object quality.[3])

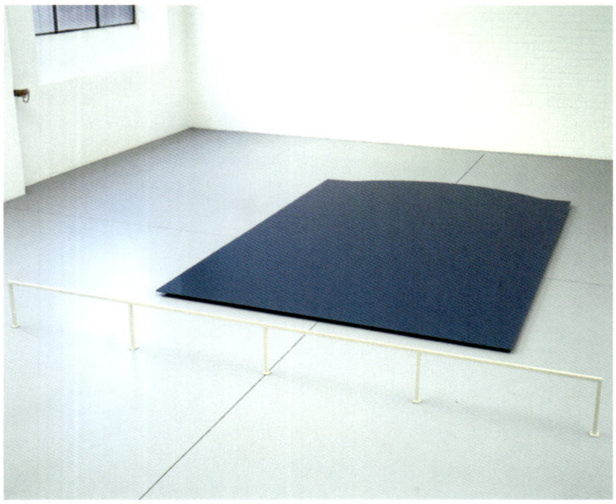

Bustamante has made the Mediterranean scrub peculiarly his own, and to learn to see these images is, I think, to learn how to see his work. If they appear unremarkable at first, the images become steadily more remarkable with time. Presented as a screen, and in this sense blind, they help us to see, and there is a sense with Bustamante of penetrating a veil that obscures not so much his art, but rather obscures our eyes.

Beyond the veil of vegetation, behind the image, beyond the lens, there will be something solid. Finding the form behind the image in front is the project exhibited here.

/

Twenty years ago Bustamante was invited to make an exhibition in one of the houses that in the late 1920s Ludwig Mies van der Rohe had built in Krefeld for Hermann Lange and for Josef Esters. These houses have fascinated many artists for their odd combination of solidity and transparency. On the cusp between the light sheetwork for which Mies is better known, and the dry brick construction of his earlier villas, the houses also seem to announce the possibility of something two-dimensional being realised in three. In this sense they were appropriate to Bustamante's project and helped him move it on.

There is a quality to German construction in general, and to Mies's houses in particular, which defies time. The excellent materials and building techniques have allowed these houses to retain a quality of newness. There is also something about their double-glazing and insulation that seems to preserve them from the outside world, as if burying all sound of change. This kind of solidification chimes well with the project that emerged here on the part of Bustamante, in which he encased more fugitive material within a solid outer form, using a limited range of distinctive materials.[4]

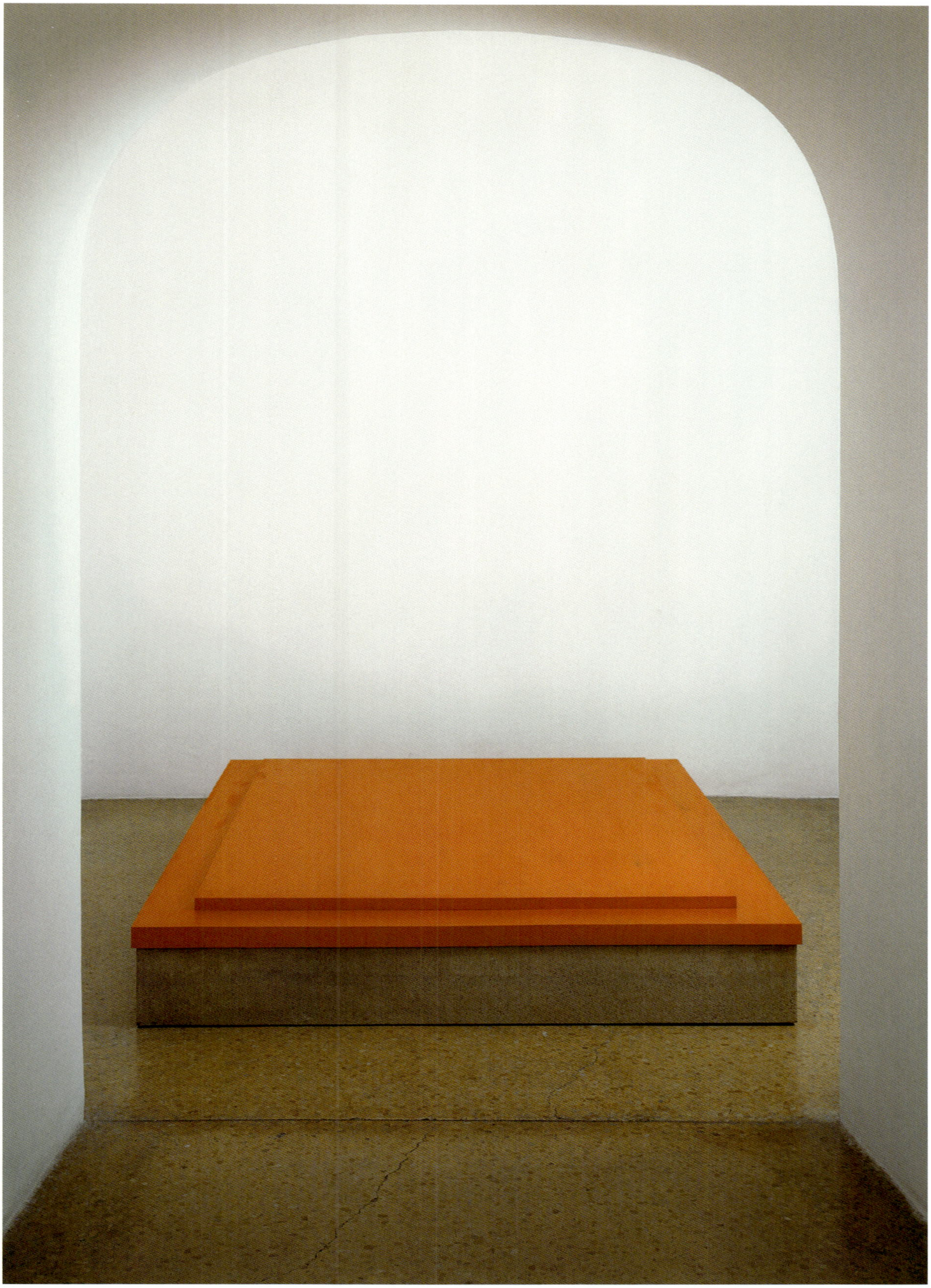

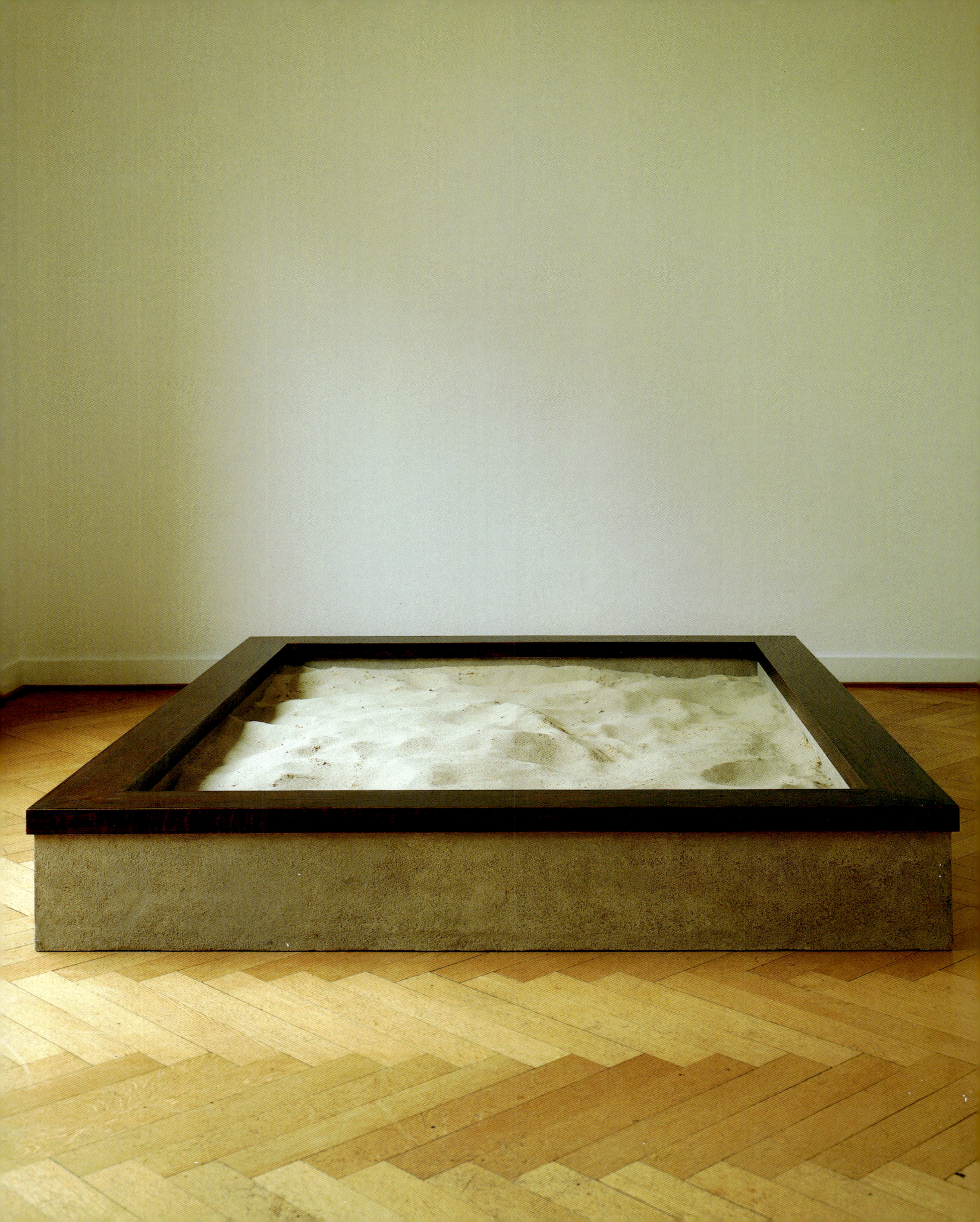

Ouverture I, 1993
Wood, C-print, 43 x 210 x 120 cm

opposite: *Bac à sable I*, 1990
Cement, wood, sand, 28 x 231 x 182 cm

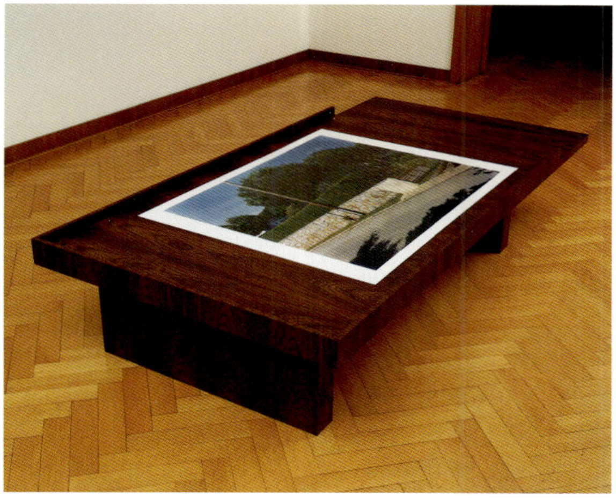

In *Stationnaire II* (1991; p. 4), twelve boxes hold twelve photographs of cypress trees; at its simplest, each box frames one image. In this way the image gains volume and durability.[5] Beyond that, the boxes allow the image to repeat itself, and to be shown as one line of images, or as one stack of boxes. The more the image gains stature, the less it can be 'seen'. In this form the boxes suggest both the archive and the memorial; referring to something beyond themselves and to themselves as well. Their repetition is puzzling; we are party neither to its arithmetic nor its fundamental necessity.

The solidification of the frame and, with it, the dissolution of the image, gains pace with *Bac à sable I* (*Sand-Pit*; 1990), which may make reference to Robert Smithson's *Sand-Box Monument* (1967).[6] Put more simply, the box refers to Bustamante's own lineage, his long-standing interest in the holes in things.

The subtly archaeological quality of Bustamante's work lies on the threshold between image and object; at the point demarcated by the image of the form that is still to be constructed. Put one next to the other and the foundations become visible. This kind of solid tracery – a seal or outline – goes back to the earliest photos and acquired actuality through the floor plans and brick courses of Krefeld such as in *T.25.79* (1979; p. 27). Here Bustamante allowed himself to give his images the weight that they were missing, jointing or sealing them with materials that were consonant with Mies's fine interiors. Now the something/nothing (solid/empty) axis becomes clearer.

The Krefeld project brought not only a certain architectural solidity but, more particularly, a way of dealing with the frame which, by allying it with interior furnishing in works such as *Ouverture I* (1993), dealt also with the question of function.[7] In this way an image could be open or closed, like a drawer or a desk. In use or out of use.

In the case of *Stationnaire II*, the nature of the image's frame meant that it was more of a box than a mount, and that one looked into it rather than at it. Changing the nature of the viewer's address was achieved surreptitiously, with great restraint, and with an openness as to front and back. At the same time the shift was meaningful, bringing with it as it did another set of associations. While many of these evoked the sense of looking at things from the past (the image in the box), there was also a more physical link in the form of the pool into which one looks, and which returns us to Bustamante's earliest work. In this way the sky becomes a pool, and the little bit of blue among the trees a reflection from above.

/

Turning to *T.11.78* (1978) and *T.50.82* (1982) the pools of days gone by remain still; their waters unmoving. Untroubled, perhaps, because they lie empty. These pools take us back to the period of their construction, a period that dwells in the memory, as if the pools would never be filled or, at the very least, never used.

T.11.78, 1978
C-print, 103 x 130 cm

opposite: *Intérieur I*, 1988
Wood, lacquer, steel, 30 x 210 x 180 cm
Haus Lange, Krefeld, 1992

In *T.50.82* the still water reflects the image above and obscures what is below. The empty pool of *T.11.78* speaks rather of the earth out of which it has been dug. We are offered the sense of either the hole or of its lid, the dry earth or its liquid filling; of the way in which the water meets the sky, in which the sky obliterates the earth. The thinnest of coverings disguises the depth of the container, the pool beneath.

Bustamante's photographs seem to present us either with the water's surface stretched over the depth beneath or with the hole awaiting its water. Neither state is fully satisfactory; in each, something is withheld. To my mind the photographs hint at this withholding and as they oscillate between one state and the other, between depth and surface, they underscore the impossibility of its being resolved. The glassy surface of the pool returns us to the picture frame and to the glass, which both protects the image and prevents us from seeing it properly.

/

In Bustamante's photographs of cypress trees from the *Tableaux* series the cypress hedge seems unbounded, repetitive, a nearly flat motif against the lens. A first inspection makes it clear that each section is different; most obviously the section of wall at the bottom is never the same, and perhaps the images are not in fact contiguous but intermittent.[8] There is clearly some overlapping, somehow like a curtain pulled loosely across a screen. As a tree that is tall and shallow, the cypress fits this project well, and these apparently simple photographs come to represent the very nature of the artist's capture and our interpretation of the image in front of our eyes, in all its insistent banality. The repetitive image is a gift to the photographer and one that is used sparingly. It is amplified here through the diptych, which makes reference both to an historic art form, and one which, like a book, can be open or closed.

One of Bustamante's most enigmatic works is *Intérieur I* (1998), speaking as it does both of an interior *ameublement*, and of the repetitive image, open to view. Its surface, scored with a grid, refers us vaguely to a book as well as a bed, but speaks most fully of the tension between surface and depth, image and object. Bustamante finds very thin forms of sculpture (platform, trellis, bed, cage, frame) and very dense forms of image.

The wood of the cypress can be used for furniture-making. As a tree it is also used to furnish the environs of cemeteries, given its ancient associations with death. How effectively these vague associations are brought together in a project that is tightly conceived but only loosely animated. Bustamante captures his image and, on occasion, goes so far as to enclose it. The sealing of the image in the box, as in *Stationnaire I* and *II*, has a quiet desperation. It is what we do with images when they matter, and this is clearly visible in the forms of memorialisation. The second version of the sand pit is sealed, and its tombal aspect surely suggests a final closure. The hole is filled.[9]

Pool, Box, Tomb; diptych, book, table; open or closed; dead or alive. This project leaves us with a *genius loci* that stirs the memory loosely but insistently, linking it, again and again, to the image in front of the eyes and the form to which it tends.

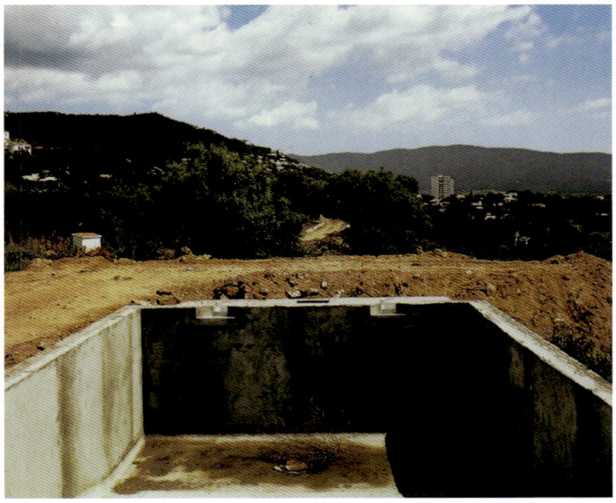

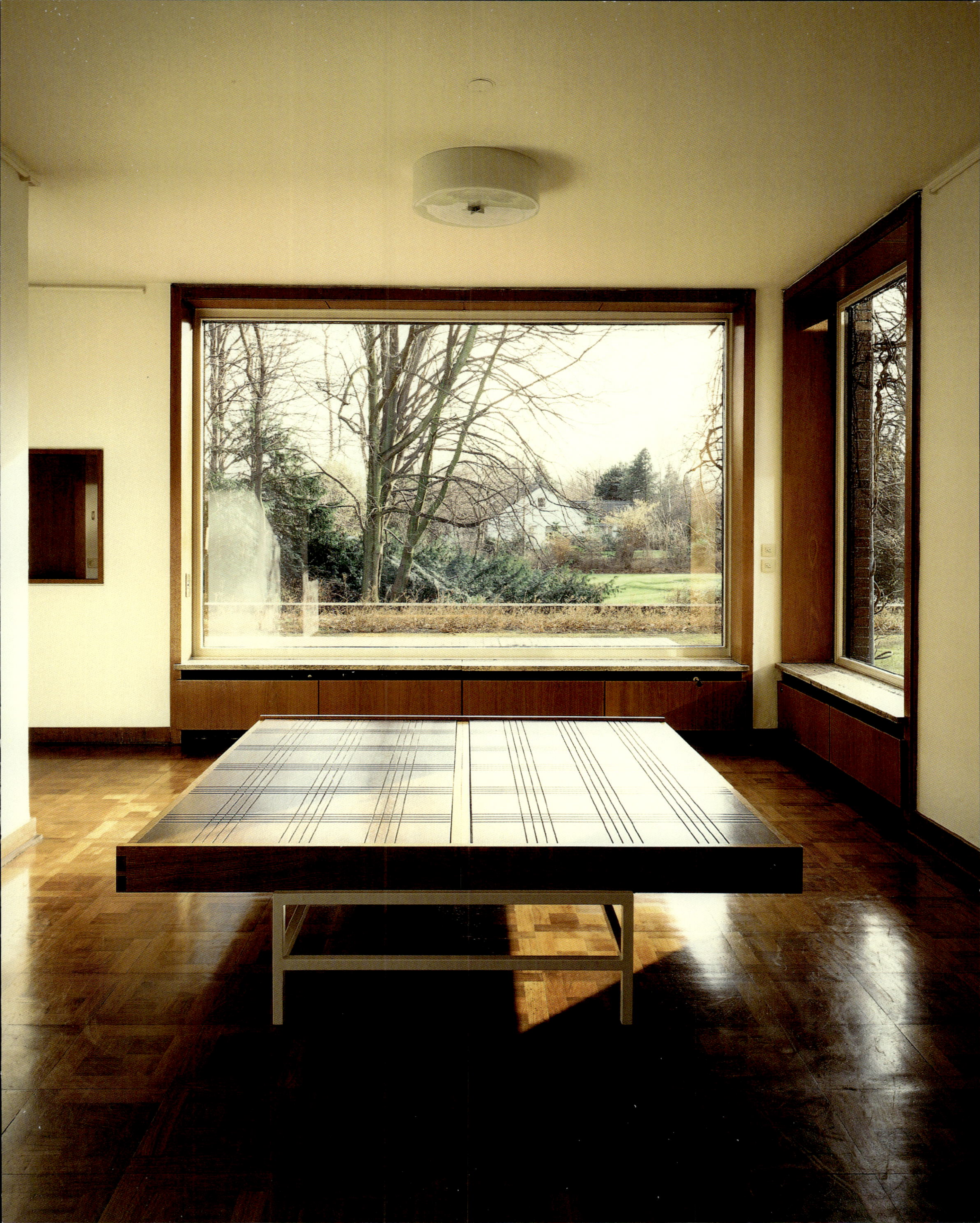

T.133.91, 1991
C-print,138 x 111 cm

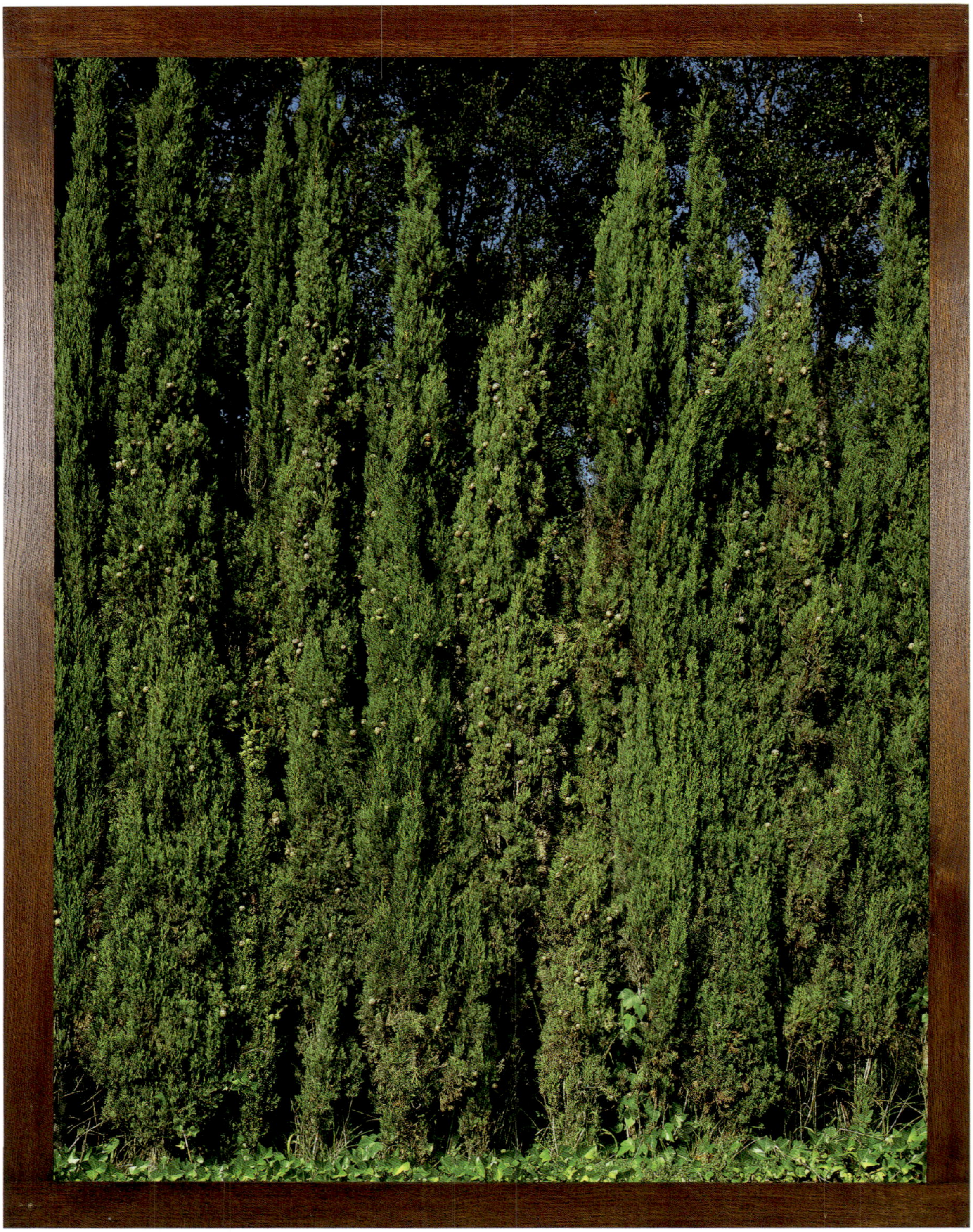

T.151.91, 1991
C-print,138 x 111 cm

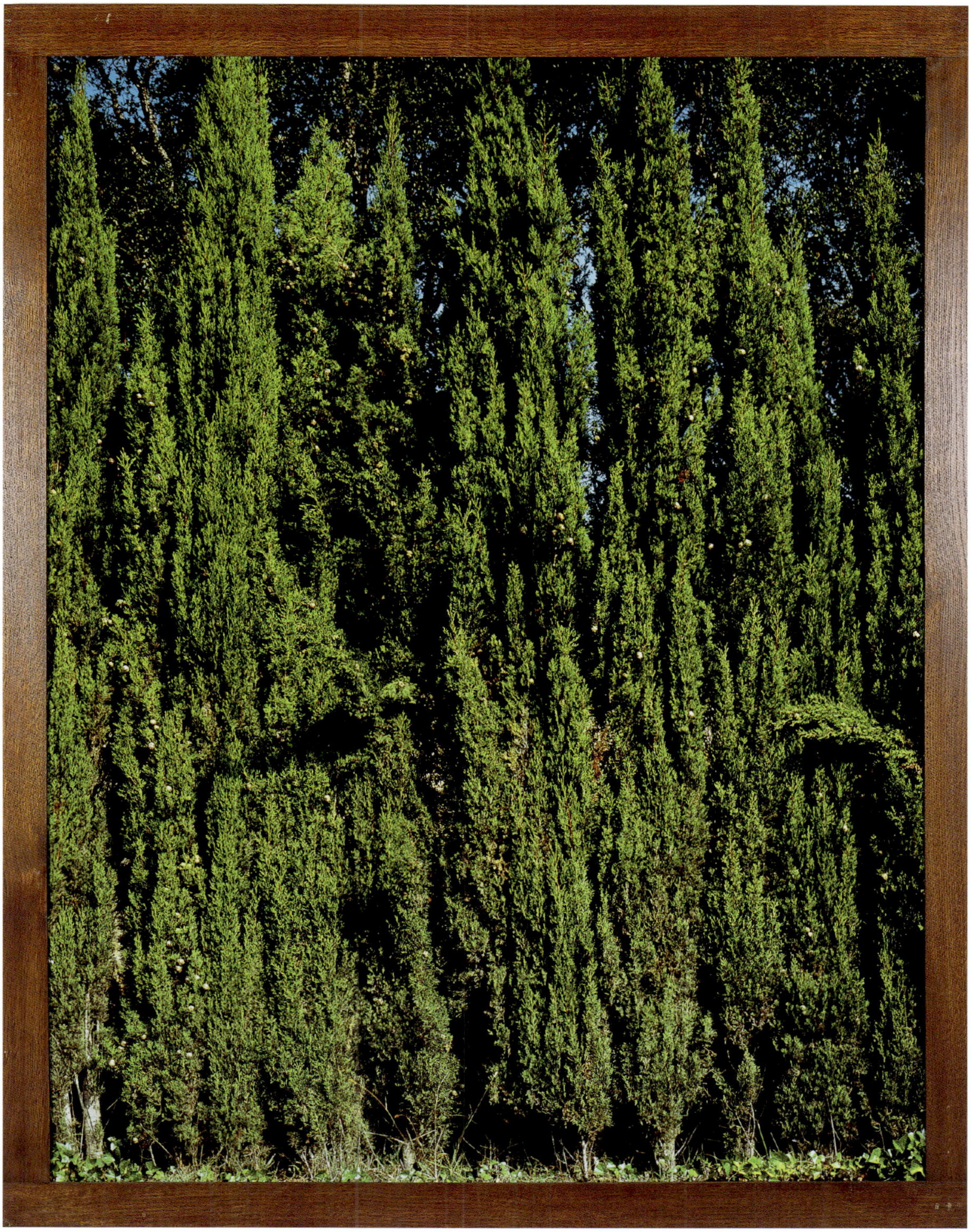

Site II, 1992
Steel, minium paint, wax, 41 x 456 x 430 cm
Matthew Marks Gallery, New York, 1997

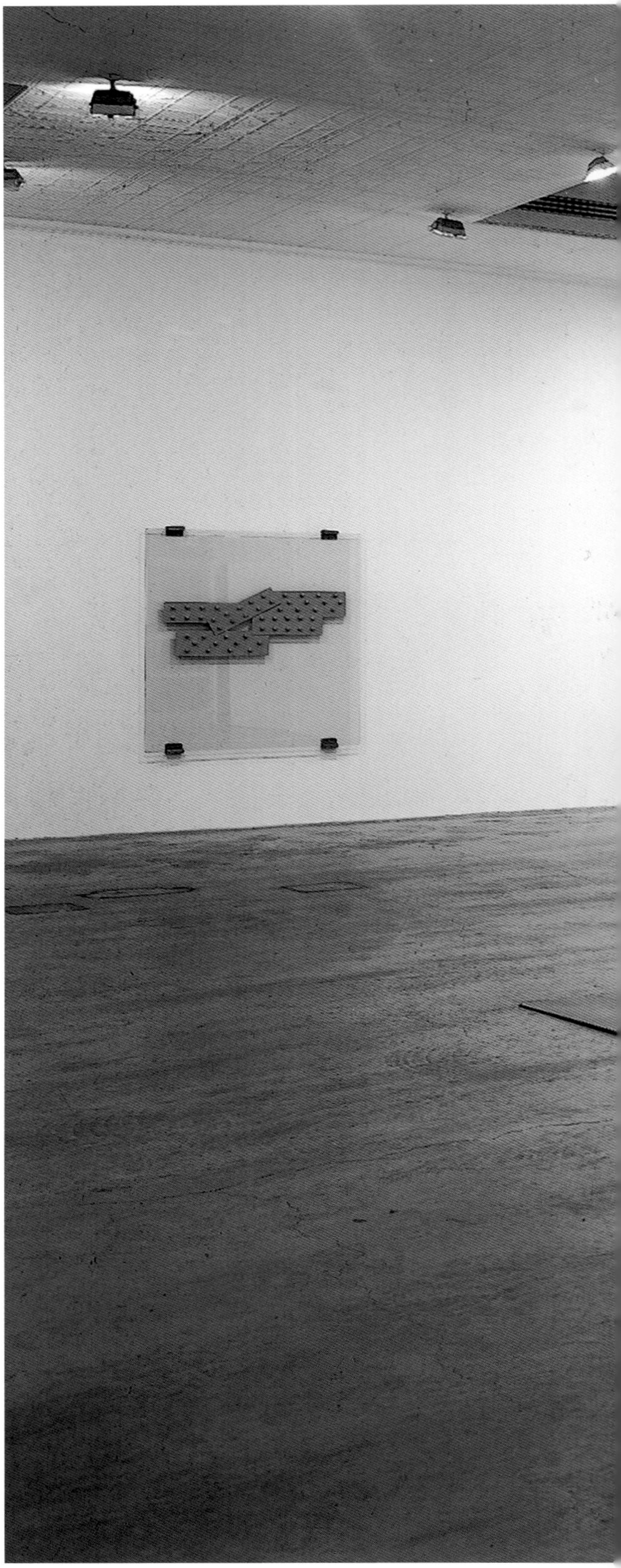

NOTES

1. The status of photography has always provoked Jean-Marc Bustamante. Despite attempts over the last thirty years – his own and others – at challenging its capacities, he is disappointed to concede that it remains a 'poor medium' (conversation with the artist, 2 October 2010).
2. Most of these were taken in the area around Girona, in north-east Spain, where his father had had constructed a modernist villa in the late 1960s.
3. Bustamante points out that the blackboard (*tableau noir*) is our first '*tableau*'. The link is all the clearer in French. Incidentally, Michael Fried, in his recent book on photography (*Why Photography Matters as Art as Never Before*, Yale University Press, New Haven and London, 2008), makes much of the 'grand format' as chosen by Bustamante in terms of the claims it made for photography as art. In a recent email (16 August 2010) the artist too underlines the importance of the 'grand format' in terms of the two-dimensional.
4. Such as acajou.
5. Much of Bustamante's motivation can be understood in terms of a kind of periodisation of his work, starting with a spontaneous gesture that is progressively transformed into a studied result at several removes from the point of departure. This distancing is often effected through shifts in material means.
6. Robert Smithson took 24 Instamatic photographs along the Passaic River, which were published in *Artforum* in December 1967 as *Monuments of Passaic*. The last photograph was *The Sand-Box Monument* (also called *The Desert*) and showed a frame set on a bed of sand. With Bustamante, however, the sand is so fine as to resemble talc and reminds us that sand takes the imprint of animate or inanimate matter, and serves as a mould for a form to be cast. Bustamante's chosen forms of sculpture, at this time anyway, have an affinity with the vocabulary of Minimalism. He makes links with the contemporary interest in qualifying and diverting the Minimalist aesthetic, whether through surface finish, through a relationship with the image (as with Richard Artschwager) or by means of domestic association (as with Robert Gober).
7. *Ouverture* exists in three versions, each one in a wood from a different tree, and in this way there is a kind of transfer between the motif and the frame, the subject and the object.
8. The earliest photograph of the same hedge, in a much less mature state, dates to 1978. The 1991 sequence numbers 22 photos; those included in *Stationnaire* did not include the wall and another set did.
9. Smithson had written, 'This sand pit somehow doubled as an open grave – a grave that children cheerfully play in.' See 'A Tour of the Monuments of Passaic, New Jersey', 1967, in Jack Flam (ed.), *The Collected Writings*, University of California Press, Berkeley and Los Angeles, 1996, p. 74.

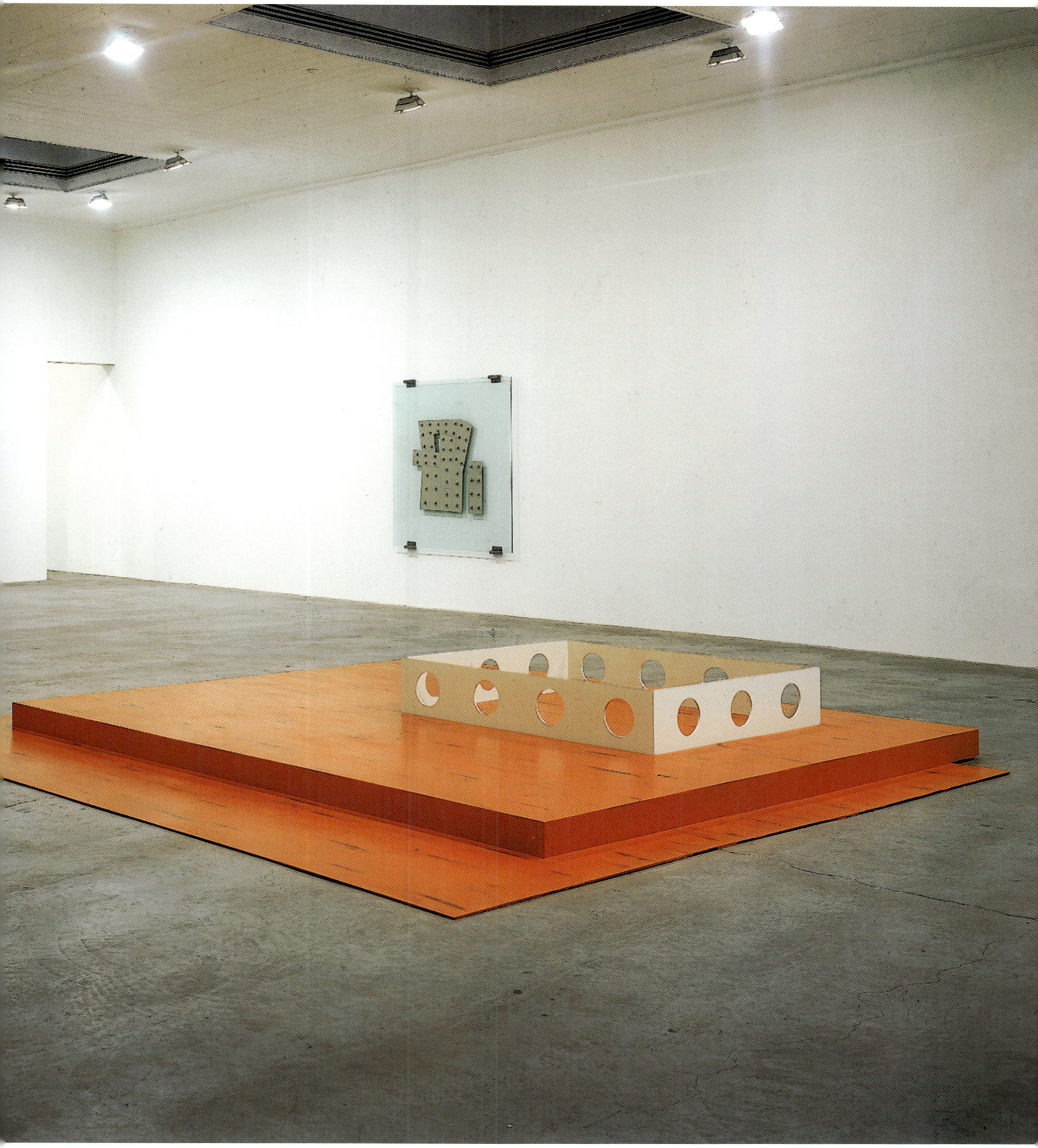

A CURIOUSLY RAPT GESTURE

/

DENYS ZACHAROPOULOS
OTTERLO, 1995

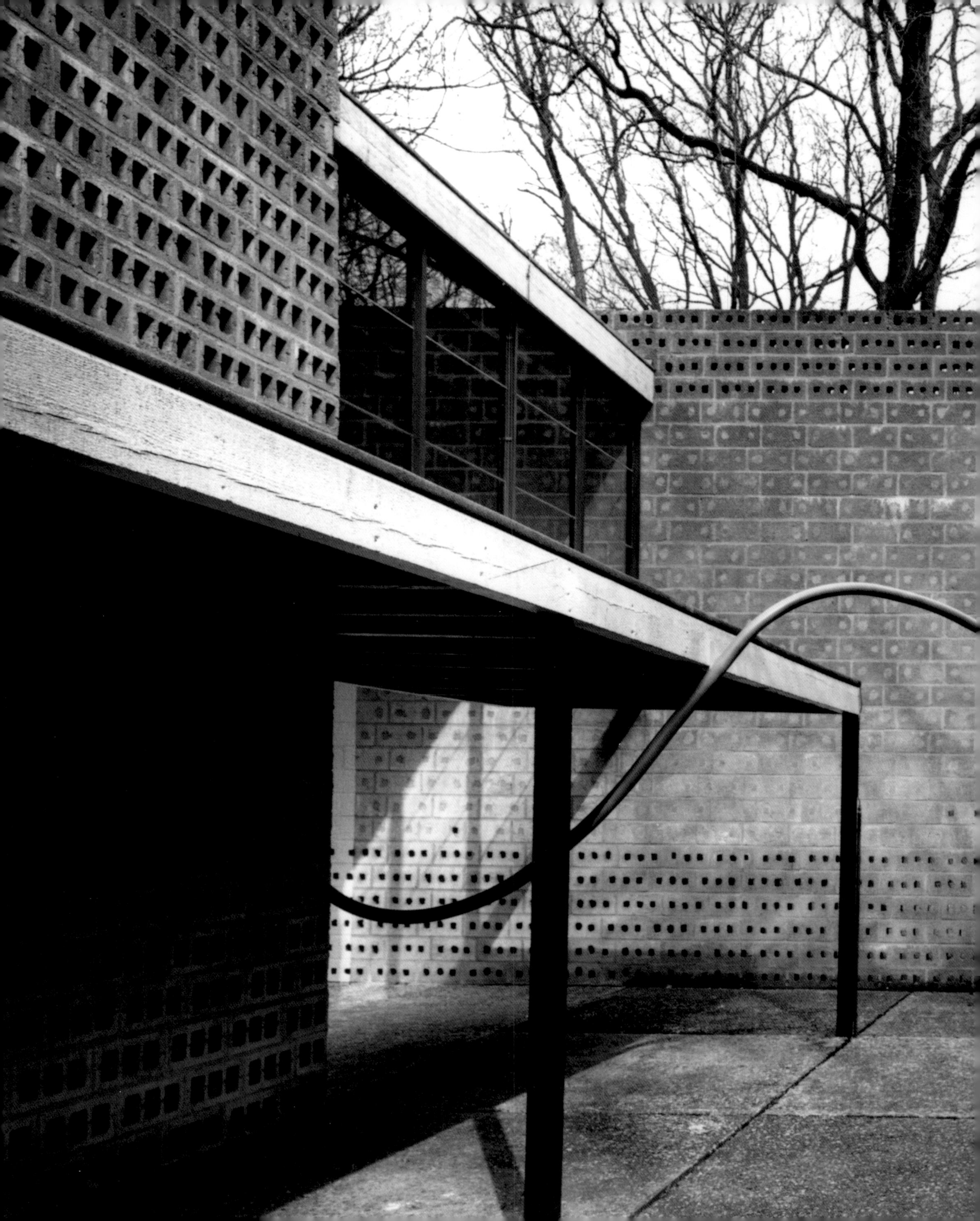

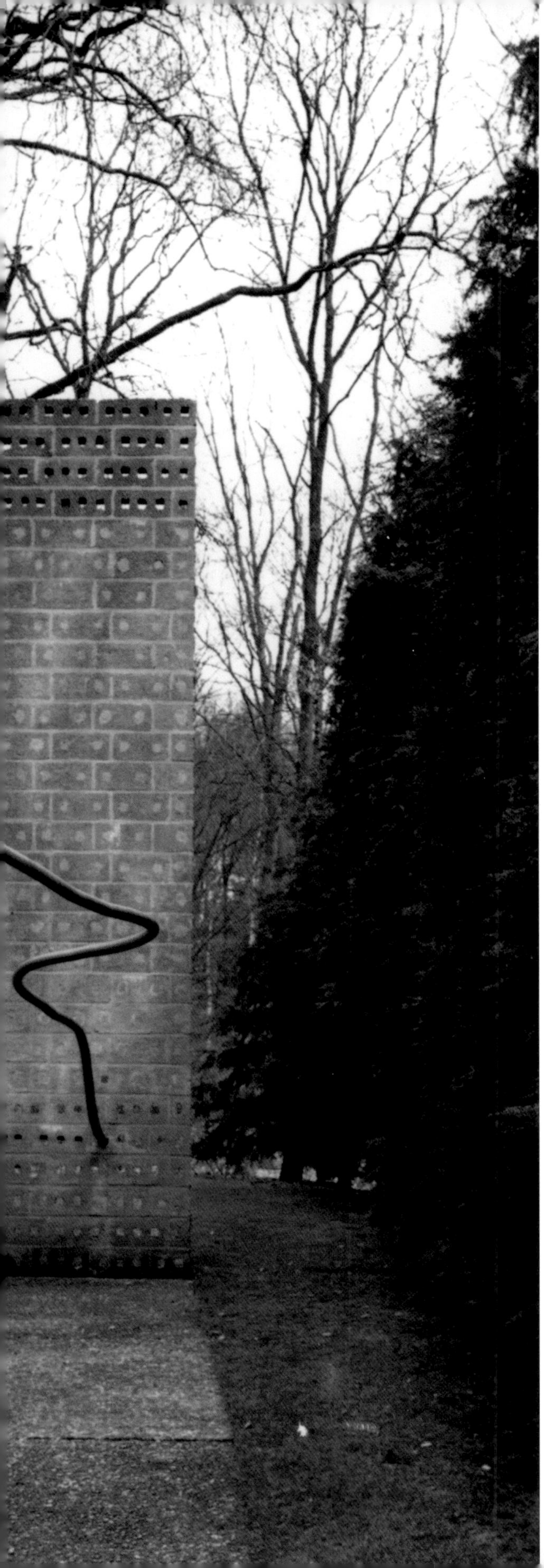

Serena, 1995 (detail)
Vulcanised rubber on steel, 7 x 12000 cm
Kröller-Müller Museum, Otterlo

I

The thing doubled or, to be exact, double of the thing: architecture. Abstract, perfect form, exactly delimiting interior and exterior, to the extent that we would be unable to discern any other division of the division itself. Beside it, we discover only the existence of a separation, defining place with an infinitely fine line that underscores the real as if it were its shadow, dividing it from the thing and from the real. It separates them, the one and the other, by a series of demarcations (concrete covering, frame, glass walls, pillars). The contour of the object imposes its rules on the surrounding world and places itself in front of us, at our feet. What other form could give rise to a project that challenges the light of day the better to absorb the night in the dazzling transparency of its daily being?

For modern architecture is not made for the night. It does not yield to night because it receives it like the most precious present. As a solar form *par excellence*, it affirms its verticality between sky and earth, absorbing and articulating everything that surrounds it. It marks the position of the sun like all those dials that, from Neolithic alignments to church spires, have inscribed time in space, exorcising the shadow that shifts unceasingly from point to line, from the line to the point where it settles, all around, immutable, closed in on itself, dense and impenetrable yet never opaque. Like time, architecture suddenly takes possession of space or, perhaps, with a movement so imperceptibly slow that it escapes all description, partition,

Panorama transfert, 1998
Ink on Plexiglas, 151 x 247 x 4 cm

opposite: *Serena*, 1995
Kröller-Müller Museum, Otterlo

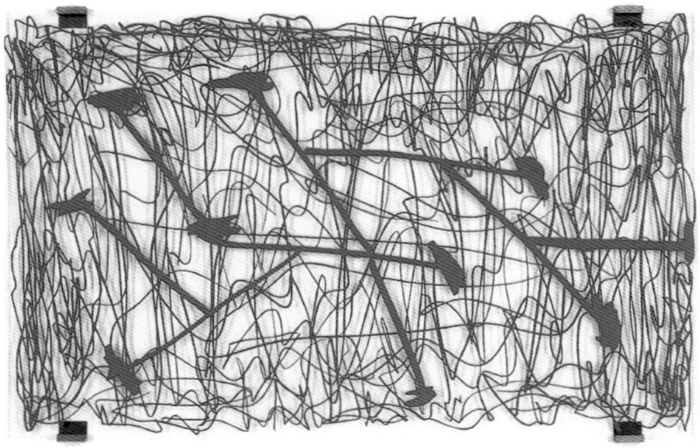

contour or delimitation, so as to be one with matter, with the element of the thing, or rather, with its double, with the thing itself.

The thing towards which we move because it leads us, where we go as if yielding to it as to the thing itself, penetrating to its core. This thing is not the *thing* of phenomenology. It is not that which philosophy dreams of, neither the kernel of reality nor the essence of the real. This thing is *the object already there*: we are already in it, in its inside. We are ourselves the description, the partition, the contour, the delimitation. We are seen through it in the same way as we are see-ers because of it. Our dark and light are already inscribed there. Defined, structured, negotiated between the thing and itself, between itself and the other, between us and ourselves, between ourselves and others: it is separation and division of being and its modes of existence. Thus architecture posits itself as the object that regulates all objects: the object that regulates all distance from the subject, itself and others; the object that regulates all division, all doubling, separation, ordering or classification of the same with regard to the other. Architecture is given thus, reflexive but not reversible, coincident but not compossible, constituent in its relation to the thing, to the real and to place.

The original foundation of architecture – the primordial construction that it contains within itself, or brings with itself (which it proposes in advance of itself as its project and challenge), forms now more than ever, an objectified foundation of metaphysics. If this foundation is objectified it is because, by doubling the place of architectures origin, this constitutes its power *in absentia*. It is more tectonic than physical. It does not belong to the order of that which appears or that which conceals itself; of that which is revealed or veiled; of that which is or is not. It is given with that which posits something or which is posited in lieu of something, which contains or does not, which stands or supports.

Normally reified, architecture is not grasped philosophically: it is not thought, nor does it give rise to or arise from thought. Rather, it is posited anthropologically so that, at the same time as it raises the question of man, it raises the question of its own existential modality and cultural condition, of its proportions and means of experience, of its symbolic systems and meanings – or, sociologically, when it comes to bear on a simple ideological object that redistributes given conditions and systems of production, substituting for every project its realisation.

This kind of construction, and also its realisation, aspire to perfection, in the sense that 'perfecting something' means bringing it to the point of self-saturation, completing it beyond its completion, finishing off its finiteness in its very finality. Beyond all virtuality, all temporality, all reversibility, architectural realisation transcends all memory, any return of the signified. It realises itself against all reversion to the origin, against any return of a provenance, any contingent circumstances or threatening arrival, any resurgence of otherness, any 'disturbing familiarity'.

To preserve nothing of the basis of architecture save the foundation of its power is merely to assemble the parts that enable it to remain standing, that give it its position and ensure its presence. In order to endow the fact of its being with full legitimacy, we must objectify this plenitude

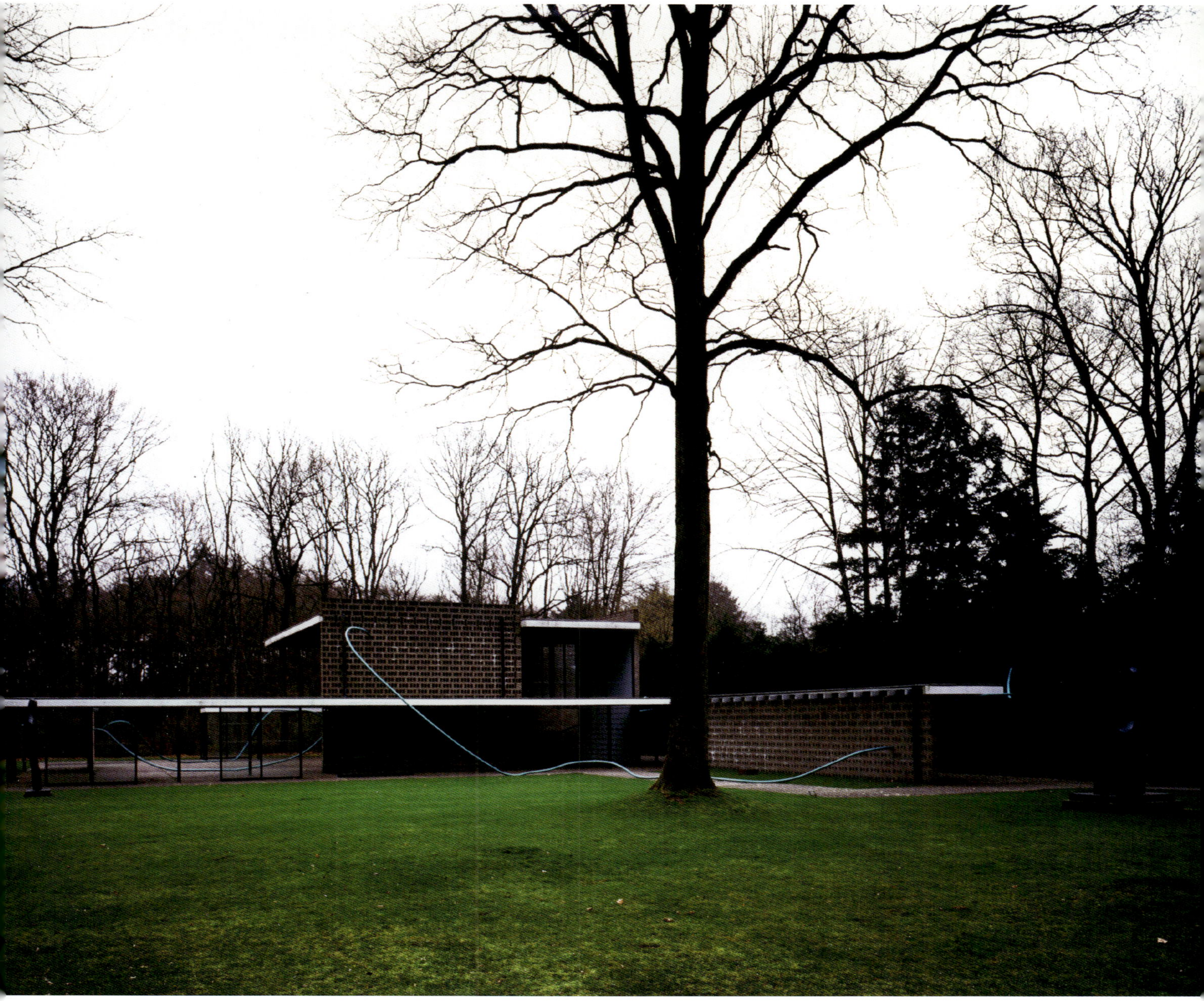

and make it the habitat of which we become the *habitus* but not the inhabitants – forever a stranger to any possibility of *poetically inhabiting the world*. Rather like the owner of a house, we benefit from our possession, are the user of our own property, formed by the combination of house and thing as both place and double of the place: the object placed there containing the given subject, a parcel that gives the present while disguising it, announcing yet enveloping it, offering itself while protecting itself.

Both the Gerrit Rietveld Pavilion and the work of Bustamante perfect and dismantle here the *arkhé* and the *tectonic*, the foundation and the power of this architecture, its *raison d'être* and its first construction, its metaphysical formation and its objectification.

II

> 'Pavilion. 1. a. A tent, chiefly applied to one of a large or stately kind, rising to a peak above. b. A tent as a heraldic bearing. 2. (*fig.*). A canopied litter. (*fig.*) Anything likened to a tent. 3. a. A covering or canopy. b. The velarium or awning of an amphitheatre. 4. A French gold coin. 5. An article of apparel worn by lawyers; a gown or cloak. 6. A light ornamental building or pleasure house, such as those common in parks and public gardens. 7. a. A projecting subdivision of a building or façade distinguished by more elaborate decoration, or by greater height and distinction. b. One of the several detached or semi-detached blocks or buildings into which a hospital is divided. 8. A flag or ensign, esp. the flag carried by a ship to indicate her nationality. 9. The spreading part of the corolla of a flower. 10. The part of a brilliant-cut diamond between the girdle and the collet. 11. a. The pinna or auricle of the ear. b. The fimbriated extremity of a Fallopian tube.' *Oxford English Dictionary*

> 'Pavilion. 1. A building at a sports ground, esp. a cricket pitch, in which players change. 2. A summerhouse or other decorative shelter. 3. A building or temporary structure, esp. one that is open and ornamental, for housing exhibitions. 4. A large ornate tent, esp. one with a peaked top, as used by medieval armies. 5. One of a set of buildings that together form a hospital or other large institution. 6. One of the four main facets on a brilliant-cut stone between the girdle and the culet.' *Collins English Dictionary*

This work began with a project, discussed at length and fully debated, prompting and partaking of the thought of place. It epitomises the active frontier between the nature of law and the actual nature of men and things as they are constituted between horizon and territory, between speech and silence, between memory and history, between experience and necessity, between structure and that which exceeds it.

After multiple detours at all stages of a debate and an enquiry both into the work of Bustamante and into the inventory of differences that contemporary creation has drawn up around the question of place in its relation to art and architecture, subject and landscape, interior and exterior and even between the classical categories of all binary, dialectical or dualist divisions (which may bear the name threshold or bridge, balcony or balustrade, atopia or tomb madness or cell, movable or site-specific, maquette or model, theatre garden or park, kiosk or bunker, standard or vitrine, etc.), the project seems to be summed up in the term 'pavilion' (or, in the French, '*pavillon*').

Clearly, in each of the many definitions, the word 'pavilion' refers to that which makes it possible to envisage an internal organisation of the exterior, a point of rest or mooring before absolute otherness, before – or almost during – the movement beyond the limit, this effect of contiguity at distance which, like an irremediable moment of final vigilance, gives rise to an almost impassable, schematic prehension, before chaos descends, one step away

T.36.80, 1980
C-print, 103 x 130 cm

Serena, 1995 (detail)
Kröller-Müller Museum, Otterlo

from darkness. As if backtracking suddenly while set on a steadfast course, a pavilion appears as a goal which, before it is reached, and independently even of any will to reach it, makes itself felt as if by reverberation so that which is distant feels extremely close, while this proximity is projected outside its constituent body, its founding expanse.

And thus the questions raised by the pavilion embrace its place and role in history and in architecture, in the conception of space and the distribution of power, in the order of representations and in the constitution of place, in the juridical grounds of truth and in the conventions of law, in the inventory of functions and the use of figures, in the organisation of rationality and the distribution of experiences, in the administration of sites and in the foundation and urbanisation of territories, in the totality of conditions that engage sense and signification, in systems of measurement and means of legitimising public space, in the distribution of interiorities and exteriorities, of openings and closures onto the world and things, in the contribution to the implementation of the modalities of presence and absence, and of aesthetic experience.

As a project of war or geography, of sovereignty or topology, of foundation or navigation, of power or constitution, of totality or fragmentation, of poetry or narration, of institution or solidity, of representation or meaning, of law or convention, of unity or discontinuity, of direction or deviation; a pavilion stands on a natural or mental frontier, on a ship or in a park, in a camp or in the countryside, above a bed or between the gaze and the horizon, on the site of an exhibition or in the work of art, on a sheet of paper or in the world. It both gathers and separates, separates and gathers, without adding or removing anything in relation to that of which it engages the participation, vis-à-vis face to face, relation or compossibility.

Considered as a project, a pavilion gives rise to a curve that is taut or slack, depending on mentalities and epochs, traversing the times and places of history, the events and conjunctures of meaning, the outcrops and structures of

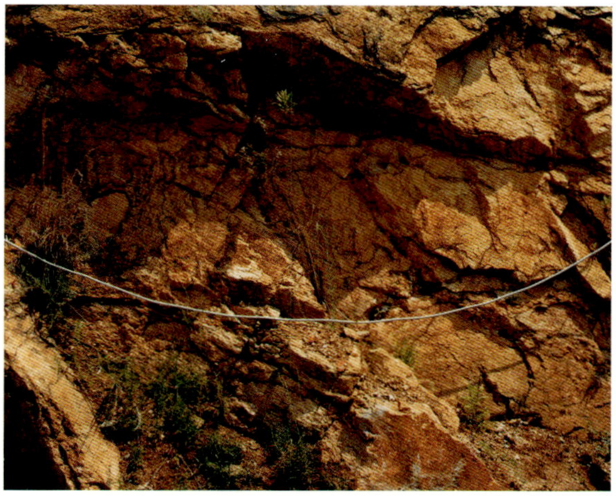

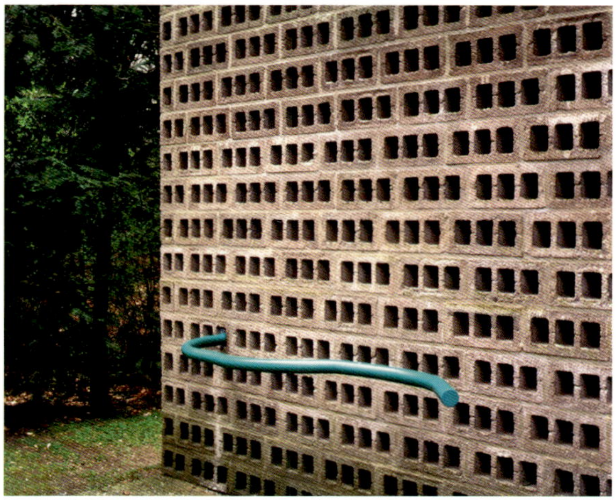

constructions, the passages and massifs of formations. It passes through everything that teems in the distance, with a gesture of reverence and prehension implied in the very word 'project': to throw forth, a jetty set forward of something as if leaving the self, throwing oneself before oneself. To *project* oneself, to throw oneself suddenly between as one might plunge into the water, as one throws oneself not *towards* the other but *at* the other, *at* the otherness, *at* what is not nothing, *at* what *is there*.

Because what *is there* is inaccessible 'for itself' and is unthinkable as a thing 'in itself', and yet it is given between the being of the thing and the thing of being, simultaneously taut and slack, thrown or projected there in the one place where neither you nor I, neither angel nor beast, neither master nor slave – *nothing among things* – could exist. Place without the possibility of foundation, where beings and things throw and project themselves, and where beings and things come from and are given, neither among us nor among themselves, but among others, between-times and between two places, for *there is* being: two infinities, two unthought-of things, two origins – neither double, nor dialectical, but reversible.

III

On a sheet of paper, Theo van Doesburg sketches a pure form, a perfect measure of intensity and extent. On another sheet of paper, Mies van der Rohe projects the structure of a pavilion, that same measure now relating the four corners inside to whatever may surround and open up around it. In a park, Gerrit Rietveld chooses building materials and erects a pavilion which, in a series of relationships, doubles measure, angles and openings, movements and pauses, interiorities and their constantly renewed projections. Between the structures of this same pavilion, sculptures form the lines of demarcation, the partitions, contours and delimitations of volumes between interior and exterior, between structure and what exceeds it, between the site and the element of living, between matter and its double. A brief history without apparent detour or anticipated surprises: drawing, project, realisation, architecture, enclosure of a place, of a collection of work of art – a date that becomes an epoch, an epoch that becomes a monument, a monument that becomes an institution. History is too linear to be equal to the analysis, to resist, for the time it has to withstand. Time. The time of those who worked to make it possible. The time that measured waiting, both day and night, through all those decades the time like all that teems in the distance, while remaining present precisely under each footstep, over each head – a double foundation *in absentia*.

For many years, this expectation was the very incarnation of the prevailing idea of art and architecture, of collections and of museums, like sleeping beauty in her purest virtuality, like this haunted territory inhabited within by the work of art in its contemplative sovereignty, in a distance enveloping all surrounding reality, in its own being, which, like a work closed in on itself, warm-hearted like a body, upright and vertical in its measure and weight, stands suspended in space and keeps us from falling. Idea whose foundation and *arkhé* partake of the same strain that persists up to the teeming of modernity, to its classical or even Greek constituent, whose uncompromising directness and inexorable verticality link Phidias, Thorvaldsen and Theo van Doesburg, Callicrates, Gottfried Semper and Mies van der Rohe.

This waiting was also our virtue and our impossibility until the moment when a familiar and curiously rapt gesture removed the film formed by things between themselves. Out of a mental image, this film produced by memory issues out of itself, like a sheet round the edge of a sleeping body, keeping out the disquieting absence from itself and the other. Its being, which is neither here nor elsewhere, on a single demarcation line, is registered like a musical motif or a thought, whose gesture, addressed to the person waiting, marks out a place with a single movement, as if casting a die, so transforming contingency into chance, abstraction into necessity, the project into a form of life, into its being-there.

Bustamante began exploring this exteriority on the edge of the urban space long ago, in the first photographic works of the 1970s. There where space tautens and slackens before extending, where, as with the first step out of bounds, the subject awaits a horizon and has lost its centre of gravity, outside the walls, in the situation of the pavilion – both pleasure house and guard post, guarding the frontier post and insomniac vigilance at the furthest extremity of what makes a body, what makes a *one*. From

Törless, 2008
Steel, painted steel, lead, 500 x 650 x 140 cm
Le Grand Tour, Musée des Arts Contemporains, Site du Grand-Hornu, 2008

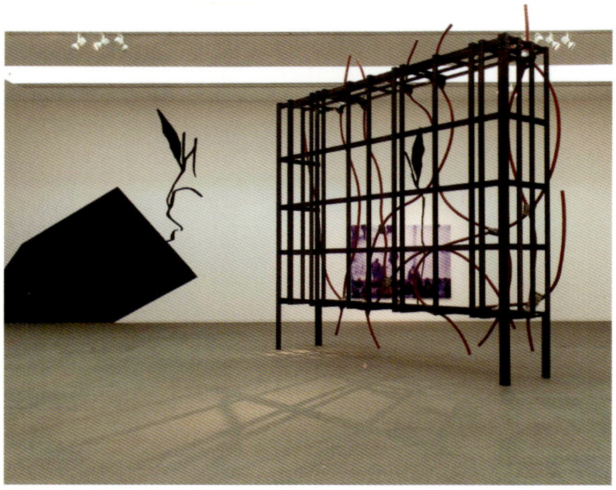

this place indicated only by movement, the subject stretches as if waking from sleep, doubling itself in this excursion from self which is not yet the other and no longer the same, but an active in-between – a free port or neutral zone, to use the terms of customs or the army. It is like the stretch of sea between two ships, the element that defines place yet belongs to no one, even if the person who traverses it retains the marks and rights of his identity, of his attachments. The law of the sea against the law of the land. Bustamante takes literally this perfect measure of the virtual liberty for self-determination of things and what links them together. Liquid element, movement and memory merging like high and low water on the banks or bed of a river. Water and dreams rise with the night to shed another light on that which the verticality of the day holds upright, balanced and contained. The landscape proclaims itself the liberator of this overflowing. Time informs space and forms experience. What is contained opens to what contains. In these terms the exterior is form. The vast form of the infinite, where the teeming profusion of what exists repeats itself beyond that which denotes it. Indescribable, the exterior offers itself to being as the very element of its original nature – not reflection but thought, not effect but cause. It is the stuff of all that appears in a nature not naturalist but without degrees, like the Greek *physis*, of a difference that cannot be measured or codified, that is not postulated (*thesis*) but is given as the very element of the living, not that which identifies it but that which unceasingly differentiates it.

If the house is the expression of a certain content, the pavilion becomes the unhoped-for container of the dweller in the world. Like a street corner or forest clearing, the pavilion belongs to the meeting between interior and exterior, day and night. And this pavilion is not the project of the architect – for this, a single one of the various definitions offered by dictionaries, histories and cultures would suffice – but its realisation in the strongest sense of the word, as the work by Bustamante has shown. It is no longer a question of a simple building term but of a range of possibilities offered by the idea of construction, along with that which constantly differentiates them: that which projects it irreversibly outside itself, which is given with the otherness particular to it between its fractal being and the profusion of its existences, that which makes it ceaselessly *exist* – come forward, be outside itself, ahead of itself, in its momentum and its project, but also in its loss, in its danger, its slippage, in its rejection. Devoid of romanticism, this pavilion has nothing of a ruin, nothing of that which forgets itself or endures, nothing ecstatic or ironic. It is neither the one nor the other, nor even a regulated in-between between the one to the other – neither moment, nor twilight, nor excursion. It is a mathematical catastrophe, biological attrition, in the vast time where infinitesimal space is measured against the time of light. On the edge of the abyss, this pavilion, as it is exposed to the project of *dwelling poetically in the world*, exists as a suspension, a *mise en abyme*.

If classical sculpture was the art of setting the body in motion and space, the art of Bustamante suspends both movement and space, and projects them to the infinity of their differentiated and differential being. Neither sign nor symbol, this line in which the corrosion of metal, the liquid

Serena, 1995 (detail)
Kröller-Müller Museum, Otterlo

opposite: Jean-Marc Bustamante and Denys Zacharopoulos during the installation of *Serena*, 1995

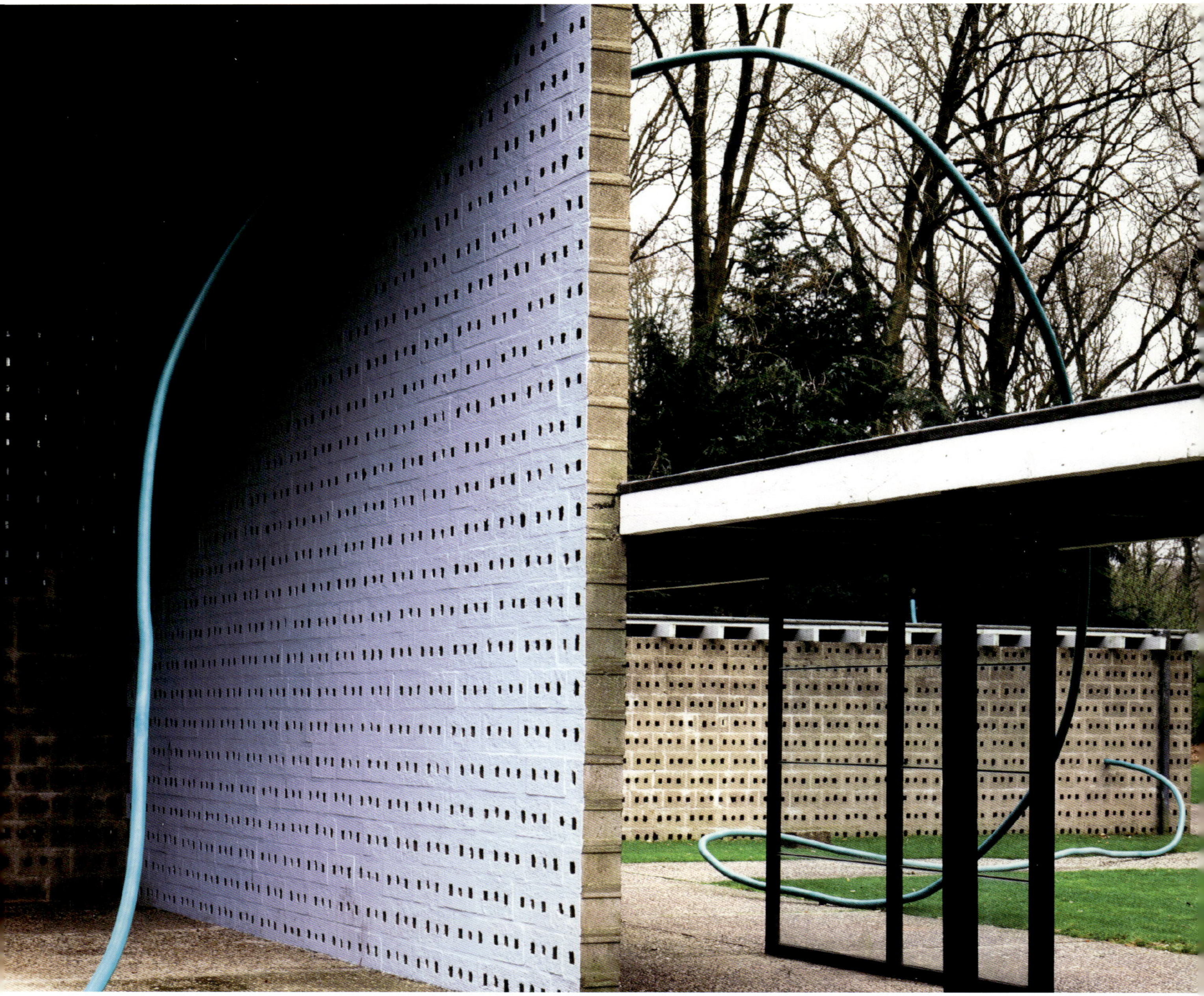

density of rubber, the absorption of colour, the continuous projection towards the end of all elevation, the oblique crossing are constantly displaced towards the point where all regimes of meaning are suspended, where silence and weightlessness become the mode of existence, the dimension of the work, make this index the element most appropriate to the world *poetically inhabited*. From *Inventaire* (1989) to *Ottoneum Garden* at Documenta IX, 1992, Bustamante had already begun to displace structure towards its excess. He has transformed the classificatory isomorphism of analogous terms – sets of shelves, mirrors – into a differential allomorphism in which every process was annulled before the infinite transformation of conditions of possibility that were far too complex and vigorous to make do with any single register. Already, in this work, one could say with the disarming simplicity of a Jean Rostand, that 'theories come and go, the frog remains': a statement of the generous failure of all ideological abstraction, of all lexicographic selection of a degree sufficient for experience, for the grasp of theory. As if there were no longer any means of seeing without at the same time being seen – by whom? By what? 'Guess!' as Blaise Pascal would have said.

Just as one slips between two pages of the same book, between the two sheets of the same bed, between the two bodies of the same half-light, so we meet between this double ex-: that of our ex-istence and of what ex-ists, the double exteriority of self and the thing. Double infinity of what is not yet other and is no longer the same. This ex-, like a pavilion facing the final edge of the expanse that carries and contains it, is already an address. Not an address *where*, but *addressing* the other: a place where the classical notion of place as topos is not a-topian but ek-topian. Ek-topism is what a body displaces from place, what is moved by its passage as in the case of immersed bodies, vessels defined in terms of the amount of water they displace, forming a complex relation between volumetry and movement, what is immersed and what is above water. This ek-topia measures fullness by the void it creates, the container by the removal of contents that in turn become

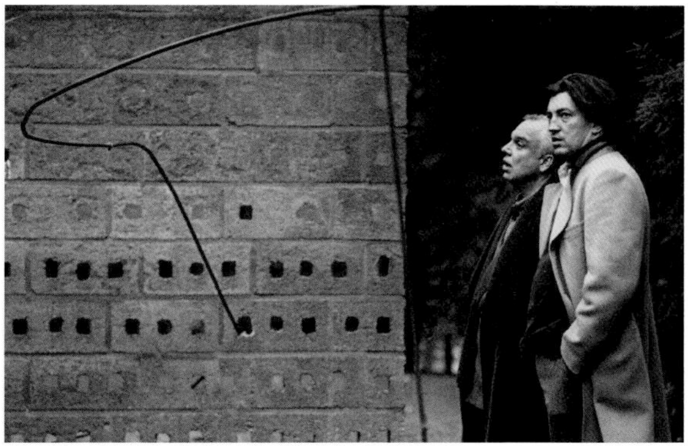

container, presence by what it makes absent. In the same way, the work by Bustamante in the Rietveld Pavilion in the park of the Kröller-Müller Museum sets in motion, along with all its concomitants, a constantly proclaimed otherness: the *in absentia* address of a constituted power, of structure and what exceeds it, of architecture and that which contains it, of the institution in the time of experience, and of the profusion of the world and the floating of sense, and of law and liberty that makes it virtual. In this infinite reversibility, art and architecture are situated on two sides of the same river, not like a bridge, but like that which bears on one side the rising water and on the other the river bed, where this fabric 'rising to a peak', this 'canopied litter', is today taut and slack between sky and earth, or rather between the infinite universe and the untenanted orbit of its possibility, its condition.

Dismantling the foundation of its power and the objectification of its metaphysics, Gerrit Rietveld's pavilion and Bustamante's sculpture have captured the project and origin of this *arkhé* and its *tectonics* with a curiously rapt gesture and a movement of reverence.

Translated from the French 'Un geste étrangement ému', in
Jean-Marc Bustamante: Serena, *Kröller-Müller Museum, Otterlo, 1995.*
Translated by Donald Gardner.

LA MAISON CLOSE

/

MARIANNE LE POMMERÉ
PARIS, 2001

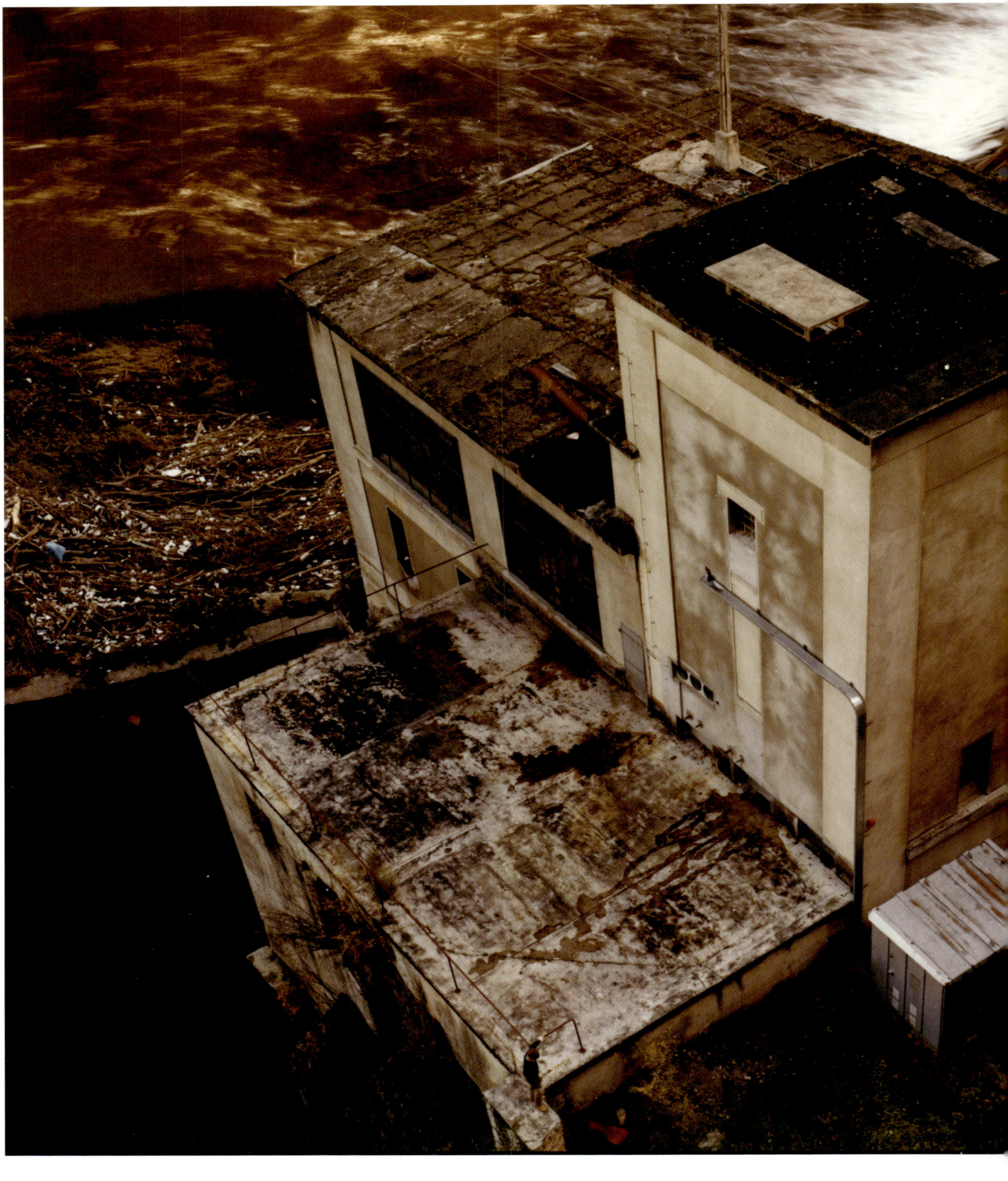

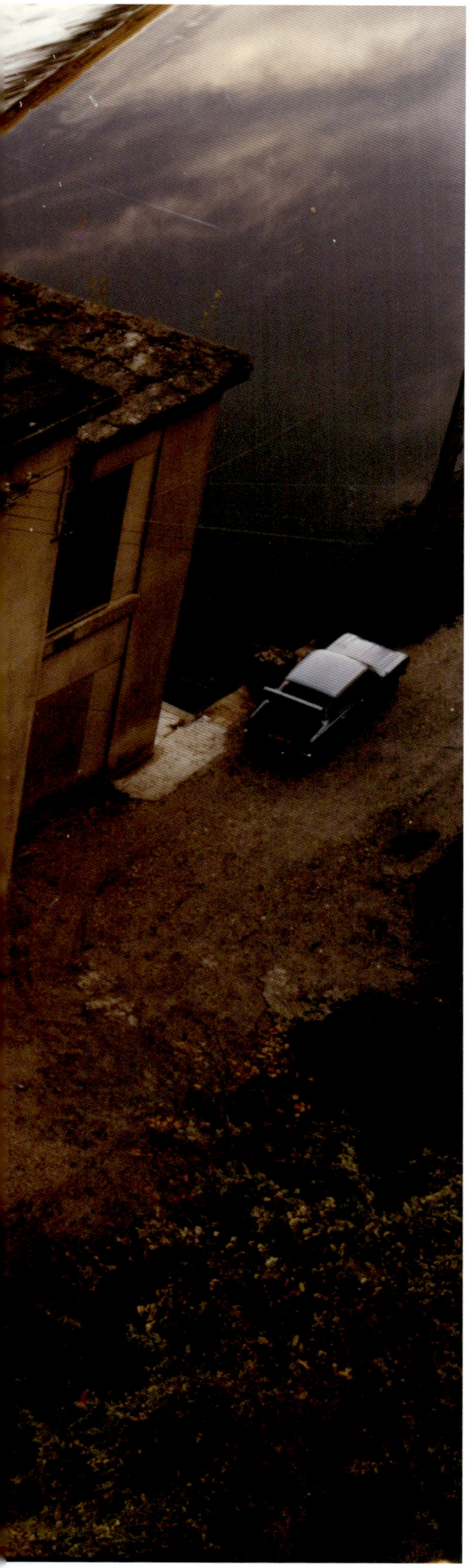

T.52.81, 1981
C-print, 103 x 130 cm

'A third table, smaller still, held a Swedish lamp and a typewriter with a waxed cloth cover. At the back there was a narrow bed with an ultramarine velvet spread covered with multicoloured cushions'.[1]

A visit to Georges Perec's house of 'dreams' is perhaps the best introduction to the construction *La Maison close* made by Jean-Marc Bustamante on the edge of the rue de Saint-Amand, as part of the redevelopment of the tramway in Orléans in 2000.

This construction takes the form of a little dwelling – a villa – which is a parallelepipedal volume measuring 3.75 metres high by 8 metres long, raised on 3 metre *pilotis* over a volume fairly square in plan. It has two functional elements: a simple chimney-stack and a balcony on the façade. There is a large frosted glass wall at the back of the balcony, which has a balustrade made of a beautiful white stone.

The minimalism of the volumes, the sophisticated finish given by the smooth stone, the economic relationship between the materials and colours determine the style: that of 1920s avant garde. Le Corbusier's housing at Pessac would come to mind, if a guardrail had been added, like the modifications carried out by the first occupants of the workers' estate. The planting, on a patch of ground edged by a wood, is conceived in a cultivated spirit, with stones and plants making reference to Japanese gardens. The system of thought into which Bustamante's

left: *S.i.M.1.01*, 2001
C-print, 40 x 60 cm

right: *S.i.M.2.99*, 1999
C-print, 40 x 60 cm

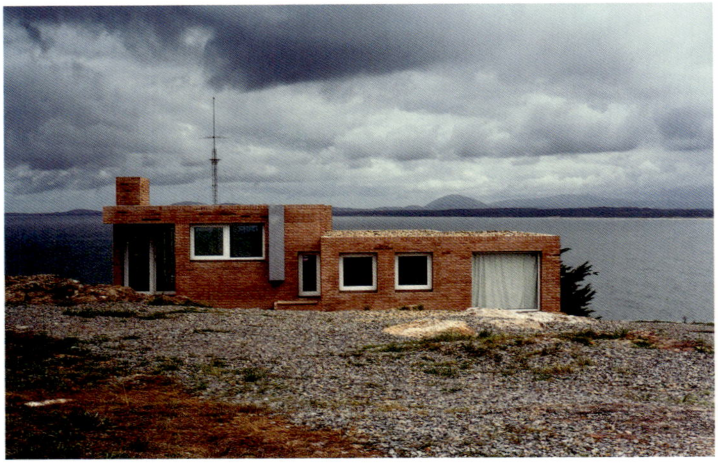

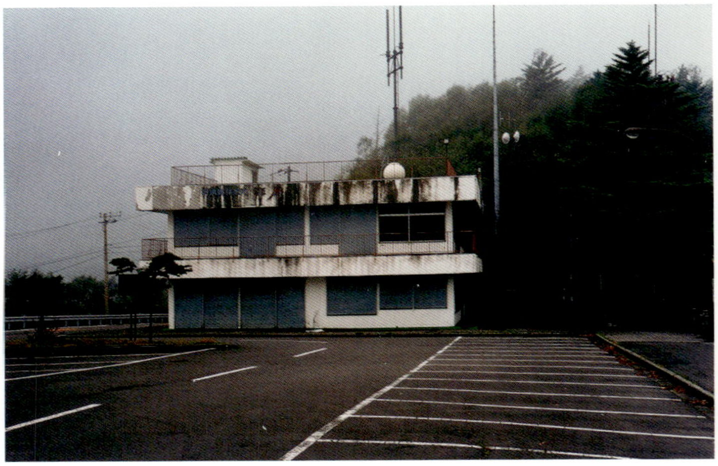

house is set may not be decoded without taking into account the urban environment by which it is framed. Orléans' university campus, like all new places of this kind, is essentially made up of large buildings. Both the avenue that crosses the campus and the rue de Saint-Amand itself carry lots of traffic, which is increased by the regular passing of the tram. The house of Bustamante cannot but appear unusual in such a context.

One is reminded of Robert Musil's description of the house of *Der Mann ohne Eigenschaften* (*The Man without Qualities*, 1930–42), which sprang up in the suburbs at the end of the long, sinuous arteries that wound round the outskirts of the town: '... partly protected, a garden from the eighteenth or even the seventeenth century; passing through the wrought iron gate, one could see through the trees, on a well-tended lawn, something like a little château – a hunting pavilion or a folly from an earlier time.'[2]

Bustamante's house, small in scale, disorientated, stylistically dislocated, is as much of an enigma as the house of *The Man without Qualities*. It has the same 'sense of being a photographic double exposure'[3]: a collage, in itself and in relation to its surroundings.

On approach, the viewer realises that Bustamante's house is completely impenetrable. In the evening, a light comes on. An electronic system is programmed so that the frosted door lights up at a time that cannot be predicted in advance: the closed house becomes a house of light, a living, autonomous organism with a heart that beats.

And yet nothing may be seen of the inside. Unlike the surrealist dream of André Breton, it is a house with a secret, completely private, totally opaque. Unlike collective housing, it retains its rights to privacy, to modesty. When the light comes on, the opalescent door becomes for the waiting visitor a virtual frontier, a gateway to dreams.

In contrast, and particularly by daylight – the balcony. Ornate, emphatic, immodest, slightly ridiculous, its projection creates an imbalance. The house becomes uncertain all of a sudden.

Bustamante likes architecture. Whether in Otterlo in 1995, when he was invited to make an exhibition in the Rietveld Pavilion,[4] or in 1990 in Krefeld in the Museum Haus Lange built by Ludwig Mies van der Rohe, the works he made and the way he installed them bear witness to this love. At Krefeld, he privileged 'the presence of this house, emphasising its presence by the way the sculptures were installed'.[5] Thus *Intérieur I* (1988; p. 47), a slightly elevated large platform, was installed opposite a picture window: covered in a network of lines, it was at once a picture and a landscape, from which the geometry sprang from that of the place, like a window open to the landscape it frames. Between *Intérieur I* and the window, Bustamante proposed a melodic continuity, a game of echoes.

Bustamante's photographs bear the strongest witness to his fascination with architecture. His earliest works, and most notably the series of very large colour photographs begun in 1978, show 'wastelands, transitional spaces, the edges of towns, unstable places' and endeavour to 'bear witness to a particular quality of photography, which is not about freezing a rapid movement, but a slow movement, that of the earth, but also that of decivilisation'.[6]

Soon designated uniformly as *Tableaux* (*Pictures*) and displayed on the wall as such, these works are differentiated by the date on which they were taken. They show plain dwellings, ground dug up for foundations, cut across with the traces of machinery, building materials scattered all around, stationary vehicles, the sky, sparse vegetation.

Several themes emerge within the series: the passage, in intermediary places, between nature – more or less wild – and the built environment;

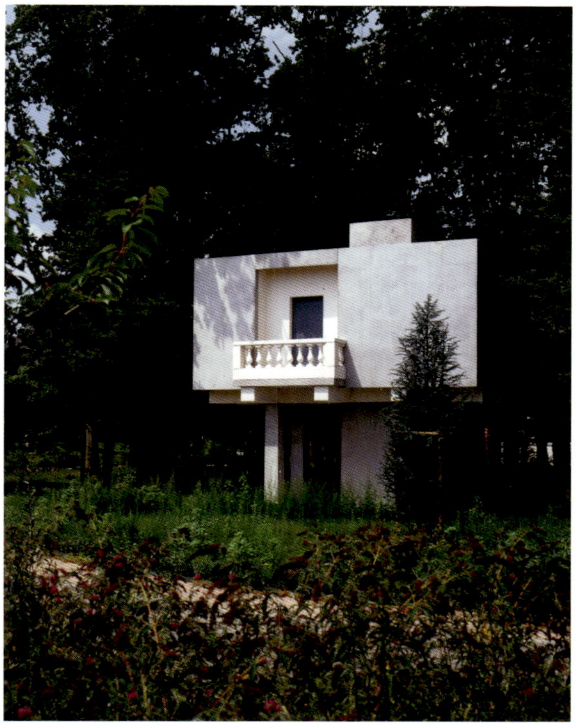

La Maison close, 2000
Cement, glass, light system

the development of living spaces and of architecture. The angle of view is always the same, with the camera at eye level, with no intervention made at the negative stage, nor any retouching. The force of these images come from the fact that they express neither a political nor sociological opinion, but rather a willingness to see certain aspects of reality in a specific language and a plastic form. As Marius De Zayas declared: 'The photograph is not expressive but true.'[7]

Critics have not stressed enough how the glazing within the frame allows a whole range of values to be exploited; the precision of the printing and, as a result, the sharp definition of the image; the style given by the distance the photographer takes from his subject; the seductive clarity of the colours rendered abstract by the medium, which in itself makes them works to be pondered.

From *T.17.79* (1979; pp. 20–21) to *T.45.82* (1982; p. 30)[8] there is the same resonant glow of ochres and siennas, of the Mediterranean light. If Bustamante is a conceptual artist, he is also a landscape painter as attached to the countryside of the South as Caspar David Friedrich was to the shores of the Baltic. 'For me, these landscapes are not banal at all. I love the light, the colours, and I try to make the objects radiant.'[9]

The *Tableaux* are themselves radiating objects, characterised by precise drawing and a clear light that reveals a multiplicity of forms, with intense colours. The realism of their image acquires through these formal qualities a subjective value that gives them a new objectivity. As such, Bustamante's *Tableaux* are objects of melancholy.

The *Lumières*, begun in 1987, bear further witness to this melancholy. They are black-and-white photographs, found in architectural books and magazines, screen printed onto Plexiglas so that the exhibition wall reveals and redoubles them through projection. They all show the eruption of light, whether natural or artificial. Bustamante has rediscovered through making them the art of painting shadows,[10] which, as the history of his production has shown, he has used for meditative and serious work. The work of René Magritte comes to mind. There is in Bustamante's work, as there is in the Belgian artist's, a fascination for 'the empire of light'. Magritte represented many times 'a landscape seen by night under a daylight sky. The landscape evokes the night, and the sky the day.'[11] It is just this type of poetic surprise that animates the *Lumières*. One example in the series also suggests a parallel with Georges Seurat's *La Parade*, (1888) with its lamps, its pure, stylised silhouettes, and its spatial construction, which evokes the solitude of the man in a fairground in the painting.

The genesis of the Orléans house may be found in these photographs: 'without qualities', commonplace and very human. The house gives to architecture that which the imagination might give form to in a dream – with its superb isolation, incarceration even, the absolute purity of its forms and the tonal rupture of its balustrade which undermines its ideal architectural beauty. Bustamante has situated it outside questions of taste: his house has sufficient irony for the questions it poses – in terms of forms of dwelling and the relation of the individual to others – to rob us of our certainties.

Repeatedly, Bustamante has declared: 'I do not want to produce new images, nor create new forms. The work must not order things, but rather make a new situation. It must above all bear witness to the existence of the viewer, who is themselves responsible for the relationship they have with it.'[12] But the questions posed by Bustamante's house arise primarily from the ambiguity of its form, and the way its form sits in space: it is a work of sculpture and not of architecture. Its ironic dysfunction – irritating, provoking even – force one to ask what makes it art, and wonder how else it might be defined. The answer to these questions would also be the answer to the sociological questions posed by the work of Bustamante.'

Bustamante's house in Orléans is a commissioned work, the programme which Serge Lemoine discusses in his introduction to the publication *L'Art Dans le Paysage du Tramway d'Orléans*, (2001). It consisted of inviting a sculptor to make a public work in response to a predetermined, formal and literary theme, that of ' a workshop'.

Bustamante thinks that his art does not allow him to make stand-alone public sculpture. In 1992 he declared:

> 'I think that the artist can work by immersing himself more in his urban surroundings. [...] Passers-by are not necessarily art lovers. They are merely going from one place to another. I would like the intervention of the artist to be both discrete and restrained, but also decisive in terms of perception.'[13]

Totally embedded in the campus environment, Bustamante's house imposes nothing: the enigma of its presence might easily go unnoticed. One cannot compare it with work by Daniel Buren or Richard Serra, which aims to reveal an existing order or impose a new one.[14] As an artist, Bustamante refuses to be progressive – an attitude and a plan that he considers naïve.

Once again, it seems appropriate to return to the description of the house of *The Man without Qualities*: ' [...] one could not help stopping in front of it with an "oh!". And when this small, white, gracious thing had its windows open, one's gaze penetrated a distinguished silence like that of the rooms of an academic, the walls carpeted with books.'[15] A folly, therefore, because enclosed within all this sweetshop prettiness and sense of the outdated, lies the study of a university professor.

There is a monumental public fountain in Paris that, because of its intelligent approach and the legend it tells, fascinates Bustamante: the *Fontaine des Innocents* (1547–50) which partly inspired the Orléans house. It should be remembered that, first and foremost, the monument was a workshop that was on the route of Henri II's solemn entry into Paris on 16 June 1549. It was a solid construction, set on a corner, with two arches facing onto the rue aux Fers (today the rue Berger) and one facing onto the rue Saint-Denis. Above the arches was a loggia. In the eighteenth century Quatremère de Quincy saved it from destruction and made it symmetrical, with four arches, allowing it to be installed in its present position in the centre of the Place Joachim du Bellay. Research into the iconographic programme of the relief carvings, and the possible presence of Diane de Poitiers among the dignitaries in the loggia during the royal entry into Paris,[16] have given credence to a legend according to which the fountain would have concealed a love chamber, hidden in the closed part of the edifice above the loggia, accessible through a door in one of the pillars. It is this legend – a little inappropriate for a monument dedicated to the 'innocents', the children killed by Herod in the Old Testament story – which gave Bustamante the pleasant and slightly surrealist idea for a 'closed' house (*maison close* is an antiquated French term for a brothel), equipped with a little welcoming light. Here, albeit in a minor key, one of the great themes of urban utopia is played out. Did not Claude-Nicolas Ledoux, in the Royal Saltworks of Arc-et-Senans, an eighteenth-century monument to the ideology of happiness, construct a pleasure pavilion?

Bustamante's *La Maison close*, a house that mingles both fantasy and gravity, and is yet very human, is a work of desire.

Translated from the French 'La Maison Close', in L'Art Dans le Paysage du Tramway d'Orléans, *Réunion des Musées Nationaux, Paris, 2001. Translated by Fiona Bradley.*

La Maison close, 2000
Cement, glass, light system

NOTES

1. Georges Perec, *Les Choses*, Gallimard, Paris, 1965.
2. Robert Musil, *Der Mann ohne Eigenschaften (The Man without Qualities)*, (1930–42) (trans S. Wilkins and B. Pike), Knopf, New York, 1995.
3. Ibid.
4. Gerrit Rietveld created the pavilion in 1955 for an international sculpture exhibition in Sonsbeek Park, Arnhem. In 1965 it was reconstructed in the sculpture garden of the Kröller-Müller Museum in Otterlo.
5. 'Fragments of an interview: Jean-Marc Bustamante, Jan Debbaut and Yves Gevaert', in *Jean-Marc Bustamante*, Van Abbemuseum, Eindhoven, 1993, pp. 10–11.
6. See the catalogue to the exhibition *Jean-Marc Bustamante: Lent Retour*, Jeu de Paume, Paris, 1996, p. 12.
7. Marius De Zayas, 'Photography', in *Camera Work*, no. 41, January 1913, p. 17.
8. Reproduced in the beautiful exhibition catalogue *Jean-Marc Bustamante: Tableaux 1978–1982*, Musée départemental d'art contemporain de Rochechouart, Rochechouart , FRAC Languedoc-Roussillon and Kunsthalle Bern, 1994, p. 69 and p. 73.
9. Jean-Marc Bustamante in *Jean-Marc Bustamante: Lent Retour*, op. cit., p. 25.
10. As Jean-Pierre Criqui has observed in his 'Bustamante photographe (notes pour un portrait inachevé',in *Jean-Marc Bustamante: Oeuvres Photographiques 1978–1999*, Centre National de la Photographie, Paris, 1999, p. 13. See pp. 18–37 of this publication.
11. Quoted in Harry Torczyner, *René Magritte: Signes et Images*, Draeger, Paris, 1977, p. 177.
12. 'Fragments of an interview', op. cit., p. 11.
13. Ibid., p. 16.
14. See, for example, Buren's installations in the Place des Terreaux, Lyon, and the forecourt of the Palais Royal, Paris, and Richard Serra's *Clara Clara*, 1983, in the Jardin des Tuileries, Paris.
15. Robert Musil, op. cit.
16. See Naomi Miller, 'The Form and Meaning of the Fontaine des Innocents', in *The Art Bulletin*, vol. L, March 1968, p. 270. She shows how the series of nymphs sculpted by Jean Goujon puts into relationship the forms of beauty and love.

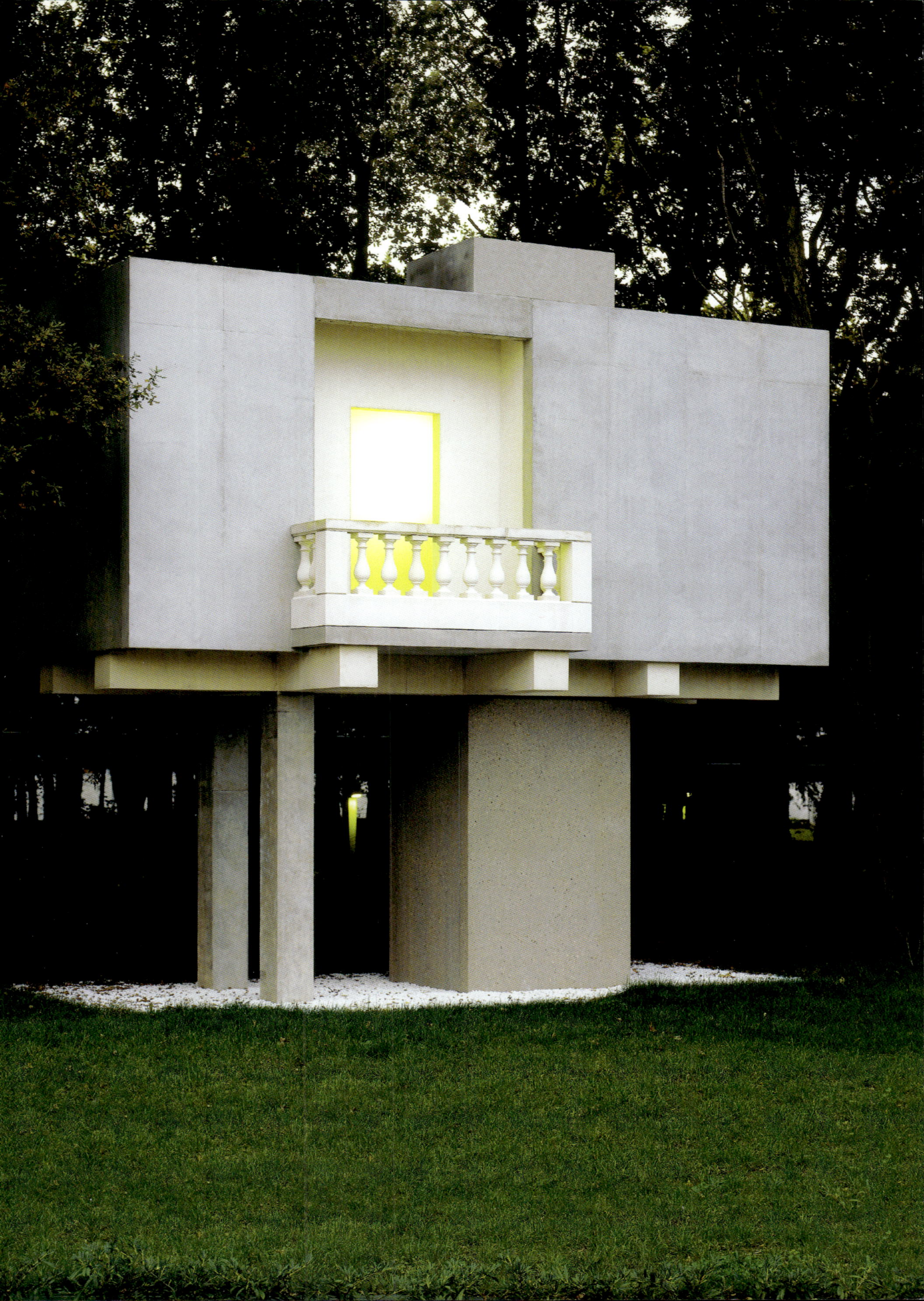

FROM THE MUSEUM TO THE TOWN: ESTABLISHING PLACES

/

JEAN-MARC BUSTAMANTE
MONTRÉAL, 1995

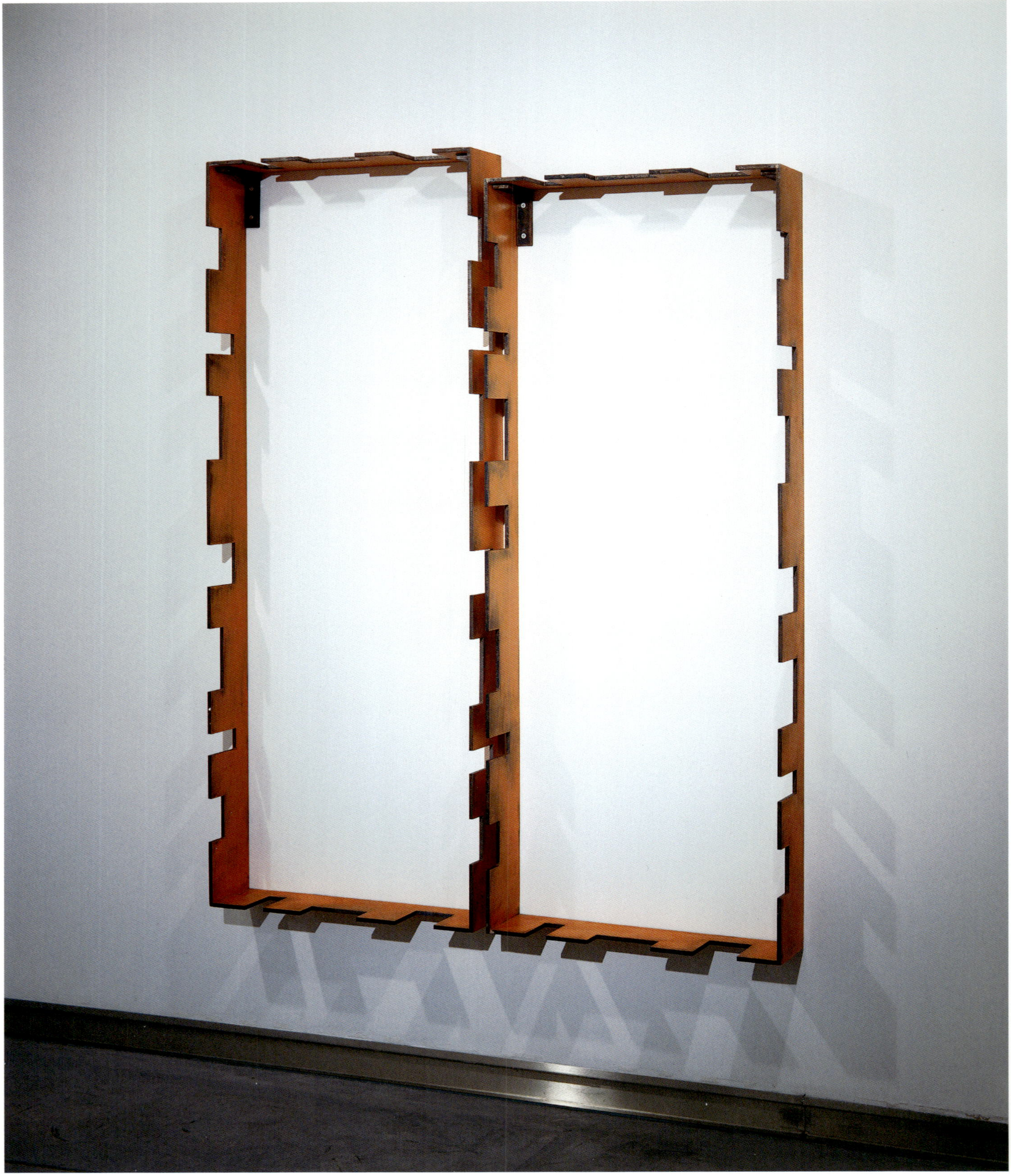

Double miroir, 1991
Steel, anti-rust paint, 185 x 100 x 20 cm (left);
175 x 100 x 20 cm (right)

As we know, the links that united artists and architects during avant-garde periods no longer exist. Since then, there has been no proper reflection on the development of art in the public realm. The architect carries out his work, responding directly to social, economic and cultural demands. The artist, having no real function outside the museum, always comes last. In public commissions, the artist is brought on board only when the site has been defined, planning permission obtained, the project all but completed. At this late stage the artist is required to produce a proposal in circumstances defined by politicians and the architect. This situation attracts only mediocre artists, the results of whose endeavours we are familiar with from the '1% for art' schemes in France and Québec – the policy of allocating 1% of the construction cost of new buildings for public artworks. The architect becomes the sole interlocutor and he does not shrink, in the service of his own self-expression, from the most flagrant borrowings. The relationship of architecture and the museum is also very telling. A museum has no real function for architects. That's why they think they are free to experiment with the most arbitrary forms in this context. Curators and artists just have to get on and deal with the results! In the built environment, it is the container that counts above all else.

One can certainly reproach art for evolving towards a complete autonomy that, while giving it great freedom, also cuts it off from the community. Inversely, art could be

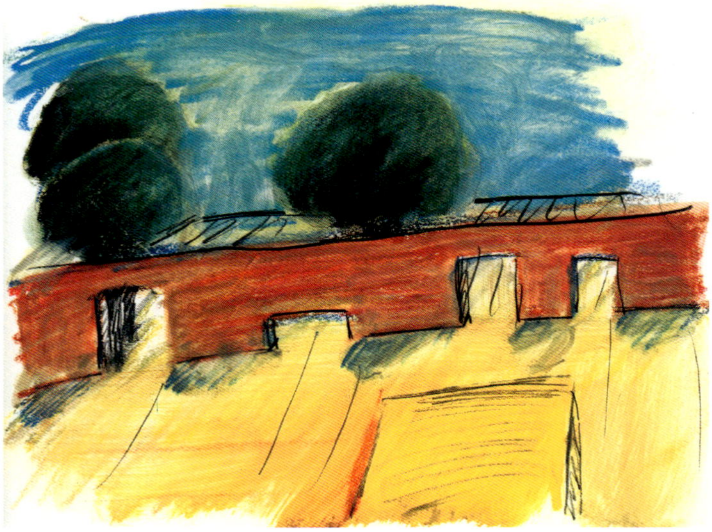

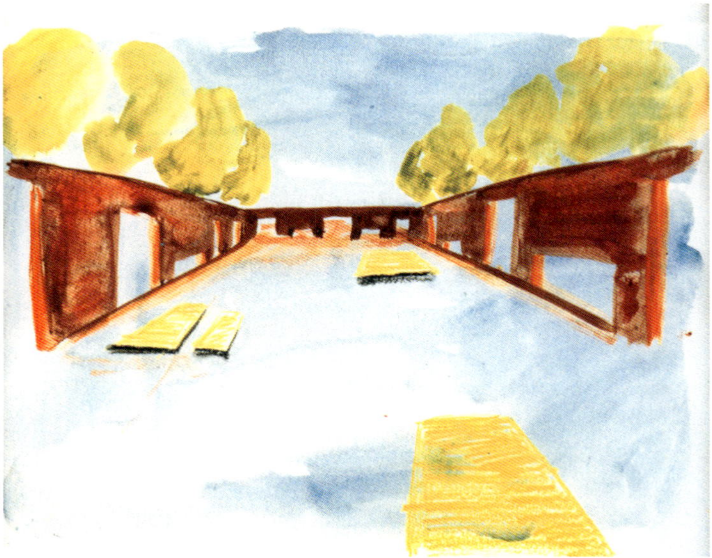

considered a victim of society. Nevertheless, if one really wants to view recent developments in contemporary art close up, its relationship with architecture is very pertinent. This rapport comes from artists' desire to engage in a new dialogue with nature, with the city; their desire to take charge of public space in a way that goes deeper than formal and decorative systems, which allows them to get back in touch with the world in a way that contrasts completely with the *in situ* and site-specific concepts of the 1970s.

I would like to propose the notion of *place* as opposed to *space*, a notion that seems to me to be best suited to art's better integration within the urban context. How can a work insert itself into the confined and discontinuous space of the real without clashing with it, putting it into question, or revealing it? Place is first and foremost about acknowledging the world. It's a kind of received idea, neither a vague geography nor a particular spot. One heads towards a spot; one goes to a place. A place is indescribable. It resists any kind of representation. It has not only a physical reality but also a metaphysical reality particular to it. The relation of place to the world cannot be disassociated from the person who has conceived it, or, more properly, made it happen, and the person who recognises it. Place is the world of others; it is understood best by the body that occupies it. For example, a vase is the place for a flower. A place is constrained by its limits, but limits that are interior rather than exterior to it; in contrast to space, which is characterised by its exteriority. Place is stable: it resists, it is the protector of the enigma, the enigma of man – upright, immobile, gazing. Far from objects, utopias, gestures, attitudes, images or arbitrary collages, place, considered in either its physical or metaphysical dimension, may not be objectivised. In the realm of place, we leave systems behind, we turn away from the idea of progress.

It is necessary to be precise about exactly what the art of today, outside of museums, can bring to the needs and expectations of a community. It is a matter of positioning oneself in favour of an art that can leave the field of

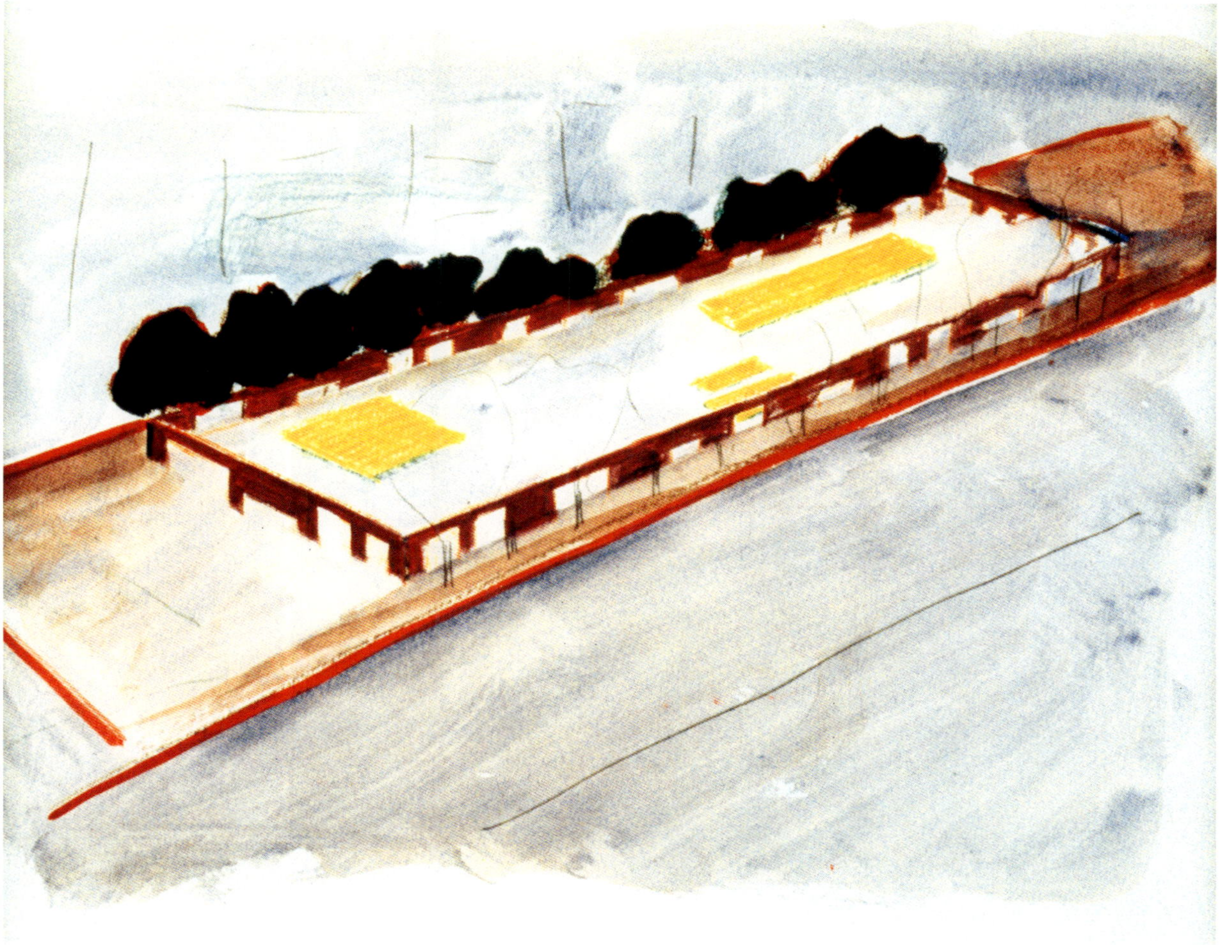

museums, exhibitions, collections, commemorations, and situate itself in a constructive way in the everyday world. In bringing with it an interest in the urban environment and the interrelationship between individuals, art and the artist can and must play a central role in the city once more, together with the architects and landscape architects who understand this primary role. Such a conception of art foresees the absence of predetermined forms and seeks a specific temporality, the fleeting interest of a passer-by, the indeterminateness of relationships.

Translated from the French 'Du musée à la ville: établir des lieux', in La place publique dans la ville contemporaine, *published on the occasion of the symposium held as part of the 350th anniversary of the city of Montréal, 1995, pp. 137–39. Translated by Fiona Bradley.*

Paysage XIX, 1990
Steel, anti-rust paint, 71 x 62.5 x 16 cm (left);
71 x 117.5 x 16 cm (right)

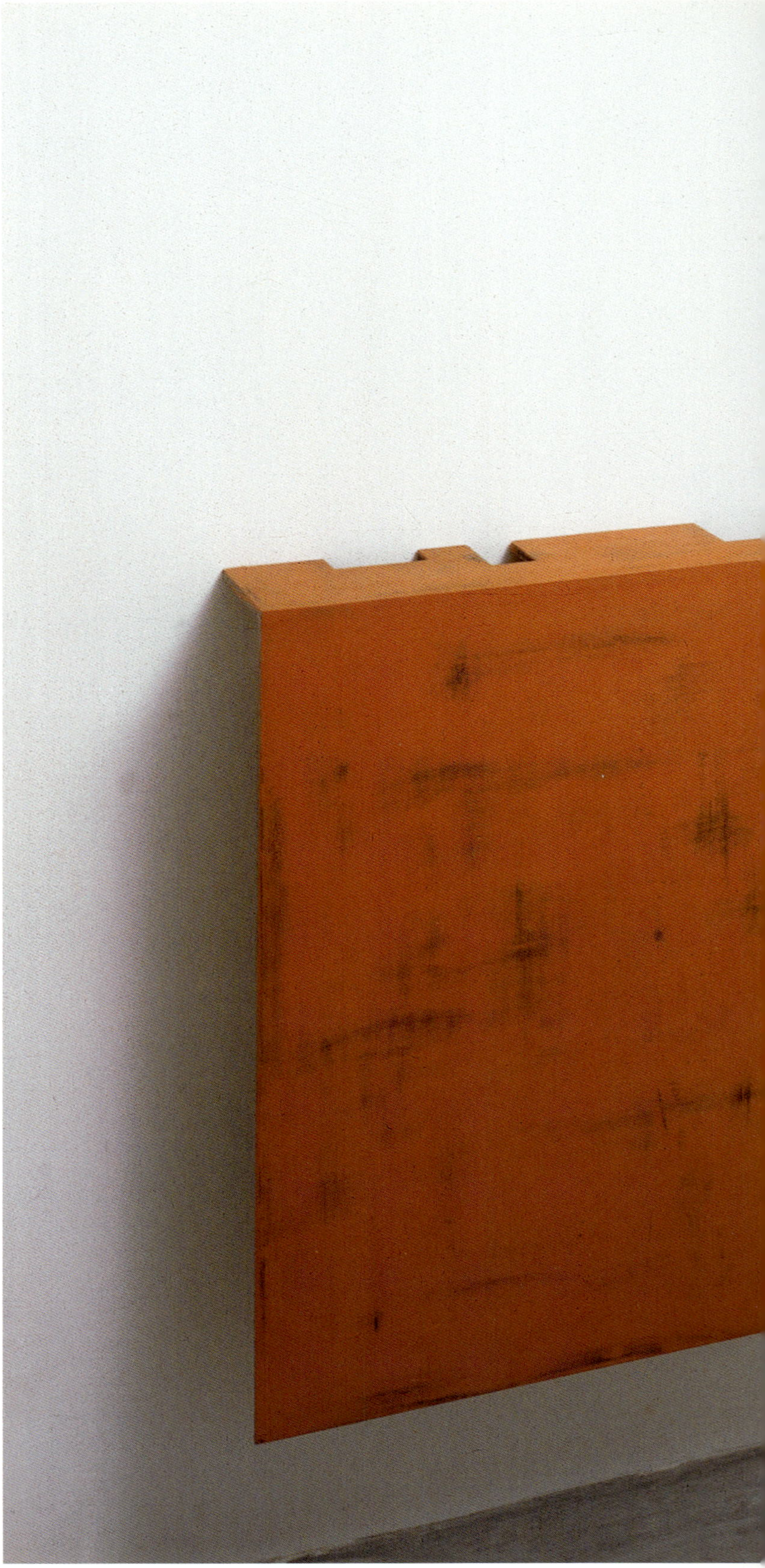

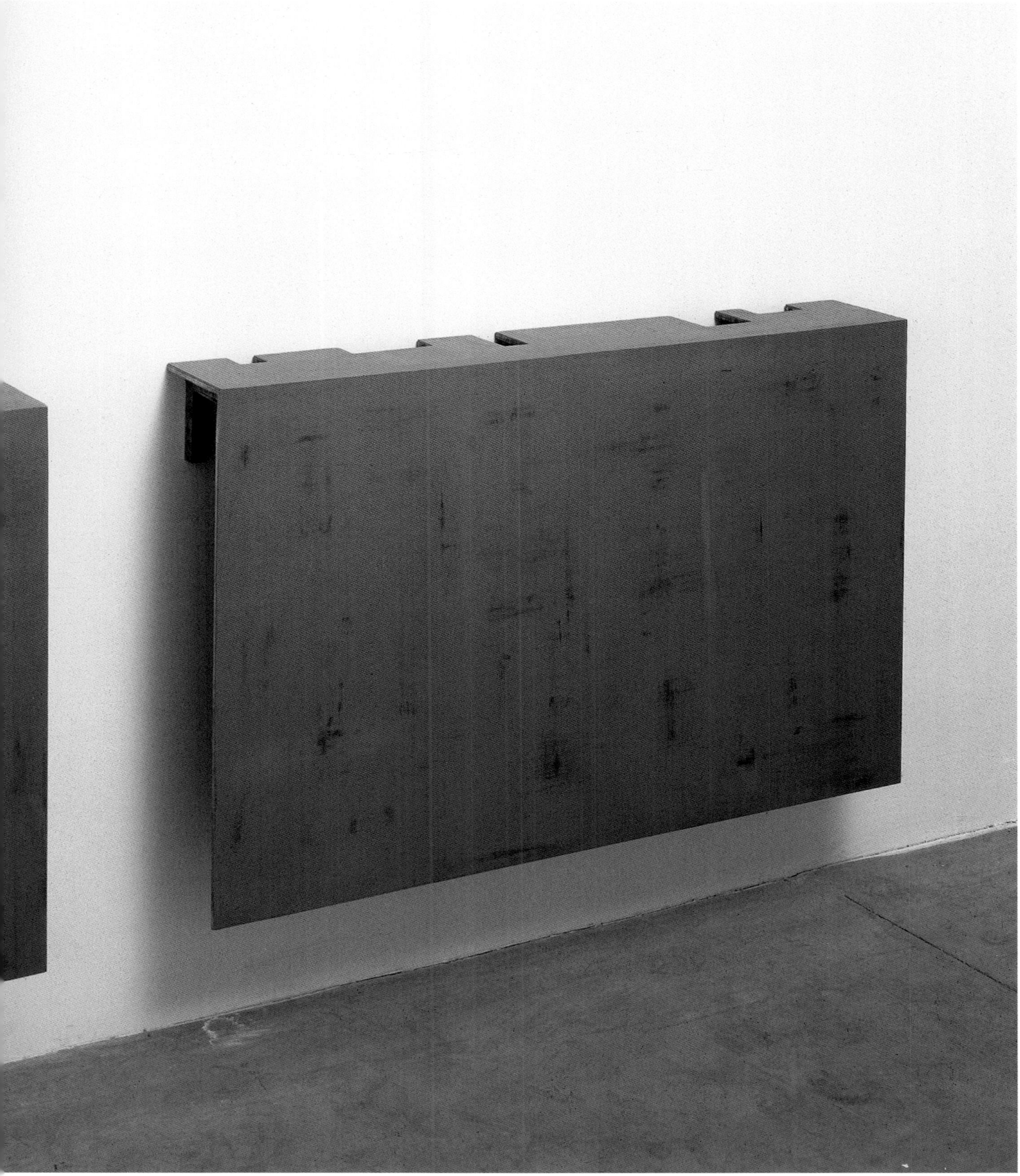

LUMINOUS MANDARIN

/

JACINTO LAGEIRA
TURIN, 1998

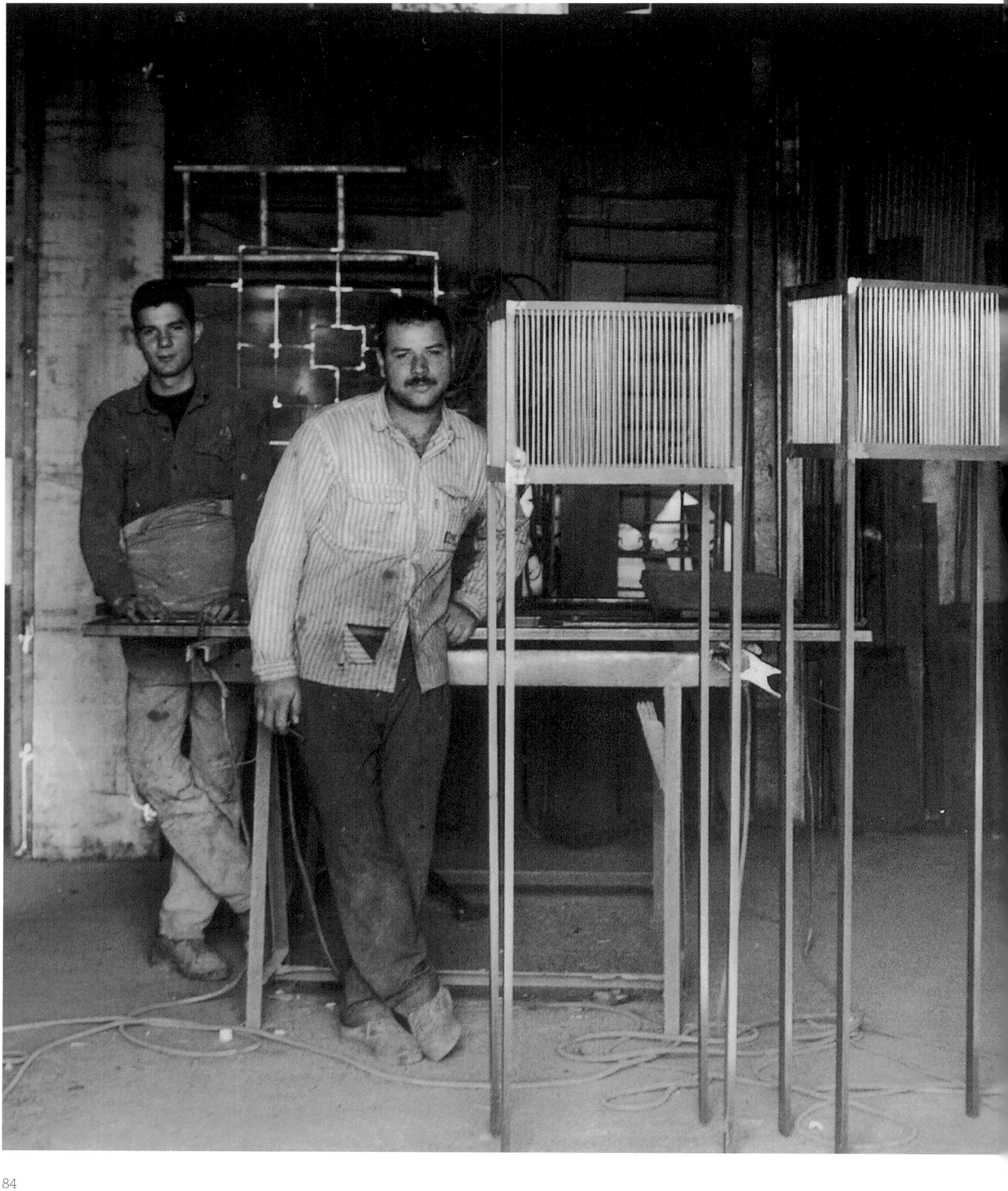

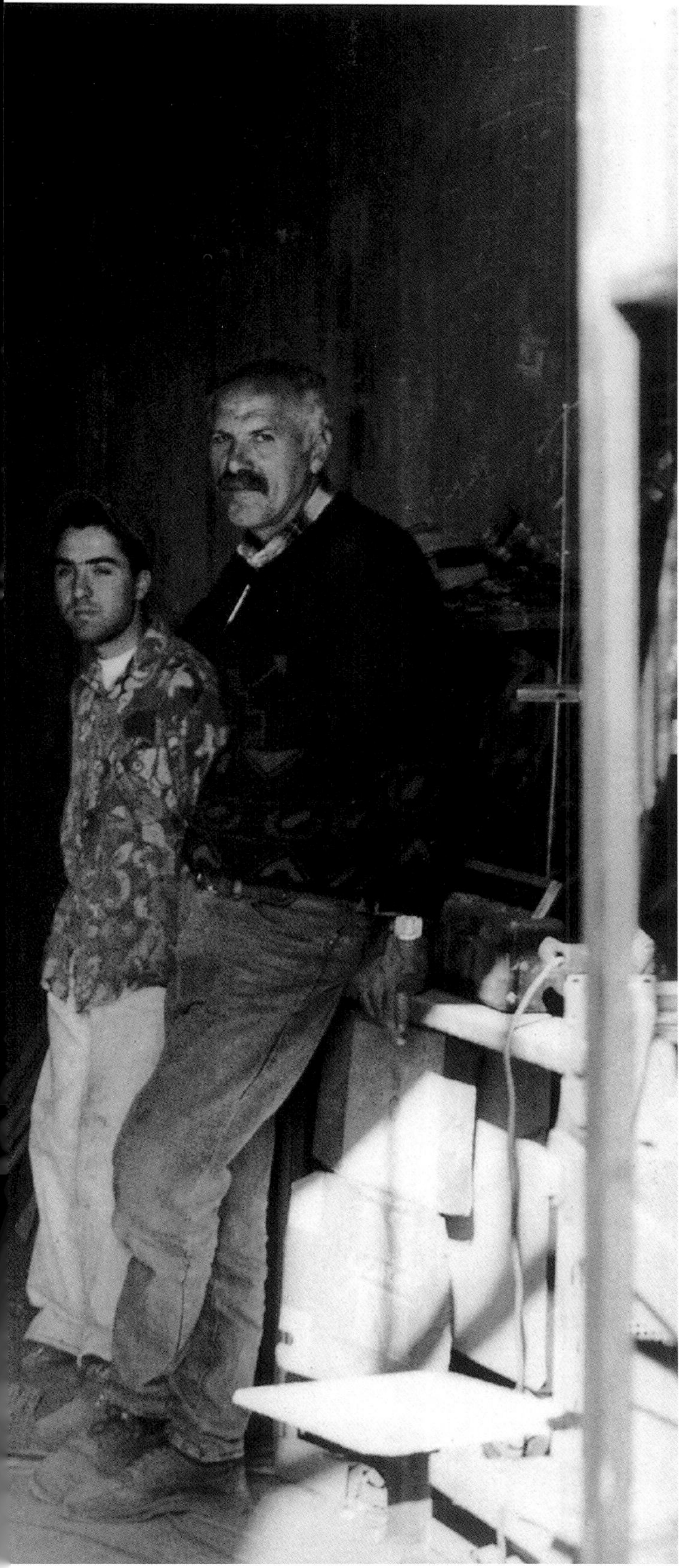

Workshop view showing the construction of cages for *Suspension I* in Palestine, 1997

There is something paradoxical about isolation since, to take shape, it requires the presence of a multitude of beings, of things and of everyday events, without which we would not feel separated from what surrounds us. Being isolated is being separated from others, but it is also being separated with others. It is not so much lack of communication or of comprehension that separate as the simple fact of finding oneself, exactly, among them. The more one seeks closeness with those one cares about, with those one loves, the more they seem to retreat like the waves upon the beach. They dig out, they erode ever a bit more, they pull away. This rekindles the desire to be closer, but very often also the desire to pull away, to turn in on oneself and, in turn, withdraw. To withdraw in on oneself, to withdraw into oneself is after all a good thing. How could we stand never being isolated? But if it is true that for some this is the prelude to relative liberation, for the majority of people it is but the beginning of the end. The smallest empty space of time or enforced inactivity, a moment of silence, and they see the spectre of consciousness of themselves appearing. And then, unhappiness prevails. Did Blaise Pascal not write in *Pensées*, 'All of men's unhappiness comes from their not being capable of staying alone in a room'? And in today's world, man's unhappiness is infinite. No one is capable of turning isolation into a living force. Stigmatised as a state that is to be systematically avoided, it is used rather as a means for breaking down the social fabric and debasing thought.

Suspension I, 1.96, 1996
Ink on Plexiglas, 145 x 185 x 4 cm

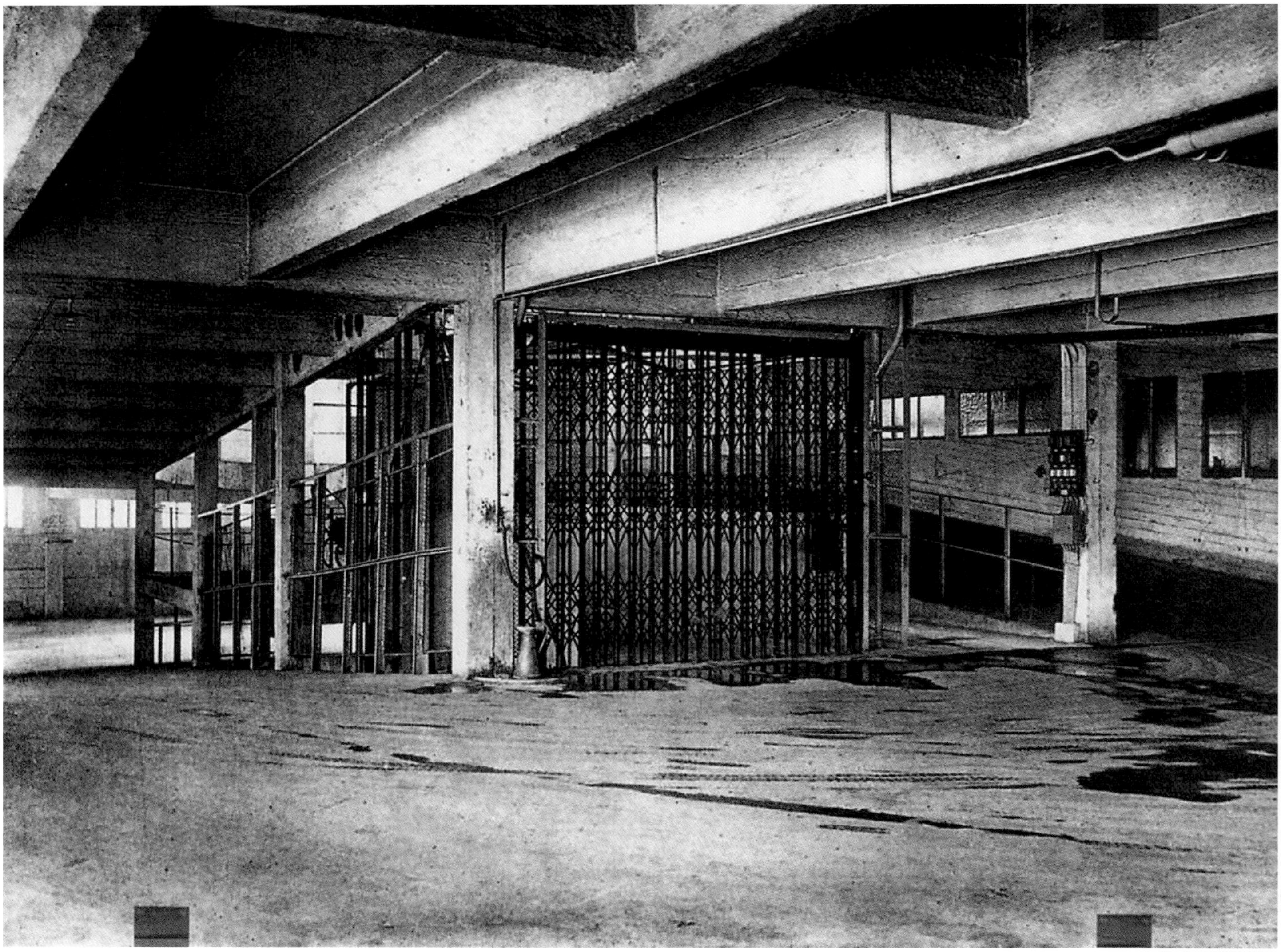

We repeat that each individual is an island, that he is no longer linked to other individuals, that he is isolated because he is surrounded by other people who also live as though isolated. Being isolated together, what a pitiful end! The field of truly lived experience is shrinking before our very eyes, to the degree that everywhere people are seeking to extirpate its sense. For a long time, one refuge was the work of art. But this last bulwark that should have made possible a privileged relationship between a subject and an object, has not only failed to rescue authentic experience but has actually precipitated its fall. Which, after all, is not so bad. In such cases, 'authenticity' always contains a residue of dogmatism, of the transcendental, of the inaccessible, of the interminable and obscure rhetoric, full of extreme formulas and conclusive words about what, in the last analysis, is defined as unutterable. Is it still possible today to speak of 'authentic experience' and, *a fortiori*, of 'authentic aesthetic experience'? What are we looking for behind those formulas, in the way we relate to others, in the glance directed at the work of art, if not the otherness that can lead us out of isolation? But – and this is the more stimulating alternative – it could also lead us back into it, like some of Bustamante's works, which secrete, which produce, isolation. Through this capacity to delimit a space which excavates a lack, virtually disgorging its very substance, emptying itself from within, many of Bustamante's works call to mind certain figures by Alberto Giacometti, or *Here I (to Marcia)* (1950) or *Broken Obelisk* (1963–69) by Barnett Newman. As must have been true for them, isolation for Bustamante is never fatality but, instead, choice. Being isolated together can thus be conceived of as a restoration of sense, an affirmation of solitude as a stage in the development of sense.

Looking at these images of Bustamante's work, these sculptures in the shape of cages, the viewer is left to himself, or perhaps we should say liberated from himself, immersed, as he is, in his isolation. Confronted with the insistent, imperious yet at the same time fragile verticality of these purified white forms, raised like other bodies in his space. Walking between these sculptures and before these images, the visitor sees all about him pieces of himself. Everything has been fabricated by human beings and for him, and yet there is nothing except these small birds with whom he shares an affinity: feeling alive. It would be tempting to see in this the metaphor for contemporary man, truly imprisoned or alienated from his very existence. The sculptures, on the other hand, had strange beginnings, as they were produced in Jerusalem by Palestinians and subsequently presented in a gallery in the old city in 1997. Each cage with its live bird was afterwards entrusted to a person who then had to look after the creature. The cage and the bird in it thus became a symbolic gift that entailed commitment and responsibility. The parallel between the human condition and that of the tiny birds seems evident, whether or not it is related to specific socio-political situations. This is even more the case since it corresponds to what for many years has been an ongoing search in Bustamante's work: the circumscription of a place. Yet looking at these images and these sculptures (or at other works), one understands immediately that all that he has ever done has been to circumscribe his own isolation.

The *Taeniopygia guttata*, whose common name is the diamond mandarin, is a small bird with a flute-like song. Here physically isolated from others of its kind, it nonetheless keeps up some exchange with them with fitful singing. The only living articulation – sound – in a habitat of geometric lines and precision drawing filled with white pebbles, the only movement among these images emptied of their occupants, it is also, in this artificial landscape of greyish or pristine shades, the only touch of colour. As a species and as individuals, at the same time similar and unique, the diamond mandarins are isolated together but, although confined in a small space, they fill the area

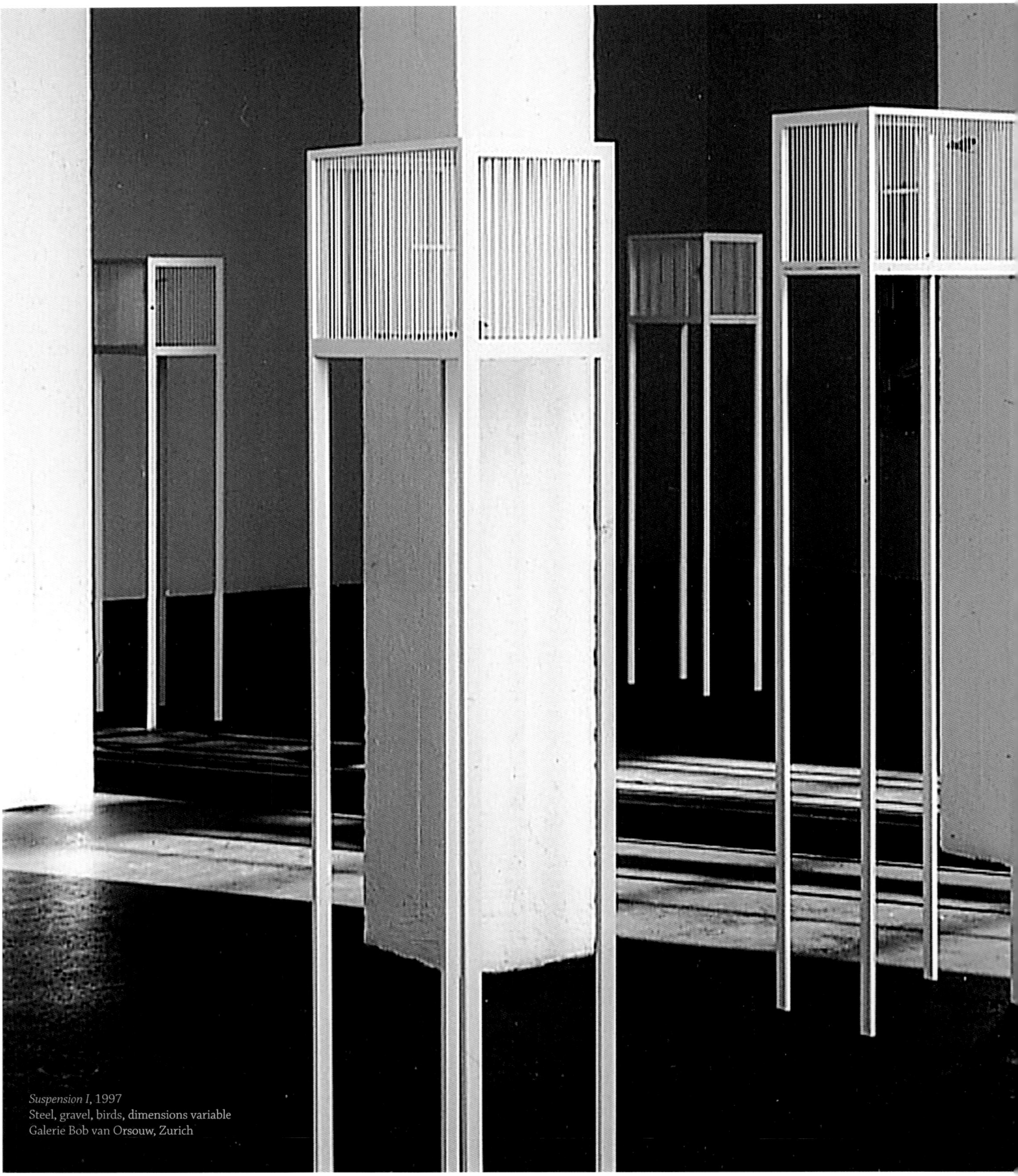

Suspension I, 1997
Steel, gravel, birds, dimensions variable
Galerie Bob van Orsouw, Zurich

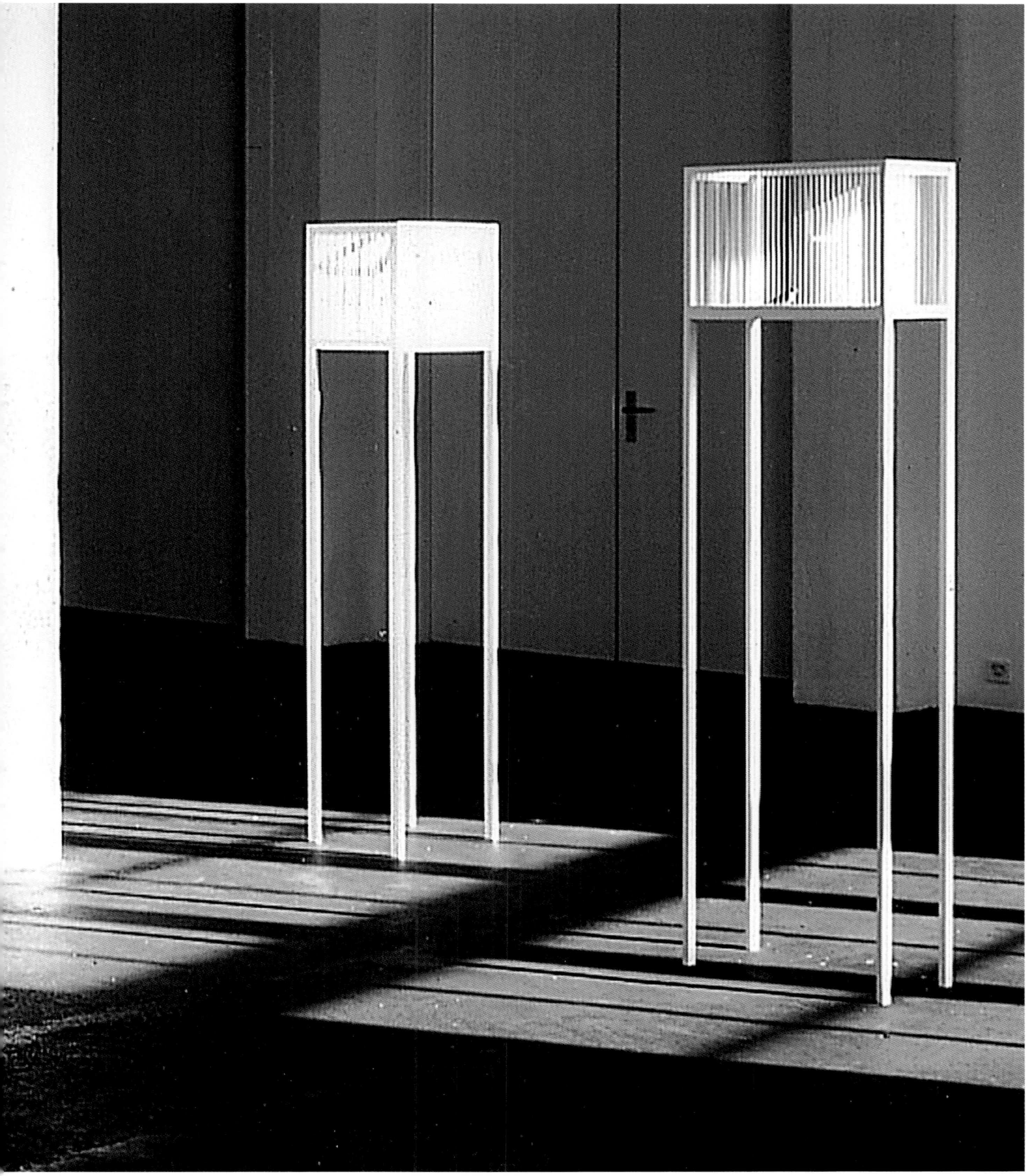

surrounding them. Separated together, by their interior and exterior position, they isolate and fragment the spaces of our movements and perceptions. Continuously moving inside a world become rigid – continuous presence within permanent absence – the mandarin illuminates the place.

Something is missing. But what? Some men, some women or some children who should be in a garage, a classroom, a lift or in showers, all defined as places for gathering? On seeing the images presented here, it is inevitable that we think of those who are absent and, even more, of the obsessive impression that they could be the *departed*. Only the places that they occupied bear witness to the cancellation of their bodies and figures, the effacement of every trace of them. Departed together. A collective, common universe has been delineated in place of human inanity. As though they were coming forth from the wall, the images give back to the supporting surface, becoming one with it, the apparition of what has already been relegated to a phantom world. At the same time, becoming one with the wall, they provoke the isolation of the viewer who, by this time, has become inextricably linked to elusive but solidly present frontiers. These images are a veritable apparition in the visitor's space; the walls, the entire room thus become the piece of paper that allows them to be revealed. But it is an apparition in which he sees himself as though dissolved in the solitude of the places in the image. Places which are out of order – temporarily or permanently – of a rather indeterminate era, they allow us to see time and space slowly taking shape. A light vibration on a Plexiglas support, porosity of grain destined almost to disappear, but also an emulsion which manifests the presence of things. Image after image, the viewer may now merge as much with the isolation of the places presented, as detach himself from them to return to his own isolation when faced with them. But he is at the same time in proximity with, in the immediacy of, what he perceives and what he hears in the room. His solitude is disturbed by the

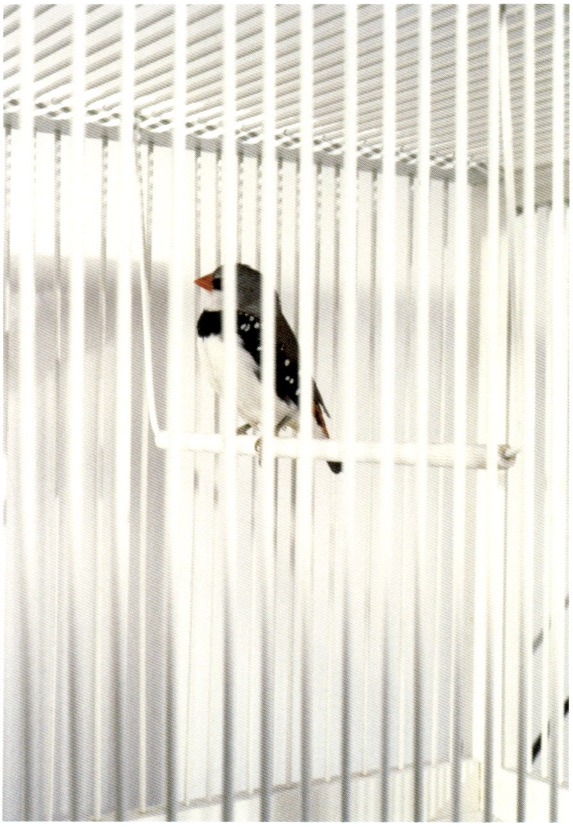

Suspension I, 1997 (detail)
Steel, gravel, birds, dimensions variable

opposite: *Suspension I, 4.96*, 1996
Ink on Plexiglas, 145 x 185 x 4 cm

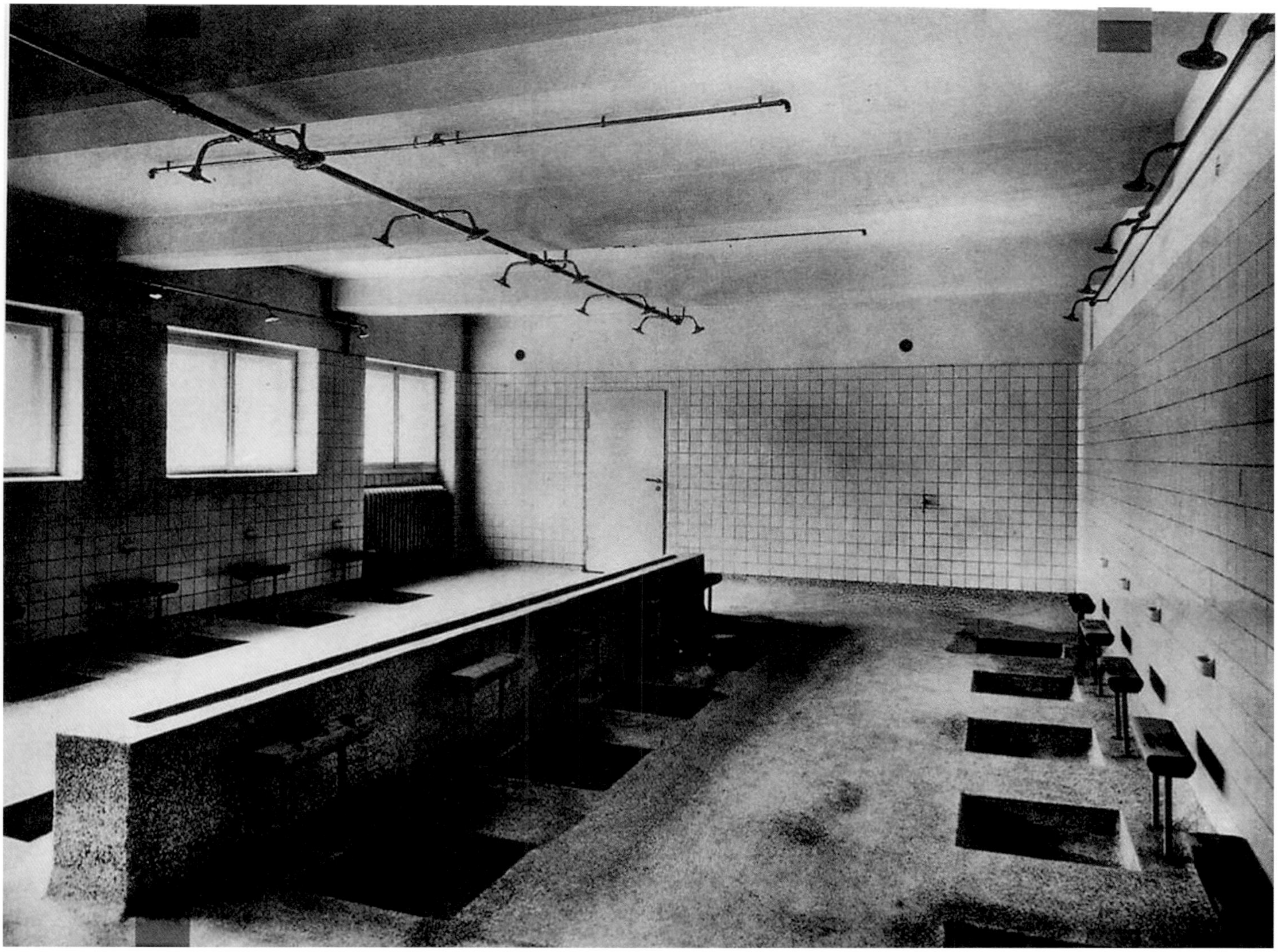

Empty cages, 2003
Steel, paint, crystal, 175 x 30 x 46 cm,
185 x 30 x 46 cm, 195 x 30 x 46 cm
shown in background: *Panorama Perroquets*, 2003
Ink on Plexiglas, 373 x 262 x 4 cm

fluttering of the birds. The cages themselves seem to move, since the mandarins confer on them a dimension which is vital, mobile, and sonorous, in contrast to colourless, frozen, silent images. The mandarins are a presence in the void of the images and the images bring certain melancholy into the mandarins' space.

Something is lost. But what? First of all, we lose a bit of ourselves. An unpleasant sensation, not merely that something is lacking but, above all, that we are feeding that lack – simultaneous consequence of the presence of the birds and the absence of human beings in the images. Might we perhaps be isolated from the places perceived, in the same way as the mandarins too are relatively isolated? But whereas in our space, a subdued presence of whistling and the flapping of wings is developing, over there, in the images, an absence, if it is right to call it that, is becoming ever stronger, ever more pregnant. And it is not so much others, still absent from the image, that create this sense of loss, but instead what they seem to have taken from us. As is true for the diamond mandarins – the attachment, the affection that we feel for our kind, for the places and the things we share with them, is inscribed within this relative isolation, inscribed as a negative image in that garage, in that classroom, in that lift or in those showers. Being isolated with others, is the feeling that we are inside places that others can share with us in reciprocal solitude. And yet these places that we could easily make our own belong to others who no longer exist, who will never exist there again. Strangely, the sign of their prior isolation, of their solitude, is anchored in these places and remains in them. It is thus no longer only the image that appears or disappears, that takes shape or falls apart, but also the isolation of this other, which has been definitively obliterated. This effacement is not an extreme or tragic end, to the extent that the choice of such interdependence between a presence and an absence, between the different states of isolation of the birds, of the viewer, of the places and of the image, marks a sort of route to follow through beneficial solitude. Some words found, completely by chance, while looking through Paul Valéry's *Cahiers*, sound like the echo of this voluntary retreat: 'I write only for the man alone – for he who rises *media nocte*, in the nakedness of his existence – as though resuscitated from the other side of his consciousness, all things seem to him both real and extraneous – as if he had come with a lamp to a dark place cluttered with unknown objects, which it illuminates and transforms at each step. At an hour when he was not expected, in a place that might be quite another ...'

Translated from the French 'Mandarin lumineux', in Jean-Marc Bustamante: Suspension I (Something is Missing), *Centre Culturel Français and Edizioni Landau, Turin, 1998. Translated by Susan Ruff.*

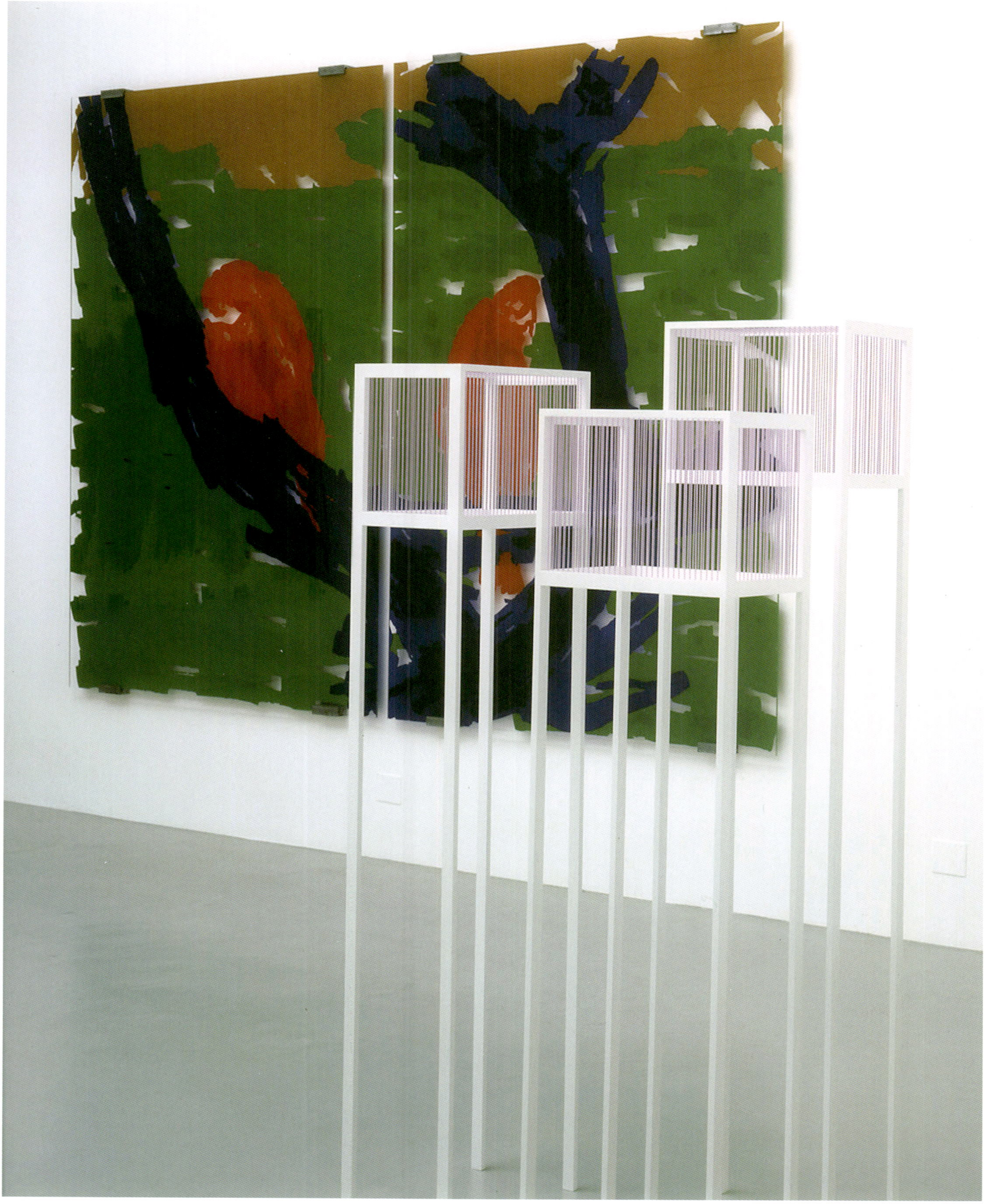

JEAN-MARC BUSTAMANTE'S
TECTONIC VISIONS

/

DENIS GIELEN
HORNU, 2008

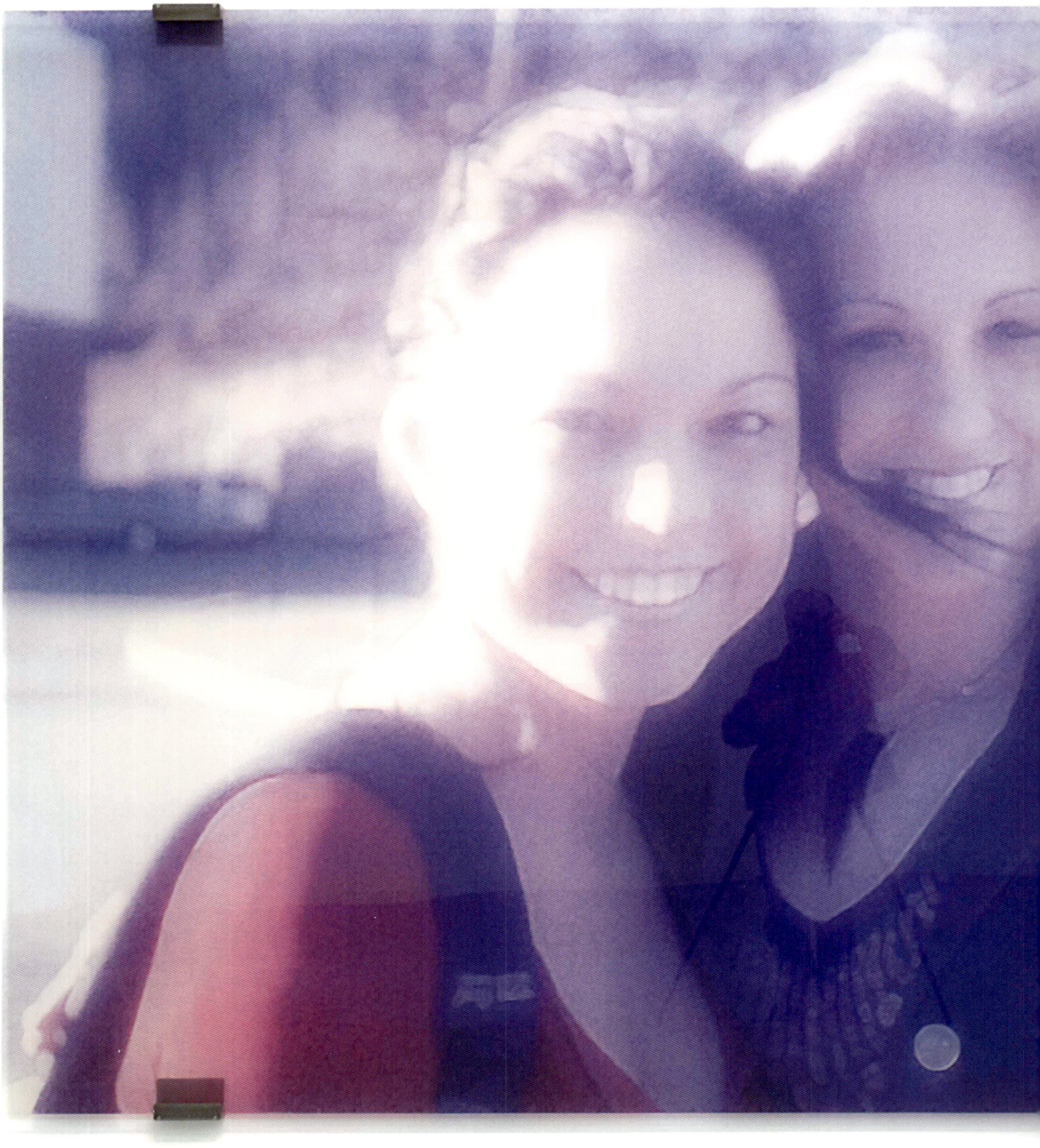

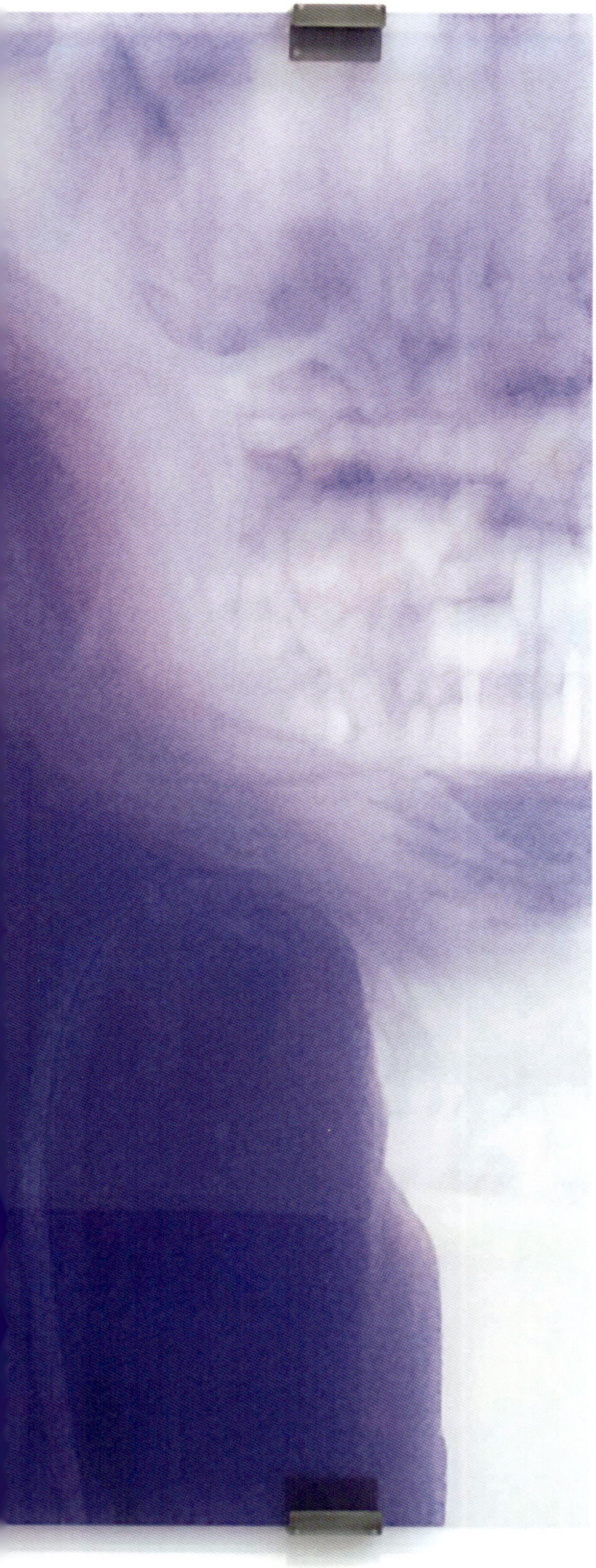

Amanda et Lisa, 2008
Ink on Plexiglas, 195 x 274 x 4 cm

'When the traveller journeys across these fertile plains, where the regular flow of quiet waters sustains its abundant vegetation, and whose ground, trodden by numerous peoples, embellished with thriving villages, wealthy cities and superb monuments, has only ever been disturbed by the ravages of war or the oppression of powerful men, he is not tempted to believe that nature also has its internal wars, or that the surface of the Earth has been disrupted by revolutions and catastrophes. But his ideas change as soon as he seeks to dig this now so peaceful ground, or climb the hills surrounding the plain. They develop so to speak with his view, they begin to embrace the scale and grandeur of these ancient events as soon as he climbs the highest mountain ranges, whose foothills cover their feet, or when, following the channels of the waterfalls that descend from these ranges, he penetrates their interior.'
Georges Cuvier, *A Discourse on the Revolutions of the Surface of the Globe*, 1825

Our ideas about the world evolve in accordance with our view of it, like the lesson, still relevant today – in science as well as art – summed up for us by Georges Cuvier, the nineteenth-century engineering geologist and inventor of palaeontology. When we think about it, we are not that far removed from Paul Cézanne's profound vision of painting: 'To paint a landscape well, I first have to discover its geological foundations. Just imagine! The history of the world dates back to the moment when two atoms collided,

L.P. III, 2000
C-print, 227 x 180 cm

opposite: *Lava II*, 2006
Galvanised steel, ink on Plexiglas, 15 x 600 x 1600 cm

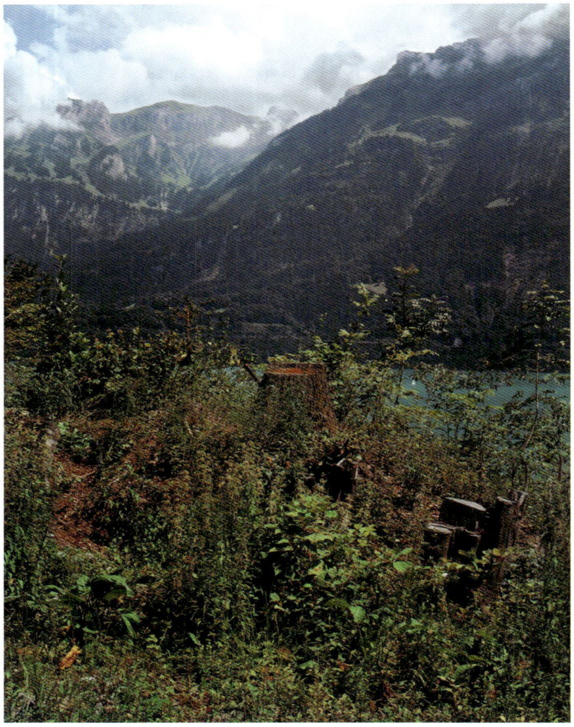

and when two whirlwinds, two chemical dances were combined.' For, as he also confided to Joachim Gasquet, the artist needed to know 'how Sainte-Victoire was rooted, the geological colour of the earth ...'.[1] Cézanne may well have been fascinated by Cuvier's discourse on rock falls, alluvia, dunes, lithophytes, volcanoes and similar incrustations, and his speculative descriptions of them. The geologist attempted to work out the Earth's antediluvian form – 'the first appearance of the Earth' – whose creation is still progressing slowly today, through the action of its four elements. 'The rains and thaws, which erode the craggy mountains, throwing the debris at their feet; the rushing waters, which carry this debris, to deposit it in the places where their course slows; the sea, which undermines the base of high coastlines to form cliffs, and which discards heaps of sand onto low-lying coasts; and the volcanoes, which pierce the solid layers and raise or spread the mass of the ejecta over the surface.' As described by Cézanne, 'It is a scientific bath, into which we have to immerse ourselves.' To do so, the artist – like the geologist – has to explore the subject and 'physically immerse himself' in it. The simple fact, as well as the complexity of our position as spectator, or sometimes seer, is that the brain is attached to the eye, which in turn is attached by the skull to the moving body. The world is never so comprehensively considered as when our legs stride across it and our eyes take it in. 'And indeed,' as Maurice Merleau-Ponty says,'it is not clear how a Mind could paint.'[2]

A history of art understood through geological expeditions has not yet been written. It would no doubt contain works that in some way resemble such earthly formations as lakes and volcanoes, crystals and grains of sand. A later chapter in this history would certainly traverse the vast territories of America that Land Art artists have explored in their time, as well as specific Minimalist objects. Indeed, geological phenomena have always inspired artists, for whom, as Guillaume Apollinaire suggested, a work of art is never as beautiful as when it does not appear 'to have been created, but to have been formed'; a thing in itself, an *acheiropoieton*, an image not made by human hand. This is not to say that effort should be banished from such creation, but rather that it needs to follow nature's logic and seek to adopt – or, to adapt itself to – these essential principles. In this way, art would necessarily evolve with the conceptual advances of science; and when entropy became (as it has today) an indispensable law of physics, we would understand clearly what Robert Smithson meant when he wrote: 'The human mind and the Earth are in a constant state of erosion'; and when he compared his sculptures, his earthworks, to a 'sedimentation of the mind'.[3]

Stratification, a geological phenomenon *par excellence*, may help us describe Bustamante's work, even though the artist is far removed, both geographically and culturally, from Land Art. We can first point to the screenprinting

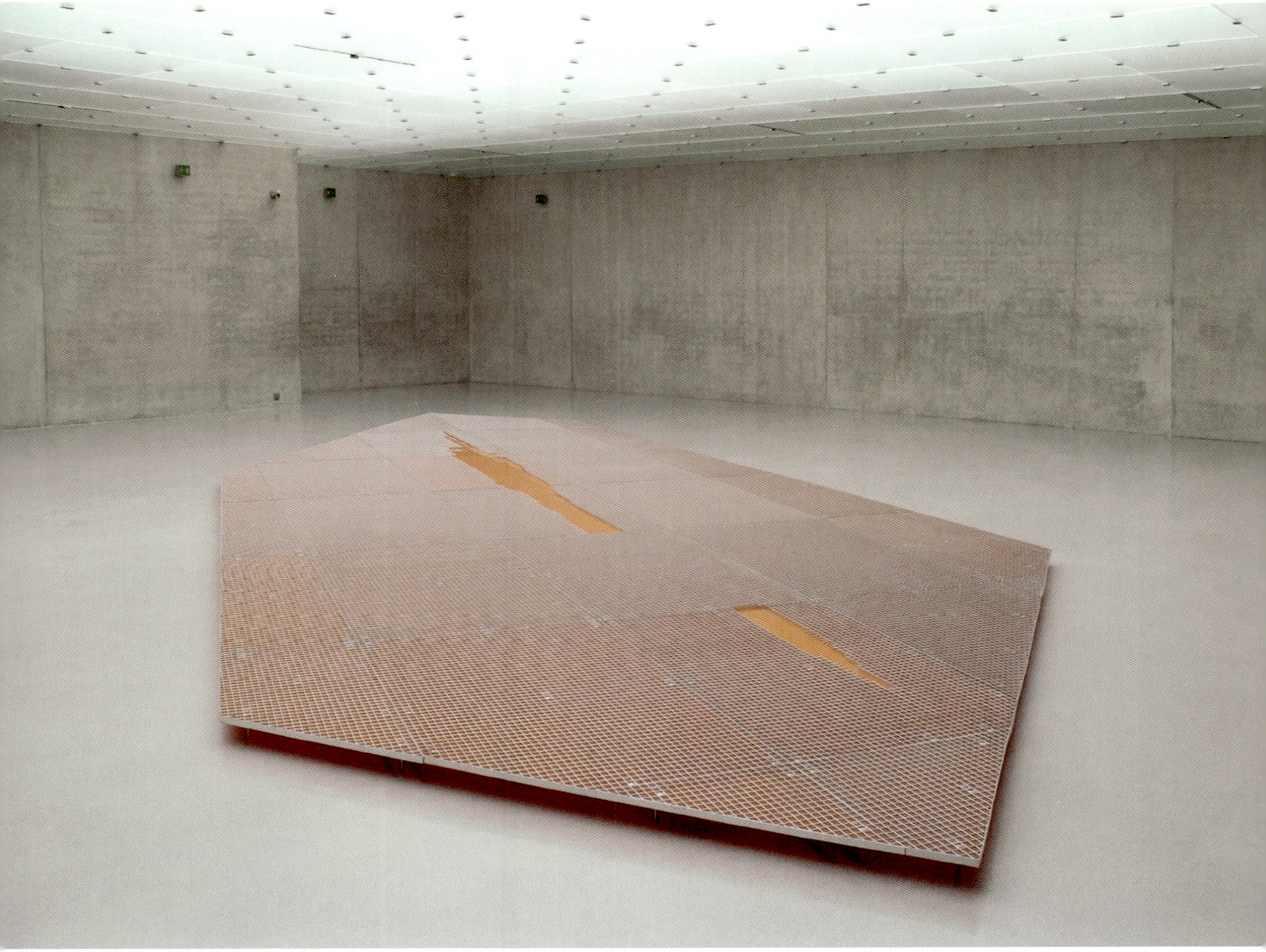

Lumière 16.91, 1991
Ink on Plexiglas, 185 x 270 x 4 cm

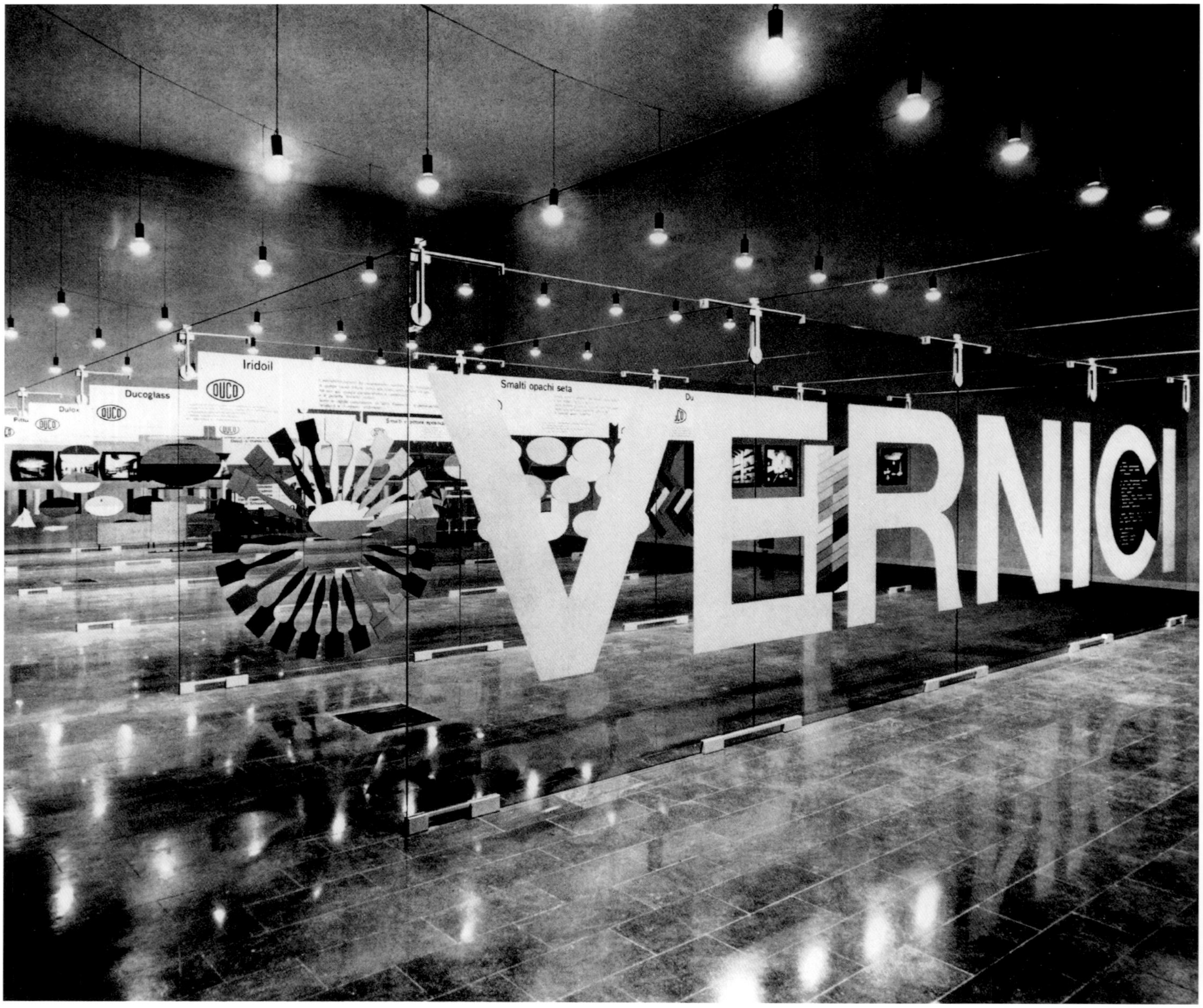

technique, which he began using on Plexiglas for the *Lumières* series in 1987, and which he still uses today to produce his *Panoramas*. When we look at these works closely, we clearly see that in certain places one film of colour passes underneath another, rather like the way fabric is woven. They record the passage of colours over the time of their production, in planes. A story, a memory, slowly emerges from these wavy drawings, which from a distance appear to be chaotic and sometimes even scribbles – this blue shows up clearly through this red, but the blue was there before. Beneath the apparent chaos, the emergence of colours on the screen is in fact governed by their order. This stratification clearly gives the painting its depth and, as Cézanne said, 'nature is more about depth than surface'. Sculptural work is no different. Here also, Bustamante suggests layers. It is most striking in the pieces treated with red lead. In certain places the sculpture's surface has been sanded to reveal the metal material underneath. Conversely, red lead is used as an undercoat in construction – as a rust protector – which suggests that a finishing coat will follow. Here, once again, is clear evidence of stratification: a layer of steel covered by a coat of red lead, which in turn is awaiting a top coat. The same is true of other materials that he frequently uses, such as cement or concrete, which are generally intended to be covered. To describe this technique in which the strata are clearly visible, Bustamante speaks of an 'agricultural finish', midway between an industrial and a crafted treatment. This expression comes from his association with the degree of finish that is found in farm machinery where, for example, welds remain apparent. Then there is the specific slowness of the stratification process: Bustamante describes his *Tableaux* as 'slow photographs'. For the point is not to capture a decisive moment, a particular, anecdotal subject, but to record 'situations captured in their constant metamorphosis'; that is to say, the image of a world always caught in the interval of the snapshot, already this and not yet that, as in the red lead plates. Hence this paradox of a slow photography which, if such a thing is indeed possible, avoids being fixed too quickly, opting instead for wandering – as Bustamante himself did in the suburbs of Barcelona at the end of 1970 – as an anti-documentary, non-typological principle. The slowness is clearly not that of the shutter, but the movement between two shots. We would also willingly suspect Bustamante of having chosen this particular landscape because he happened to stop there, out of tiredness; not so much seeking it out as finding. He stumbled across it. We are reminded of Gilles Deleuze. In nomadic (*smooth*) space as well as in sedentary (*striated*) space, there are both points and paths; but in nomadic space it is the path that leads to the point, not the reverse. Paths are not subordinate to points there: nomads do not go from one point to the next. This is why it is sometimes suggested that they do not in fact move. 'The nomad distributes himself in a smooth space; he occupies, inhabits, holds that space; that is his territorial principle.'[4] This is exactly the same as Antonioni's wandering characters of whom Bustamante is so fond: we are thinking here of Aldo's fate in *Il Grido* (*The Cry*, 1957).

When we consider this properly, the slow photographer cannot be worldly, even though his subject is the world. He has to remain solitary. His opposite would be Andy Warhol, with his quick snapshots of a world in which he belongs. The same is true of Nan Goldin and all the photographers who could be described as 'familiarists'. Generally, the rare people who appear in Bustamante's photos are in the distance, which is again reminiscent of Antonioni: 'I look at us from the outside and within, and from afar in order to see more closely.' Most often, Bustamante's figures are absorbed by the monumentality of a landscape or architecture, and/or by the intimacy of a task, like in the scenes depicted by Jan Vermeer in the seventeenth century or Jean-Baptiste Siméon Chardin in the eighteenth century. The images in the *Lumières* series abound with a similar distancing, for the people are not apparently aware of being observed, captivated as they are by their game (children playing in a ring) or any activity – be it intellectual (the classroom) or physical (the gymnasium) – which ultimately

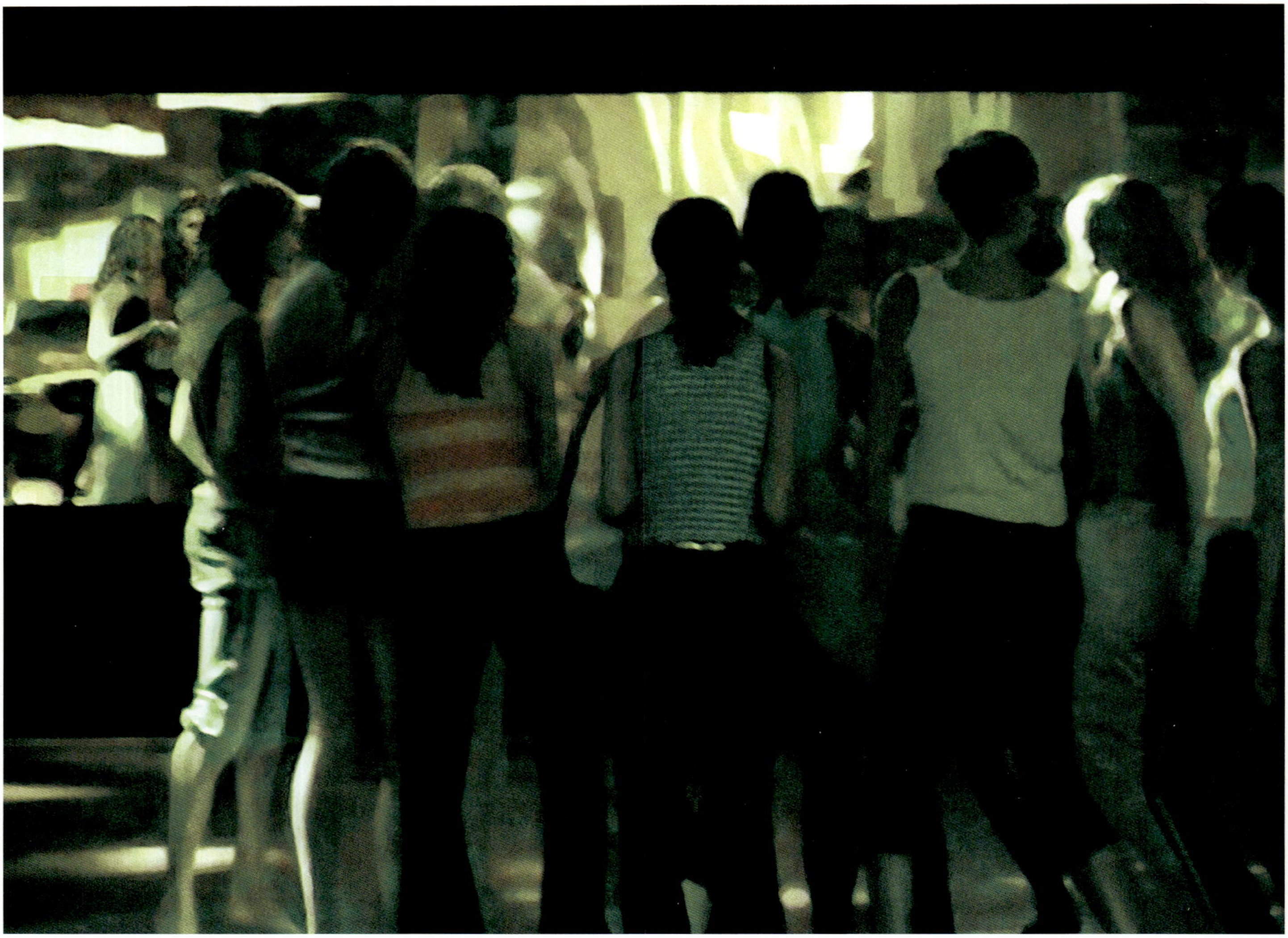

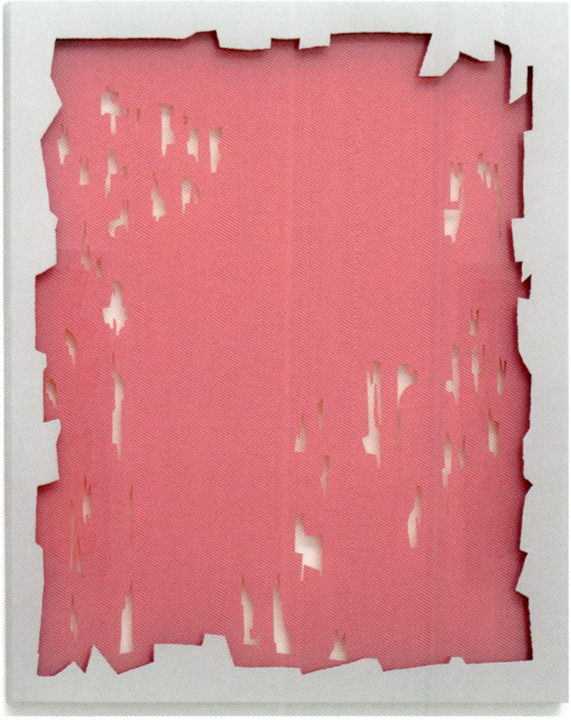

Perfect Dream 5, 2005
Galvanised steel, ink on Plexiglas, 172 x 145 x 5 cm

opposite: *Lumière 1.03*, 2003
Ink on Plexiglas, 190 x 264 x 4 cm

cuts them off, not so much from the photographer's space as from his time. Looking at these images, I feel rather like I do when I look at Albrecht Dürer's *Saint Jerome in his Study* (1514), with whom I share the same space obliquely (being on the threshold of his cell), although not the same time (not having distracted him). In his analysis of the place of the spectator, Michael Fried compared the paradoxical question of this moment of complete concentration to the presentation of the phenomenon of duration by snapshots, not isolated but connected to *the before* and *the after*, taken therefore in a stratified time. 'Chardin's *Les Osselets* (*The Game of Knucklebones*),' he notes, 'isolates a particular moment, in all its plenitude and density, from a continuum that is evoked so brilliantly by the entire painting.'[5]

If the photographic image is stratified, it is not because it has been produced like a screenprint, by layers and successive sweeps of colours (the photograph is produced all together, in a single moment), but because – being precisely timeless or beyond time (or else in an infinitesimal time) – it takes part, in fact, in no particular time. Consequently it is like a geological section, *hic et nunc*, that is able to reveal all the times of the world simultaneously. For the photograph is this vertical cut that, perpendicular to the strata, makes multiple time horizons visible. Bustamante sums this up well: 'The camera does not belong to the same reality as the accumulation of photographed things.' Through this gap, this distance created between the worldly and the photographic, the artist therefore manages to reconstruct the world's multiplicity in a single image. 'At the Kunstmuseum Wolfsburg,' he goes on to say, 'I called my exhibition *Un monde à la fois* (*A World at a Time*). I liked this formula because it is paradoxical: the singular world is put into perspective by a single instant, as though there could be several worlds at this time. An artist can only resolve this contradiction by always remaining slightly at a distance.' In this photographic slicing operation, the angle of vision – which determines the gap or qualifies the distance – becomes essential. The panoramic or high-angle shot, the

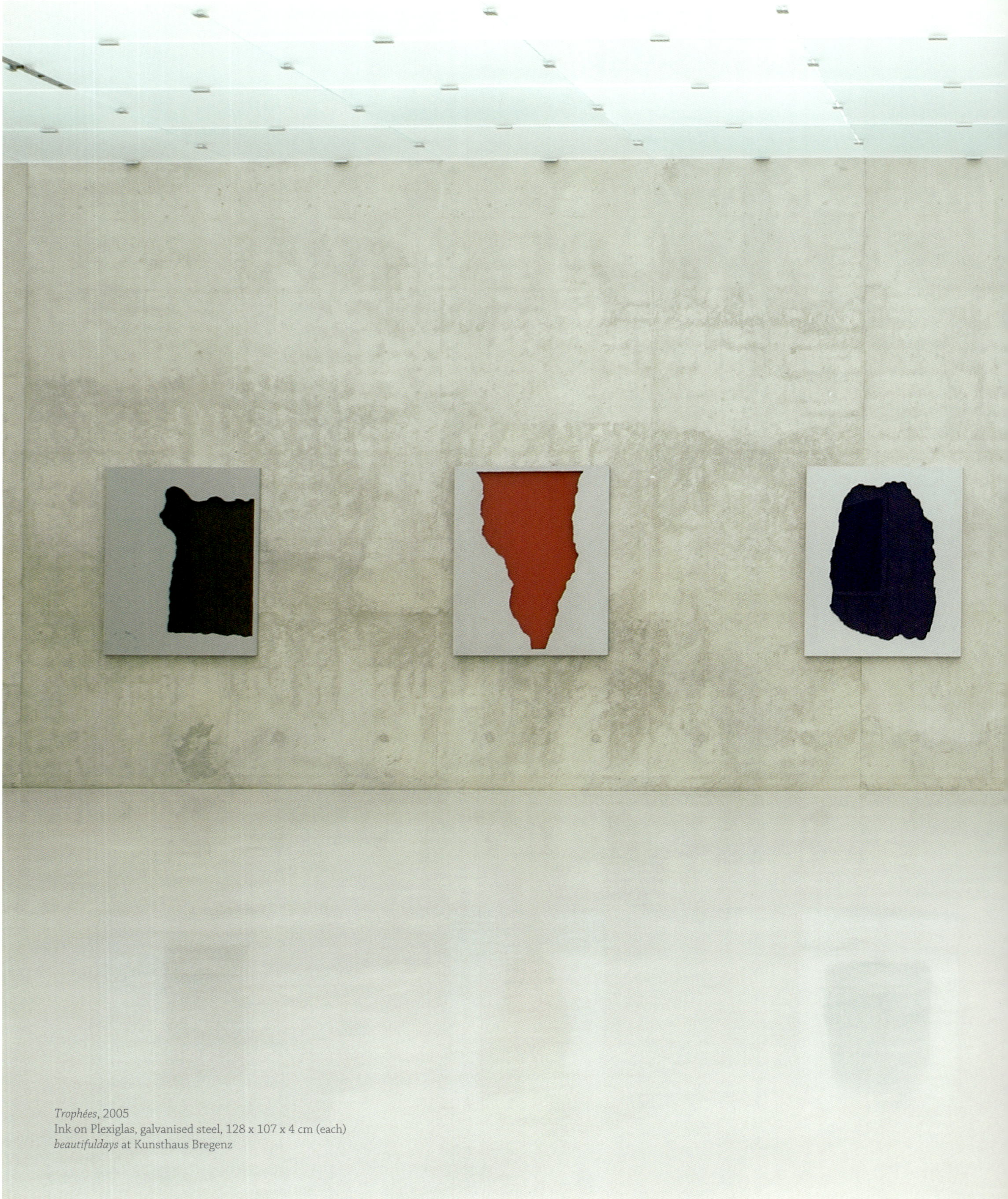

Trophées, 2005
Ink on Plexiglas, galvanised steel, 128 x 107 x 4 cm (each)
beautifuldays at Kunsthaus Bregenz

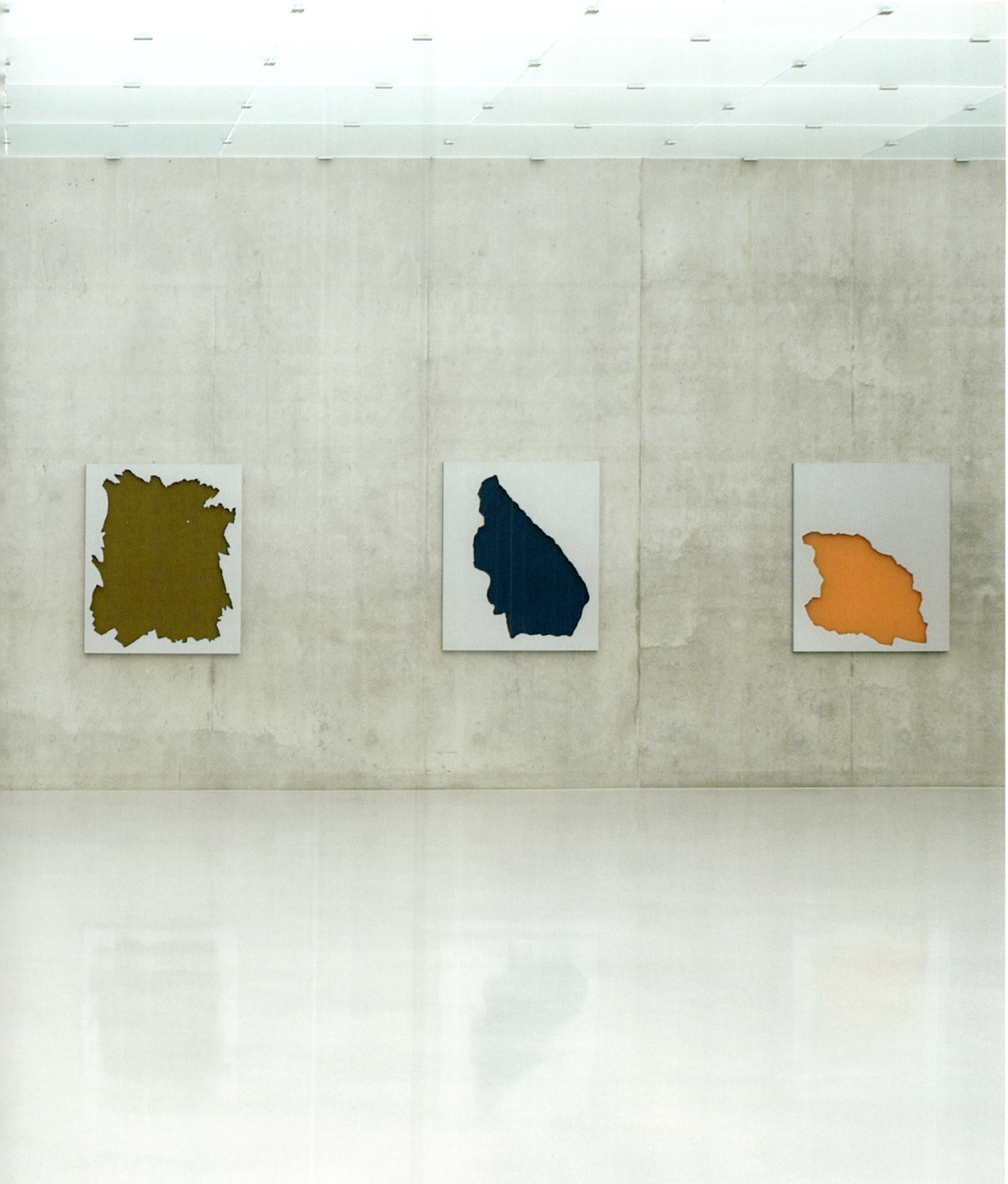

close-up or the wide angle do not address the world's contours with the same exposure effect or knowledge of its strata or tectonics. Bustamante's *Tableaux* photographs and plate-sculptures (on the ground or fixed to the wall) are powerful witnesses to this revealing, for example, the antediluvian rock under the contemporary house in *T.13.78* (1978), or the red lava under the surface of the volcano.

We can see that Bustamante's stratified work is unitary, for different times inhabit it simultaneously – the near and the distant – in a sort of depth of field. The miracle of this art – and its paradox – is that it captures snapshots over time and reconstitutes in the here and now the fleeting perceptions of durable, independent and thus, in and of themselves, 'blocks of sensation', as Deleuze said. This was equally Cézanne's aim: 'I orchestrate my entire canvas, if you follow me, all at once and as a whole. I use the same movement, the same faith to bring together all the scattered parts ... Everything that we see is dispersed, moving away, don't you think? Nature is always the same, but nothing that we see of it remains. Our art must convey the sensation of duration with the elements, the evidence of all these changes.'

We have not yet considered stratification in Bustamante's work from the point of view of the subject that is represented. At this iconological, even allegorical level, much has already been discussed, notably the fact that Bustamante regularly revisits either his own pieces – altering them each time they are moved – or works by other artists, which through a more or less deliberate choice are often much older. (The level of awareness is sometimes enigmatic: did he really intend to cite such and such an image, as he claimed, or has he simply assumed the reference afterwards? Is it purely involuntary, or even contrary to his desire?) The fact that the artist cites himself appears to be the epitome of stratification. We could simply say that he is *laying it on*. Be that as it may, we should note a sort of insistence on certain figures that recur like leitmotifs, perhaps under the impulse of an involuntary memory, a source of reminiscences; hence also the survival phenomena, with their production of archaic images. Let us take the case of the swimming pool, which we find several times in Bustamante's work, for example in *Tableaux* (*T.I.78*; p. 29; 1978; *T.42.81*, 1981; p. 24; *T.50.82*, 1982, pp. 40–41), as well as in his sculptures (*Le verre bleu*, 1987; p. 42), or even in a few *Panoramas*. Likewise we could point out in this context the recurrence of the sand pit, the tree, gates and curtains that literally haunt his work. There is probably a lot more to say on the specific meaning of each revisiting.

The swimming pool motif, for example, could be interpreted in three ways as indicated by the artist. In phenomenological terms, it is a model of depth, the 'radiance of the visible'; iconologically, it is a sociological marker (a stereotype of exoticism, an 'image' of a lost paradise – with palm trees making it even better!) and/or a historic reference (Ed Ruscha's *Nine Swimming Pools and a Broken Glass* (1968) identify this vernacular); and ontologically, the swimming pool, smooth like a sensitive plate, is indeed waiting for impressions, striations, and thus is essentially photographic (the swimming pool being equally revelatory to, 'the liquid intelligence' of photography, as Jeff Wall commented). Yet although it lends itself so well to interpretation, this genre of open work strikes the imagination more through the way the image is considered than where it is (a method Bustamante has been developing for thirty years now). Rather than focusing on its fiction or its legend, the image is seen in its reality or materiality; in the fact that it is, here or elsewhere, a projection or panorama; in short, an optical device in space.

Another revisiting, that of Antonioni's *La Notte* (*The Night*, 1961) in his exhibition at the Van Abbemuseum in Eindhoven in 1992, is also explained by Bustamante's determination that it should be possible to sense the apparent depth of the image, its true depth of field. *Lumières* operates in a similar manner, taking place in the gap between the glass and the wall. We always come back to strata, to the layers that are of interest to the geologist and the glassmaker. This iconographic stratification is even more noticeable in the works that appear, as if by chance, in the book, which we consult page by page. The sculpture *Inventaire* (1989) originates from an illustration taken from *Staatliches Bauhaus in Weimar 1919–1923*, and reconstitutes a piece of furniture – from the glass painting workshop run by Paul Klee and Josef Albers – that was used to store glass plates to be worked on by students. *Lumière 16.91* (1991) is after an image taken from an architecture publication and reworks a trade presentation – by the firm Duco – in which six glass plates were positioned vertically, one behind the other. (This image is also reminiscent of *Glass Strata with Mulch and Soil*, 1970, by Robert Smithson.) Finally, underlying this chain of revisiting and citation, there is the almost psychoanalytical or archaeological notion that an image always hides another; the stratification of art history ultimately producing a gigantic palimpsest. This aesthetic of suppression is also not far removed from the 'magic book' used by Freud to represent the subconscious, or the reminiscences and ghost images of Aby Warburg and his *Mnemosyne Atlas*.

Finally, let us take the case of a citation that was acknowledged after the event: a photograph of a building site, from the Swiss lakes series, *L.P., IV* (2000), the composition of which resembles Rogier van der Weyden's painting, *Saint George and the Dragon* (c.1432). Bustamante himself drew the parallel after having taken the picture: 'I realised afterwards,' he said, 'in spite of all the respect I have for Rogier, if we simply imagine the fight with the dragon instead of the construction site, then the bell-towers, the shimmering water, the exact division of the foreground, middle and background, everything matches, even Saint George's lance and the steel cables that subdivide my picture. The concordance is clear for me.' This example and Bustamante's precious account clearly illustrate the way in which the revisiting operated in his work like a distant echo, owing to the – quite paradoxical – fact that the revived image (of the knight) is a disappearing image, in the sense that it becomes obliterated in the reverberation and is worn away by its alternating presence and absence. This is not to say that there is no saint in Bustamante's photograph – this is quite obvious – but that he is no longer there, which opens up the image to numerous speculations. To begin with, let us imagine using the question 'why?'. As everything tallies, even 'the lance and the steel cables', why is there such a blatant absence – Rogier van der Weyden's very subject? Is it not precisely to make this absence the new subject of the work, or even the painting? *Something is Missing* (*S.i.M.*), the title of a series of photographs taken in large cities, keenly asserts this admitted affect of loss, which haunts the work: 'Increasingly I have the feeling that something is missing,' states Bustamante. The question of 'why' then moves to 'what'. What is missing? What is this absence that the artist is so keenly asserting? We could say, without venturing too far, that what has disappeared with the saint and the dragon, is nothing more than the very subject of the picture, i.e. the action, the decisive and heroic act of the knight slaying the monster. Unquestionably the action is taken in its most causal sense as it effectively serves a cause (the spirit of chivalry; that is, the principal theme of this already political iconography). This appears to be particularly true when we remember the question posed by Sartre (the true philosopher of action) when looking at the version of the same legend by Tintoretto: 'Is the saint carrying out an act or is he merely the passive vehicle of an event?' (The answer to this question is also found in the scene of the murder of the Arab in Albert Camus's *The Stranger* (1942): 'My eyes were blinded by this curtain of tears and salt.') However this may be, the profoundly philosophical reflection surrounding the act (freedom or fatality?) leads us to specify the absence: a loss of chivalry – elegance even – which Sartre detects by comparison with what is painted of the combat fifty years earlier: 'I note that he [Saint George] charges from right to left, as in Carpaccio's painting. But he is more cunning, less fearful. Rather than confronting the monster head on, he slays it shrewdly, from behind; it's safer. The lance bears witness to this, as it strikes the beast above the eye: the years have transformed the knight-errant into a mercenary leader. I can't see anything

Phantom I, 2005
Ink on Plexiglas, 345 x 550 x 4 cm

wrong with this: he has to save the maiden; temerity would be criminal. But something has been lost.' *Something is Missing*, said Bustamante ... But what exactly? In a word, style! Not yet the act, which remains (in spite of everything) free and courageous, but this aristocratic manner that distinguished Carpaccio's soldier and which is clearly no longer in Tintoretto's 'plebeian' painting, and even less in Bustamante's slow photography where the action, as we said, no longer appears. However, in this last image, the remaining landscape – rather like the theatre of an action that is long finished – has retained the traces of the battle in the form of a building site, like the distant echo of the beaten earth of the fight. We could sum it up by simply saying that we have moved from one earthwork to another, from the chivalrous levelling to the ground of the dragon, to the proletarian levelling of the building site; with the visual and sociological consequence that the landscape is doubly desolate. Already at the end of the Middle Ages when the knight was leaving the countryside to live in semi-urban courts 'in the dependence of kings and princes', paintings were suffused with nostalgia in place of landscape; worse still, landscape was sentimentalised. As Norbert Elias observed, '"Nature" and "countryside", which initially served simply as surroundings for characters, gradually took on an aura of sadness as the urbanisation or "curialisation" of the ruling classes progressed, and the rift widened between city and country life. "Nature", like the characters, took on an air of dignity and solemnity. We find a sentimental polarisation here: a distinction between what incites agreeable and pleasant sensations and what is felt to be painful or disagreeable. The same can be said of the characters. Certain things that in reality are found in the countryside, in "nature" are no longer represented for the absolutist audience at court. The hill is still depicted, but without the gallows and the hanged man at its summit.'[6]

These vestiges of heroic action – the landscape as the remains of the action – form the historic basis for the great family of artists whose work reflects duration. Deleuze identified this, in the context of Italian Neo-Realist cinema, as the shift from the *movement-image* to the *time-image*. Antonioni's films, which persistently haunt Bustamante's oeuvre, bear witness to this quite melancholic, postmodern aesthetic of the after-effect. As Deleuze notes, 'the idle periods in Antonioni do not merely show the banalities of daily life, they reap the consequences or the effect of a remarkable event which is reported only through itself without being explained (the break-up of a couple, the sudden disappearence of a woman ...). The method of report in Antonioni always has this function of bringing idle periods and empty spaces together: drawing all the consequences from a decisive past experience, once it is done and everything has been said. "When everything has been said, when the main scene seems over, there is what comes afterwards ..."[The story can only be interpreted implicitly, through images that are consequences and no longer acts].'[7] Bustamante's photographic picture, subconsciously haunted by Rogier van der Weyden's painting, which is itself stratified by other versions of the same painting, is a striking example of how the postmodern image no longer depicts the act, but its resonance after the event, its distant echo in a space emptied of its substance. This is a time-image, a snapshot that no longer captures 'the decisive moment', to borrow Henri Cartier-Bresson's phrase. This is *lentissimo* photography.

Translated from the French 'Les visions tectoniques de Jean-Marc Bustamante', in, Jean-Marc Bustamante: Le Grand Tour, *Musée des Arts Contemporains – Site du Grand-Hornu,* 2008. *Translated by Laura Austrums.*

NOTES

1. Joachim Gasquet, *Conversation avec Cézanne*, Macula, Paris, 1978.
2. Maurice Merleau-Ponty, *L'œil et l'esprit*, Gallimard, Paris, 1964.
3. Robert Smithson, 'A Sedimentation of the Mind: Earth Projects', *Artforum*, vol. VII, no. 1 (September 1968), pp. 44–50.
4. Gilles Deleuze and Félix Guattari, *A Thousand Plateaus: Capitalism and Schizophrenia* (trans. Brian Massumi), Continuum, New York, 2004, p. 420.
5. Michael Fried, *La Place du spectateur*, Gallimard, Paris, 1990.
6. Norbert Elias, *La Civilisation des mœurs*, Pocket ('Agora' collection), Paris, 2003.
7. Gilles Deleuze, *Cinéma 2, L'Image-temps*, Les Éditions de Minuit, Paris, 1985.

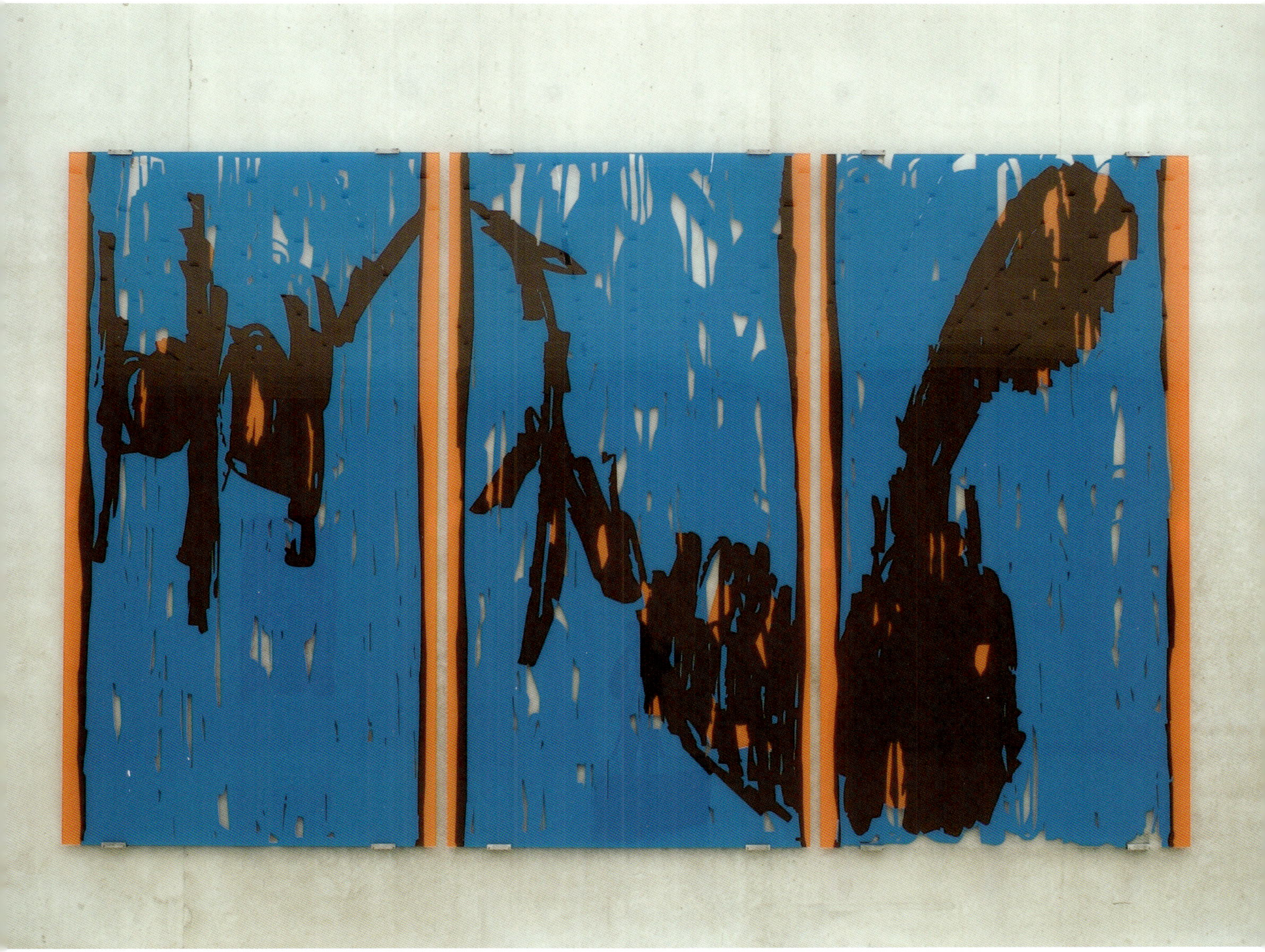

TAKE SOMETHING HOT
AND COOL IT DOWN

/

EMMA DEXTER
LONDON, 2010

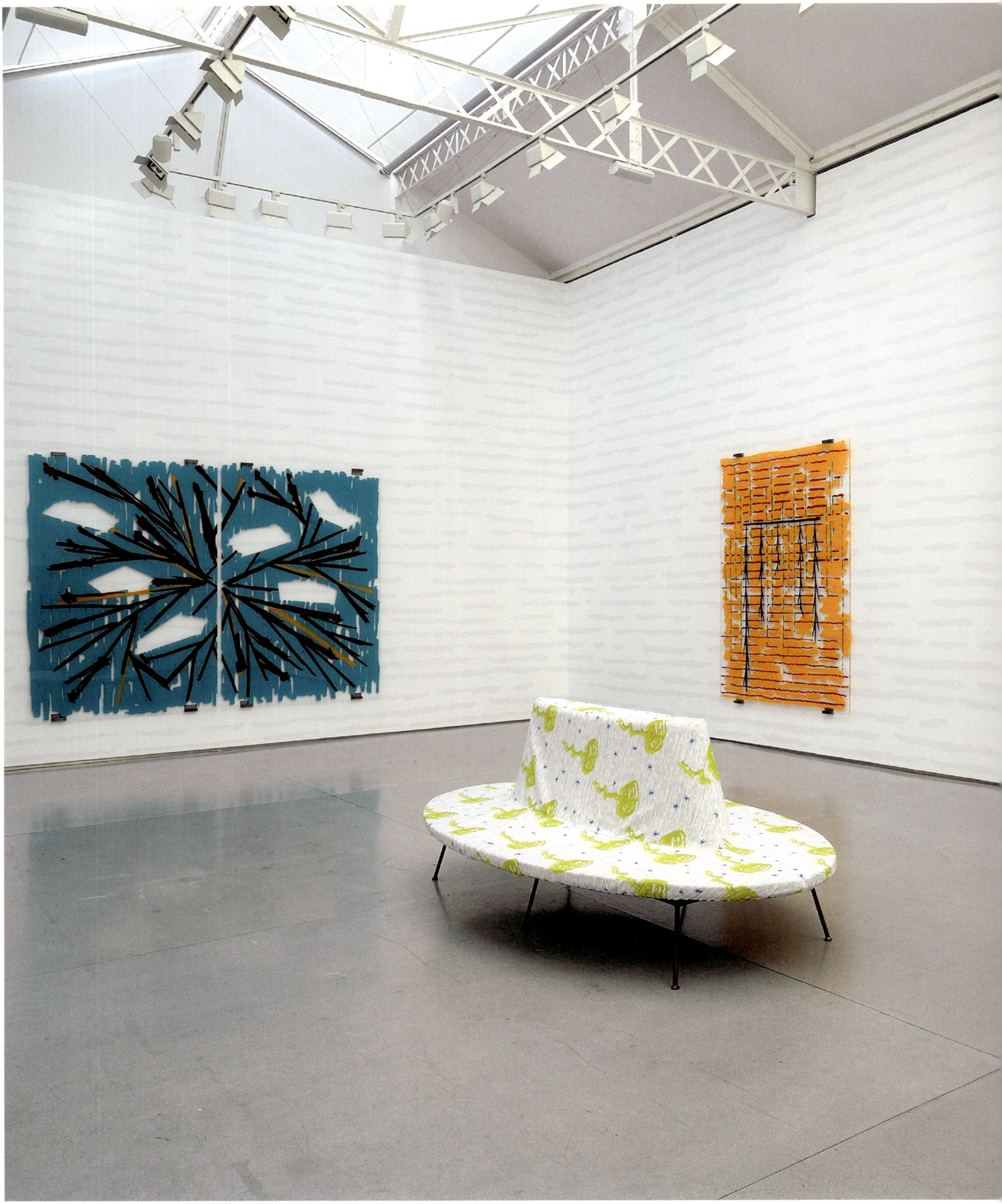

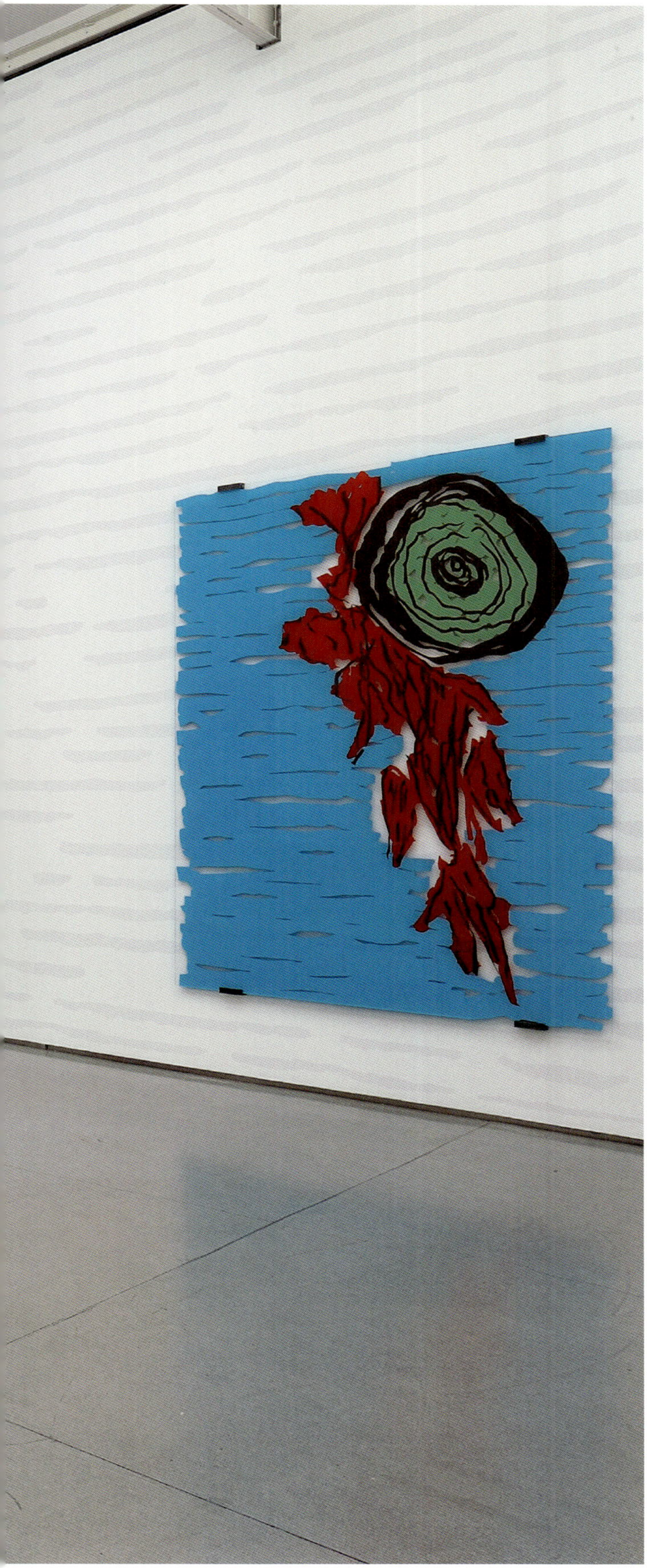

Les lacs des saintes, Boisdale, Roccou, Pouf
(in collaboration with Franz West), 2008
Ink on Plexiglas, steel and fabric
La Chambre des Saintes,
Galerie Thaddaeus Ropac, Paris, 2008

The decision to make paintings in the late-twentieth and early-twenty-first century is deeply problematic. Ever since photography stole painting's simplistic representational function in the nineteenth century, compounded in the twentieth by Malevich's end-game black square or Duchamp's readymade, painting has always seemed to be on the back foot, playing a game of eternal catch-up. Declared dead at the beginning of the twentieth century, painting has been decried by Marxist critics as the aesthetic lackey of either authoritarianism or advanced capitalism. This attitude has been nowhere stronger than in France, where the events of May 1968 fed the predominance of leftist literary theory among intellectuals and artistic élites, spanning everything from Saussurean structuralist linguistics at one extreme to the thoughts of Chairman Mao at the other.

Tableaux

It is therefore no surprise, perhaps, that the French artist Jean-Marc Bustamante came late to painting, via a career that explored many different media: photography in the late 1970s and sculpture during the 1980s. When Bustamante did embark on painting in the 1990s, these were not paintings on canvas or board, but thick, sculptural sheets of silk-screened Plexiglas that were secured to the wall with heavy, industrial steel brackets. Using ink rather than paint, the effect was a lush and brilliant colour, which, like the ground of the Plexiglas, was also see-through.

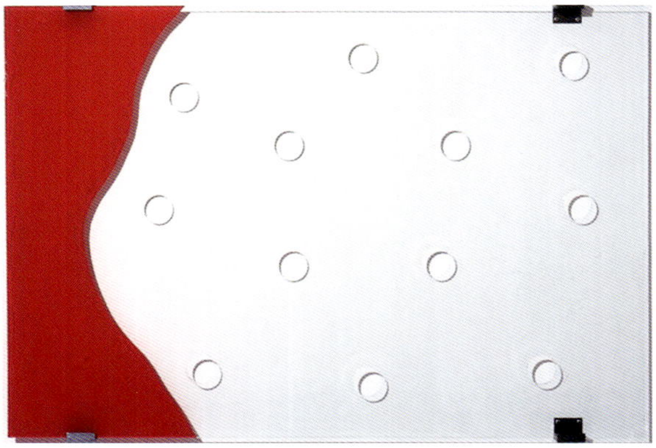

Aerogramme Rose, 1997
Ink on Plexiglas, 120 x 180 x 4 cm

opposite: *Aerogramme Miel*, 1997
Ink on Plexiglas, 145 x 185 x 4 cm

Bustamante has always paid close attention to the names he gives to his works and the types that they belong to. Calling his photographs *Tableaux* (*Pictures*) and his paintings *Panoramas* suggests that Bustamante encourages a playful ambiguity and elusiveness in his practice. Bustamante is engaged with an enquiry into the philosophical nature of each medium: intertwining an investigation into the properties of materials and processes with the theoretical and philosophical realm of semantics, linguistics and semiotics. Bustamante's approach seeks to explore the gaps, ambiguities and correspondences between media, testing the thinness or robustness of the delineation of each medium, aiming always at their redefinition and reinvention, and the typologies of his production and their names are part of that process. Thus in the late 1970s he gave the tradition-laden and bourgeois term for oil painting – *Tableaux* – to his matter-of-fact large-scale colour photographs describing abject semi-rural non-spaces on the outskirts of Barcelona. The power of the term *Tableau*, with its associations with the aura of the unique artwork and the masterly grand tradition of painting, is shattered and devalued by this linguistic *détournement*, as the viewer confronts a mechanically-produced image of an unremarkable industrial site, a location expressly chosen for being 'without qualities'.[1] Bustamante's use of the term *Tableau* for a photograph further reminds us how, in the nineteenth century, realist painting was threatened with obsolescence by the invention of photography; but it also addresses the fact that in the late 1970s and early 1980s technological advancements allowed large-scale colour photography to compete with the scopic and somatic power of large history paintings, in terms of scale, ambition and significance of content, fundamentally changing our understanding of the photographic object. Bustamante's choice of the term *Tableau* inserts here a critical discourse on material, orientation, semantics and representation into these apparently affectless photographic objects. Later, when the artist chose to make paintings, he again chose

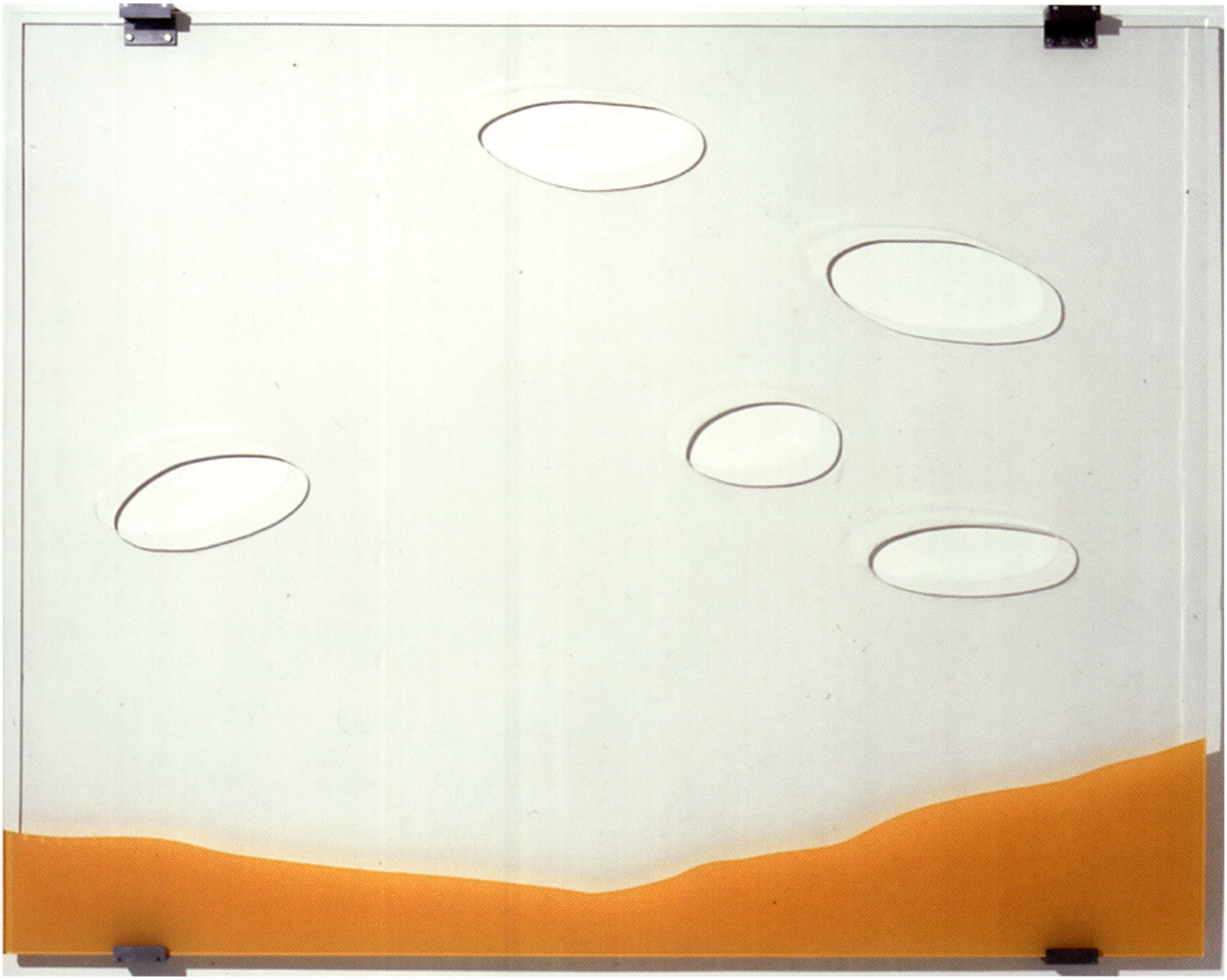

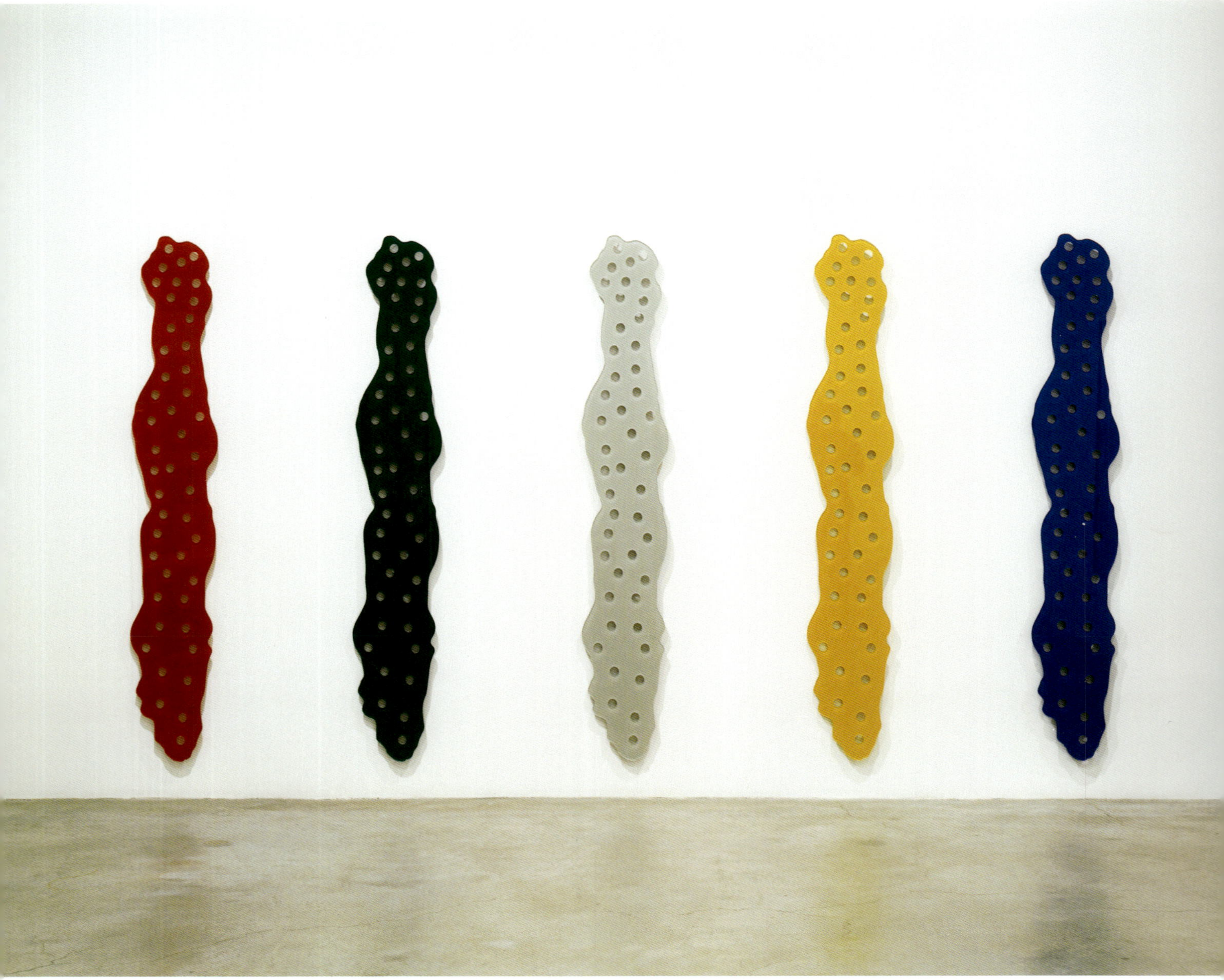

a similarly elusive yet allusive term to describe them: *Panoramas*. The term, from the Greek meaning 'all sight', was and is used for all wide-angled views, in a range of media from painting, to drawing, photography and even three-dimensional models, where the emphasis is on delineating detailed topographic information in an elongated landscape format. Here Bustamante again subverts expectations; lacking any descriptive drive these *Panoramas* are dedicated to pure sight: slits and holes puncturing the surface of the transparent Plexiglas become spyglasses to the wall behind, while the painting remains like a object vanishing on the wall in front of our eyes: a palimpsest of what and where painting used to be.

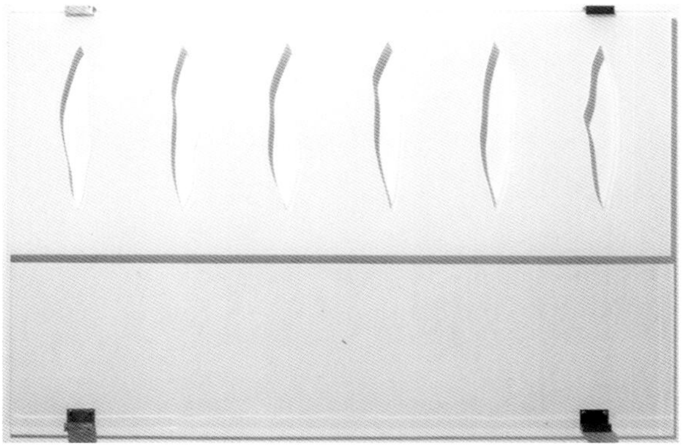

Aerogramme Lacté, 1997
Ink on Plexiglas, 120 x 180 x 4 cm

opposite: *Dispersion I, 2002*
Paint on Plexiglas, 220 x 40 x 1 cm (each element)

The Factory

Industrial and technical processes have always been of central importance to Bustamante's oeuvre: from photography, to the *Lumières* (found photographic images printed on sheets of Plexiglas), to the modernist industrial aesthetic of his sculpture and, finally, the silk-screened Plexiglas of the *Panoramas* and *Peintures*. In this, Bustamante follows in a grand tradition, forged principally in the United States, of artists such as Frank Stella, Andy Warhol, Donald Judd, Richard Serra or Robert Smithson, who either metaphorised or actually used industrial processes to make art. They aimed to create art that was far removed from direct expression or the handmade, moving towards a fully industrialised aesthetic attuned to 1960s modernity, to create a technological sublime. Bustamante's paintings are what Caroline A. Jones would describe as within the order of the performative technological sublime – where the artist has developed a process that assimilates aspects of industrial process.[2] Today's technological sublime is, however, very different to that of the 1960s, when European and US heavy industry enjoyed global domination in the mass production of steel consumer goods. Now, as heavy industries decline, the domestic sphere has been technologised, invaded by computers,

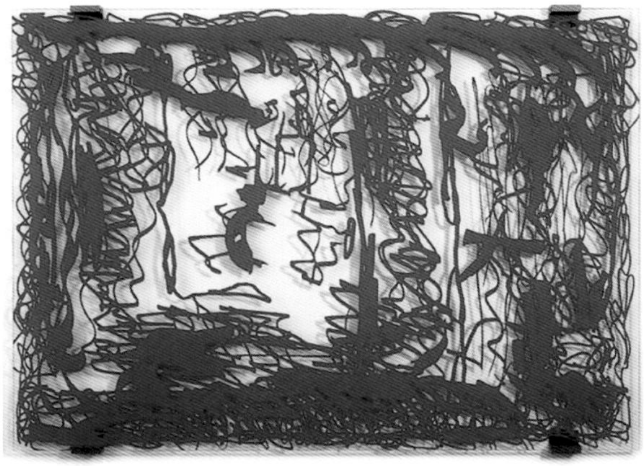

Suspension, 1998
Ink on Plexiglas, 152 x 213 x 4 cm

opposite: *Entrelacs*, 2003
Ink on Plexiglas, 210 x 328 x 4 cm

printers and scanners. Bustamante's home/studio is symptomatically the site of the first and second stages of a production process that reveals the blurred boundaries between the technological, the industrial and the domestic: the cottage industry of the information age.

Eric de Chassey says of Bustamante that 'all his work is governed by modes which can be diversely described as photographic process, painterly aims and sculptural forms', and the interchanges between them.[3] Tellingly, the medium missing from Chassey's list is drawing, and yet drawing is, like photography, at the core of how Bustamante conceives, constructs and executes his work. Drawing is the most process-oriented of all media, lowly in status, always presented as the preparatory medium for a completed sculpture or painting, rarely an end in itself. Presumably Chassey does not mention drawing because Bustamante does not exhibit preparatory drawings as 'completed' oeuvres.[4] But drawing is at the ontological heart of these 'paintings', not just as a part of the process, but because it brings with it crucial notions of completion and incompletion, provisionality, authenticity, thought and idea.

A proliferation in the past twenty years of post-Pop commodity aesthetics, sometimes acting as a critique of consumerism, has been counterbalanced in recent years by an upsurge of interest in drawing – seen as antithetical to cool, Pop-art inspired works, free from the hand of the artist. Drawing offers a sense of the authentic, the personal and the idiosyncratic, the site where the record of an act, performed by the artist, remains unadulterated and unmediated. Bustamante's paintings, therefore, interweave the uniqueness and the aura of the 'drawing' with an industrially-produced final work, which is never unique, being part of an edition, and dependent on various technologies for its creation: computers, scanners, digital photography and silk-screening. The process is deceptively simple: a drawing becomes the template for an enlarged

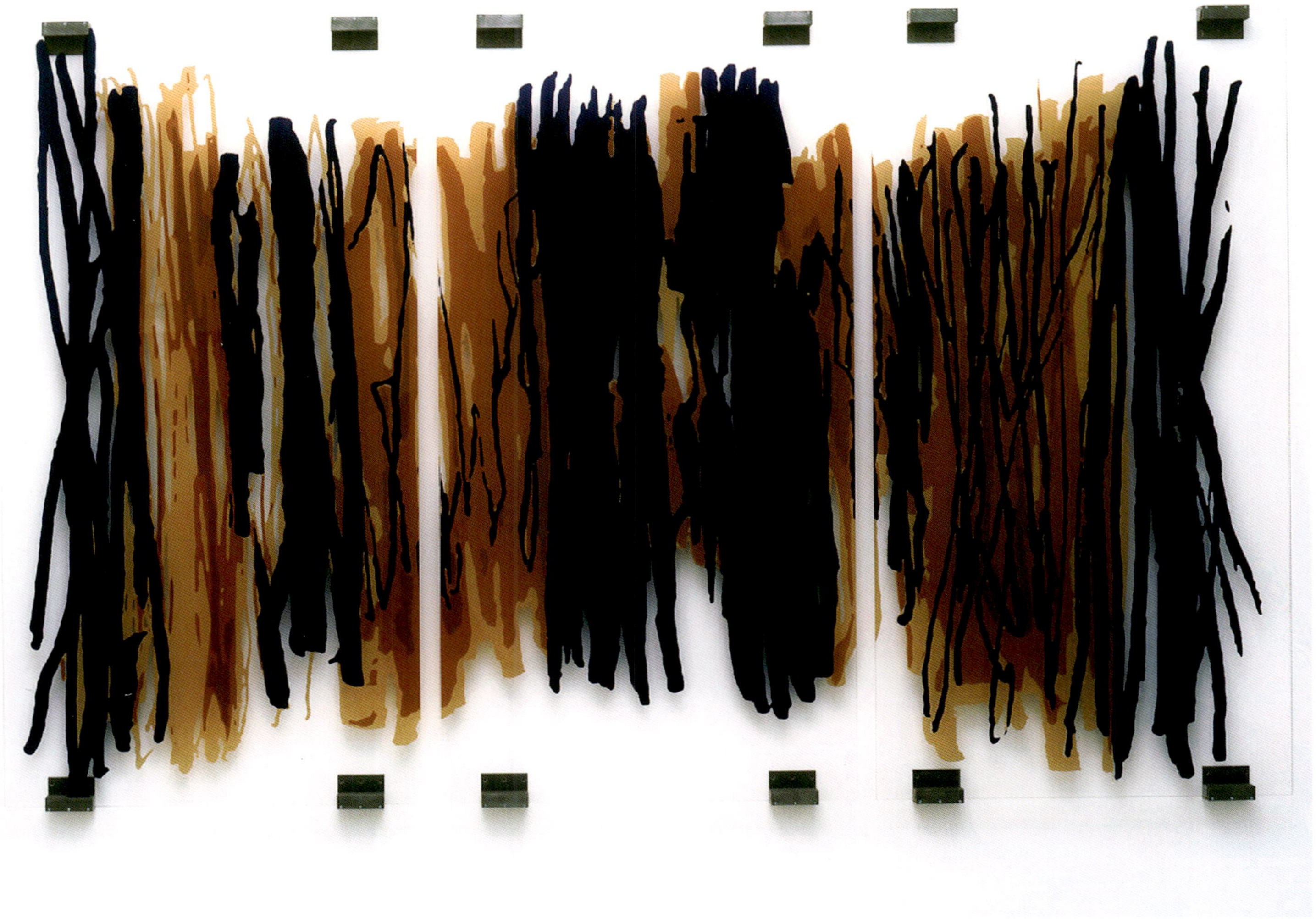

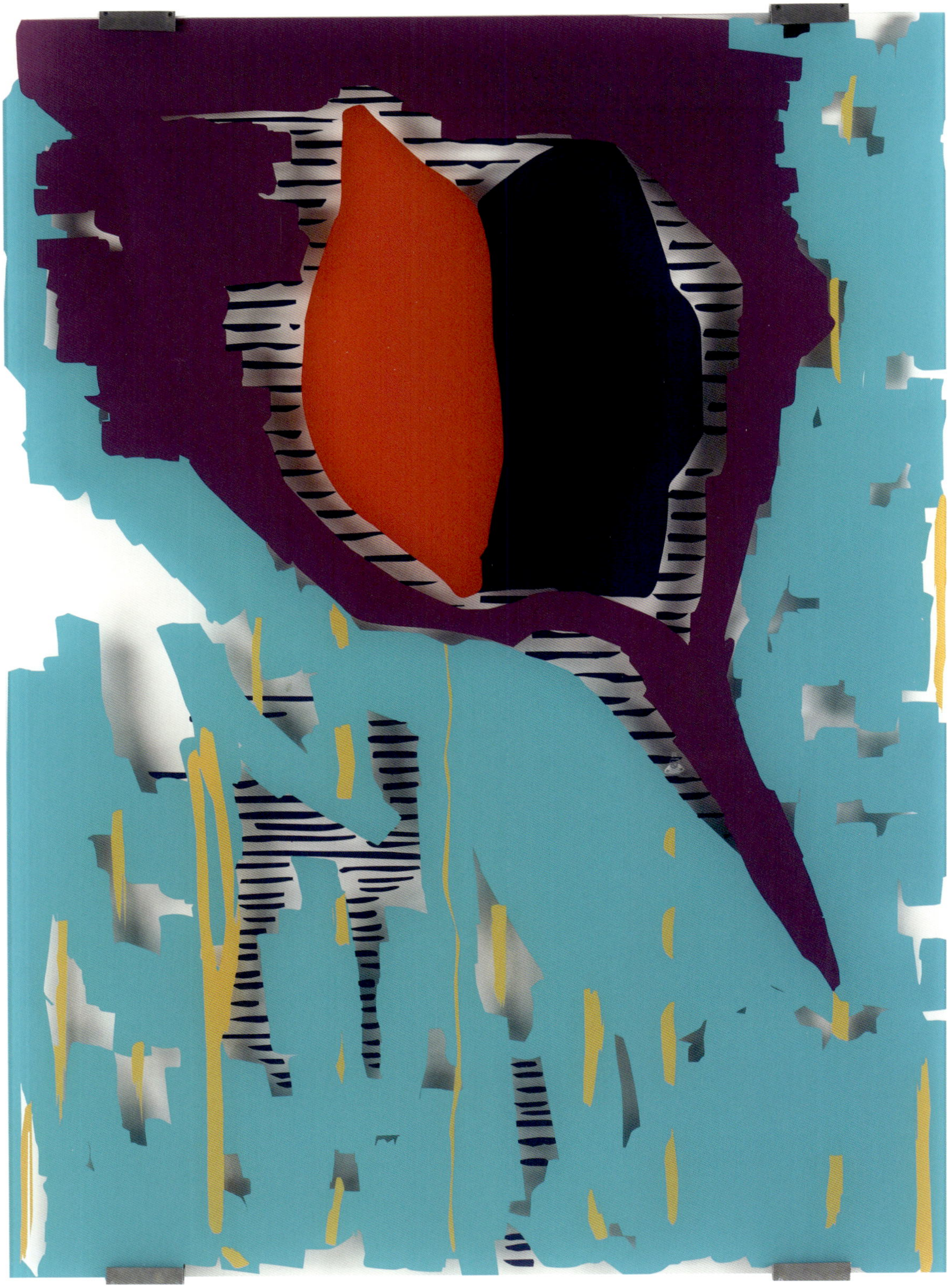

silk-screened work. These haiku-like quick doodles are made with a small brush on gridded paper. Making a selection of the most successful or relevant, they are scanned into the computer, where they are revised on screen, tweaked with subtle changes, sometimes simplified, approximated, the colours reduced: subtle gradations of tone disappear and the colours are chosen to comply with the mechanical screenprinting process that now follows – and the work becomes in the artist's own words 'a pictorial proposition' or his *cuisine personnelle*.[5] This is also the means of producing what will be the blueprint that the industrial silk-screeners will follow.

opposite: *Répliques*, 2006
Ink on Plexiglas, 195 x 147 x 4 cm

Preparatory drawing for *Répliques*, 2006

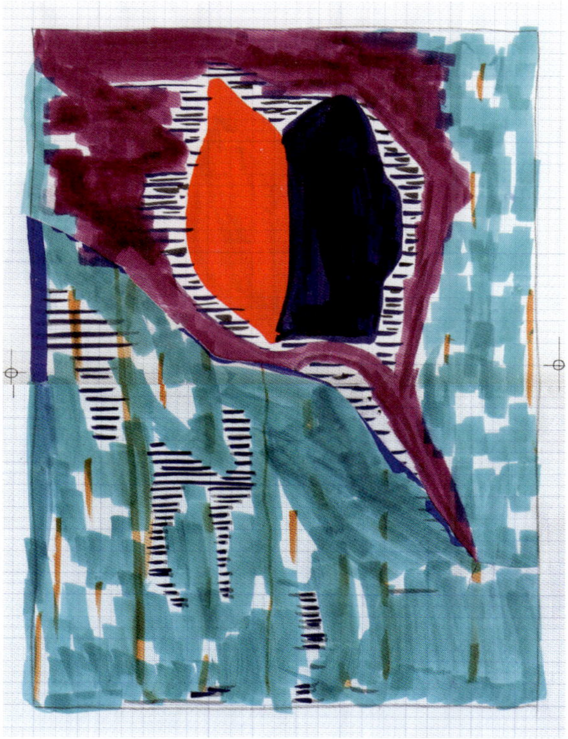

Drawing into Painting

Drawing itself exists in a unique position within media, offering innate qualities of provisionality, incompletion, transparency and temporal specificity. The association of drawing with process, combined with its tautologous and thought-like nature, offers a model of how art can still be conducted within a sceptical postmodern context. Lying at the heart of Bustamante's painting practice is the question of the difference between painting and drawing – how painting carries with it the notion of completion, and how drawing carries with it the notion of continual experimentation. Painting is an art of accretion and concealment – working in layers, errors can easily be revised and covered with new areas of paint. The essence of the drawing, however, is that errors are made visible – in that sense it is the art form that mirrors most exactly the process of thought itself, and acts as an untainted record of an act. Bustamante's transfiguration of drawing into the final painting, via the computer, overrides many of these traditional assumptions about the nature of drawing and painting. As Chassey has observed, Bustamante has 'found a way to conjure up the richness of colour and complexity of form (linked to an elevated genre of painting) with the provisionality of drawing'.[6]

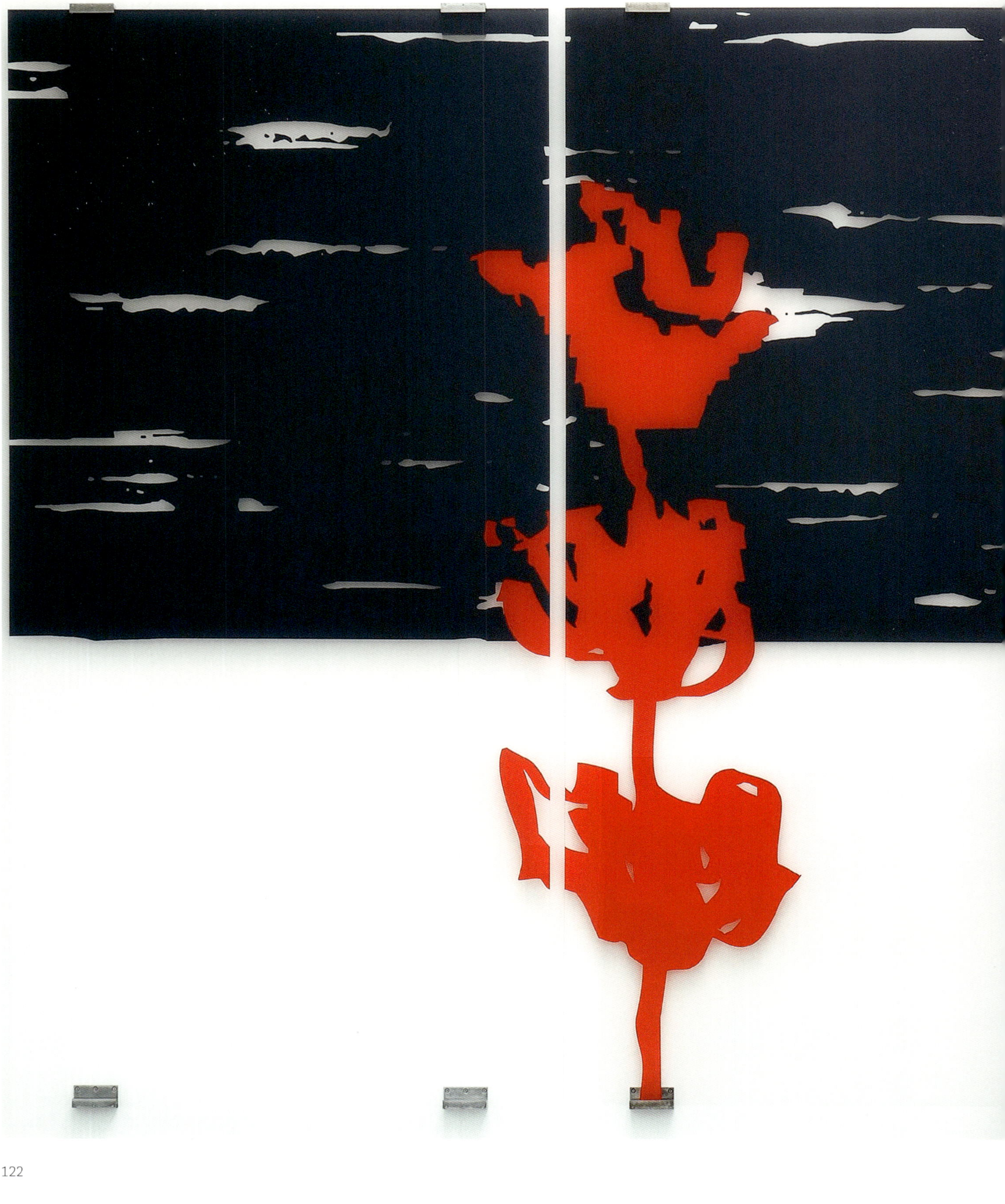

Entre nous, 2005
Ink on Plexiglas, 300 x 450 x 4 cm

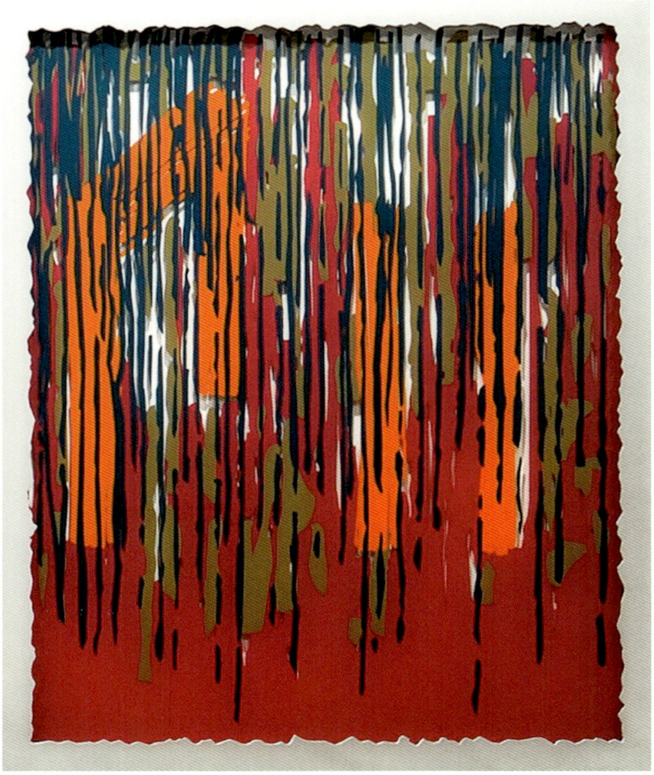

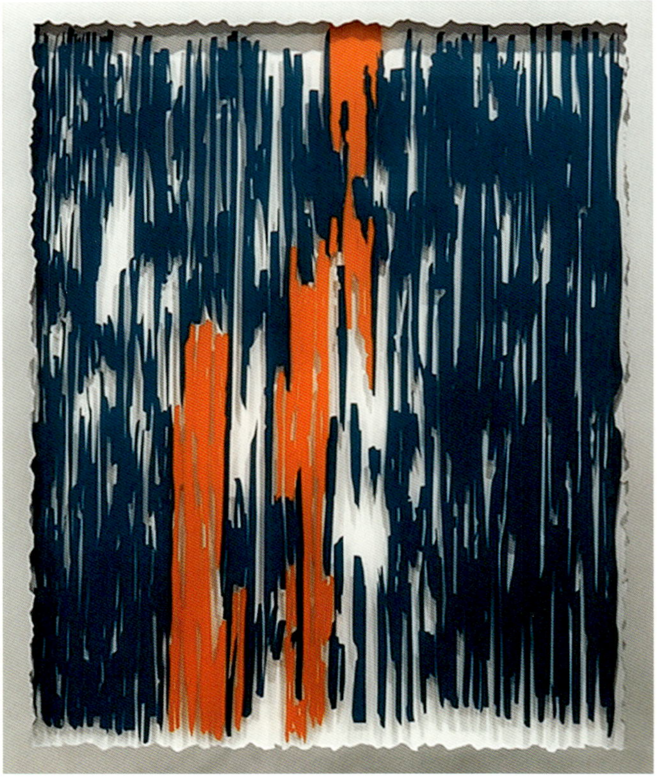

Michel Gauthier provides the most cogent description of Bustamante's achievement in this area, outlining how the original drawing or sketch and the finished Plexiglas work merge together, the final work being nothing more nor less than 'a perfect image of the sketch'[7] – drawing and final work become one and the same, but enlarged, and the role of the sketch is no longer simply a preparatory function. The process differs from the use of an epidiascope, used by Franz Kline to translate drawings directly into seemingly spontaneous larger 'finished' paintings. Gauthier argues: 'What makes the process used in producing the *Panoramas* ... so unusual is its view of the implementation phase as being one of pure representation. The work actually appears when the draft is turned into an icon of itself ... With the *Panoramas*, what we now have to discover is a work not *in* the image, but *as* the image of its rough sketch.'[8] The drawing – something that would normally never be seen and would traditionally disappear from view after it had been used – is elevated into the final version. 'It is granted the benefit of the aura attached to the final state, to the work itself.'[9] Gauthier suggests that Bustamante's project is part of a tradition in recent painting of semiological enquiry into the ontology of painting: artists such as Roy Lichtenstein in the mid-1960s made paintings of paint, in which 'an index becomes the subject of an icon, the brushstroke the image of a brushstroke'.[10] Gauthier further suggests that, rather than playing out a 'critical, ironic or de-sublimating function' as so much recent painting has done, this in fact offers a new type of painting.[11] Indeed, Bustamante's paintings on Plexiglas seem to have anticipated many aspects of how we now perceive and receive imagery and colour: via computer screens, mobile phones, iPads and other illuminated devices. Ink on Plexiglas creates special effects of light, transparency and colour. The lustrous yet transparent inks intermix with and overlay each other, creating new hybrid deep colours further transfigured by the play of shadow or light. The colours and even the forms have a sense of mutability and fluidity, due

A view, 1998
Ink on Plexiglas, 195 x 138 x 4 cm

opposite: *Suite japonaise 1*, 2008
Ink on Plexiglas, aluminium, 170 x 128 x 5 cm

to the potential for changing conditions of light and reflections affecting the paintings' surroundings. Indeed the Plexiglas itself is in fact nothing but an enormous screen through which light can pass in both directions. But what do these paintings actually depict, aside from being an image of their original sketch? Much of the surface of the earlier *Panoramas* was often covered with doodle-like squiggles over the entire transparent sheet, which, either in horizontal or vertical format, echoed the traditional formats of landscape and portrait painting. In the past three years a more figurative, lyrical and even traditional imagery has crept in: some images remain quite abstract; others represent leaves, branches or water. Neither fully abstract nor distinctly figurative, they function, perhaps, as ciphers for a residual memory of what painting once signified; are they, in fact, perfect objects of mourning for the death of painting? Bustamante, however, views them as light and playful constructs: painted on a clear surface, their transparency, playfulness and delicacy suggest *jouissance*, reminiscent of the famous film of Picasso painting on glass.

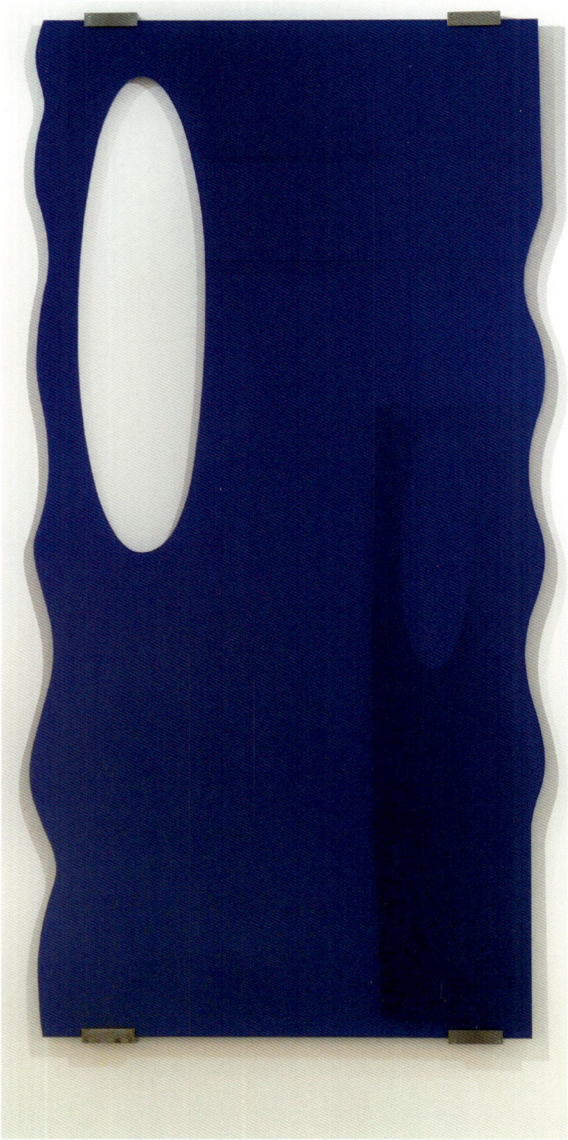

Untitled (*Blue Door*), 2005
Ink on Plexiglas, 185 x 95 x 4 cm

opposite: *Lion*, 2005
Ink on Plexiglas, 195 x 345 x 4 cm

Loss

Loss is a fundamental part of the process: the translation from watercolour on paper to computer drawing necessitates a simplification. But in exchange something else is gained, described by the artist as 'an esprit, a lightness, a simplicity'.[12] Indeed, the threat or promise of loss is close to the inherent nature of drawing as the pen only lightly touches the surface – each touch is a sign of departure, withdrawal and end – unlike painting which hides the temporal aspect of making. Michael Newman describes it thus: 'Drawing with each stroke re-enacts desire and loss. Its peculiar mode of being lies between the withdrawal of the trace in the mark and the presence of the idea it prefigures.'[13] The computer, the machine in the studio, becomes the vehicle for further evacuation of qualities, mistakes, hesitancies and the hand of the artist.

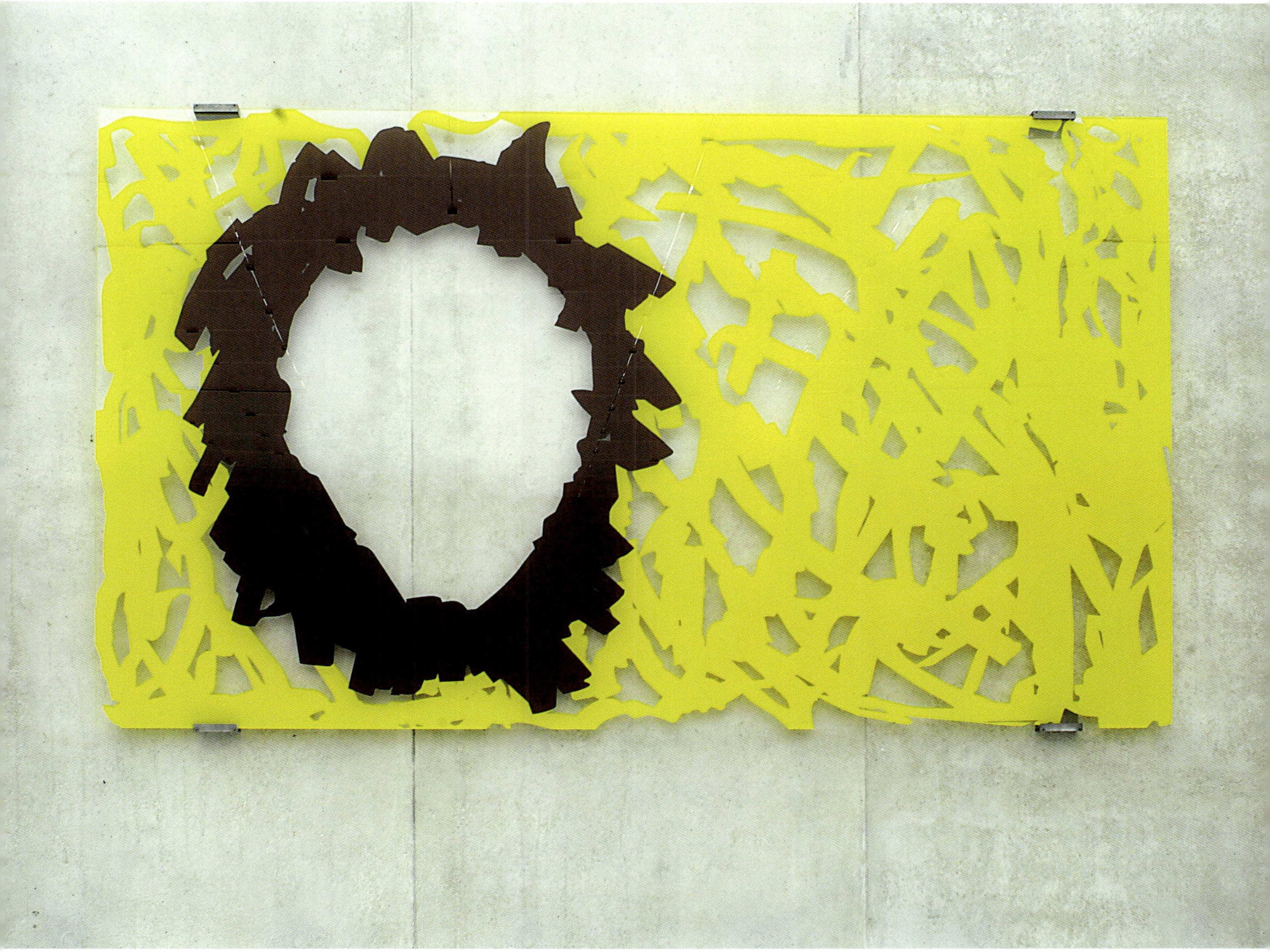

At the same time, the computer, like drawing, suggests the possibility of limitless versions, an endless provisionality, choices and changes, as well as necessary delimitation and simplification. As Bustamante's painting technique has developed, so now the computer and scanner have replaced the use of photography to capture an image of the drawing, as a means of reproduction and also enlargement. These processes have earlier antecedents, such as the use of the epidiascope, or the ancient cartoon method of enlargement using paper, chalk and pins.

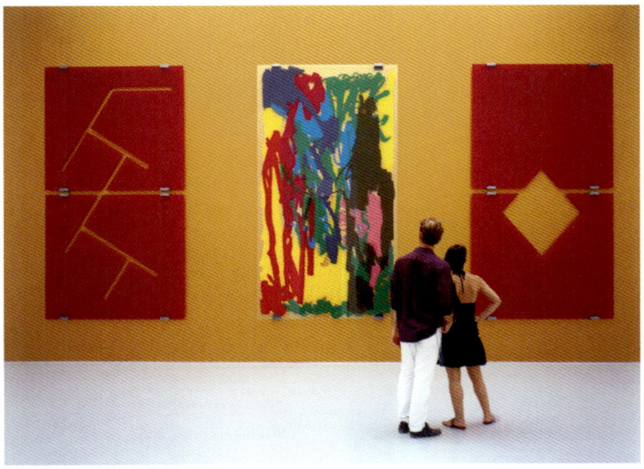

French Pavilion, 50th Venice Biennale, 2003

opposite: *Perfect Dream 2*, 2005
Ink on Plexiglas, galvanised steel, 172 x 145 x 5 cm

Painting as Object and the Ground

In Bustamante's paintings the ink is applied in layers on the transparent Plexiglas sheet, leaving much of the surface free of ink. The viewer therefore literally sees through the work to the wall behind, meaning that the wall becomes part of the work, functioning as the 'ground' of the painting/drawing. In traditional drawing, the ground – the untouched area of paper – is an essential element in the conceptualisation of the drawing. As Norman Bryson has observed, the ground acts as a reserve, a blank from which the drawing emerges. It is only given meaning in contradistinction to the line and is 'perceptually present but conceptually absent'.[14] The existence of the reserve gives meaning to the line through its absence. The reserve must remain always free of ornament in order to preserve the nature of drawing itself. Walter Benjamin further commented: 'The graphic line marks out the area and so defines it by attaching itself to it as its background. Conversely the graphic line can exist only against this background, so that a drawing that completely covered its background would cease to be a drawing ...'[15] But Bustamante's paintings have problematised the notion of the reserve – a role split in this case between the transparent Plexiglas and the wall visible behind. The Plexiglas is transparent, visible and reflective all at the same time; it is perceptually present, but in this case it is conceptually active rather than absent. It functions

Nature et découvertes, 2006
Ink on Plexiglas, 195 x 147 x 4 cm

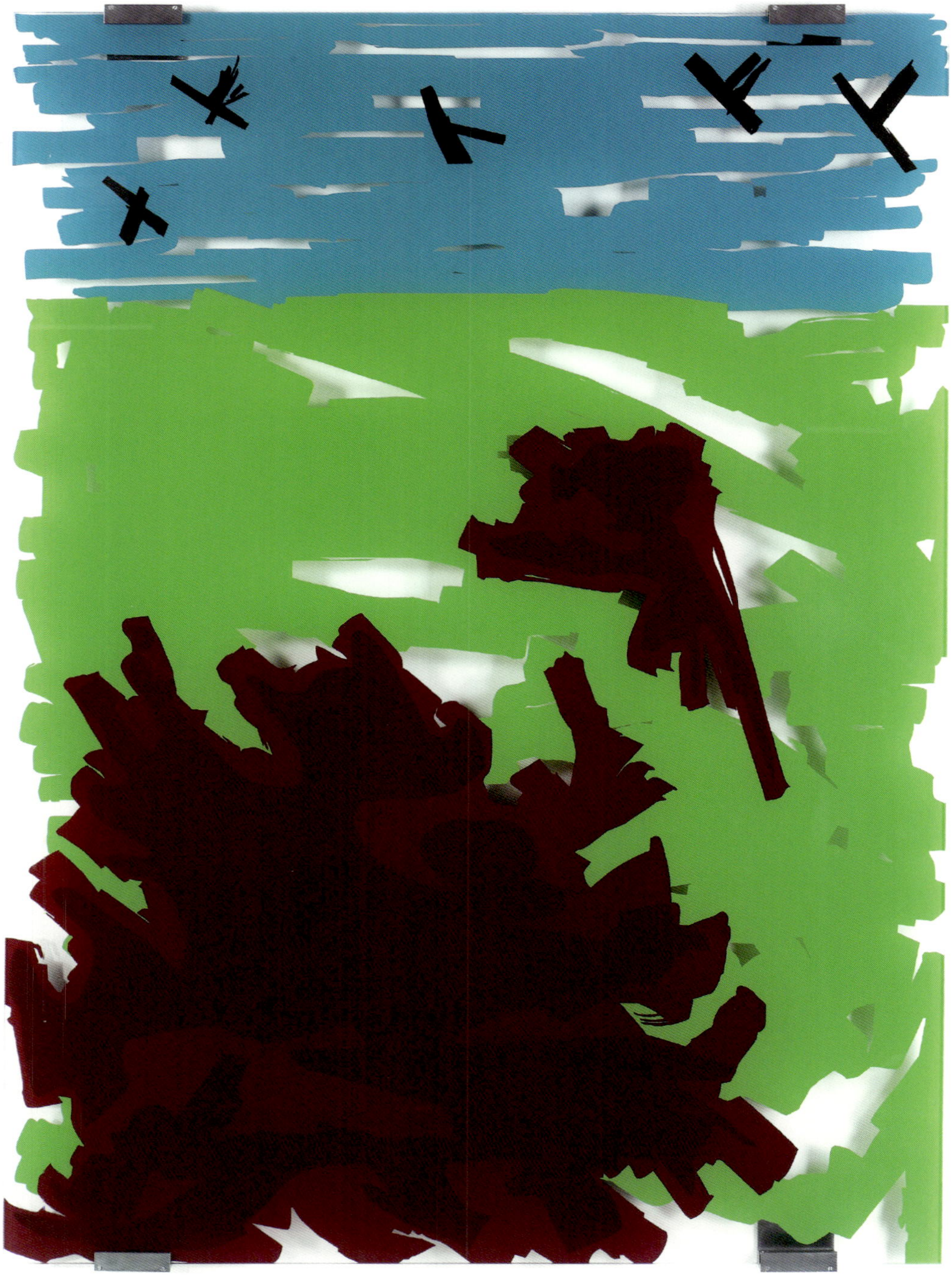

Oaxaca, 2006
Ink on Plexiglas, 195 x 147 x 4 cm

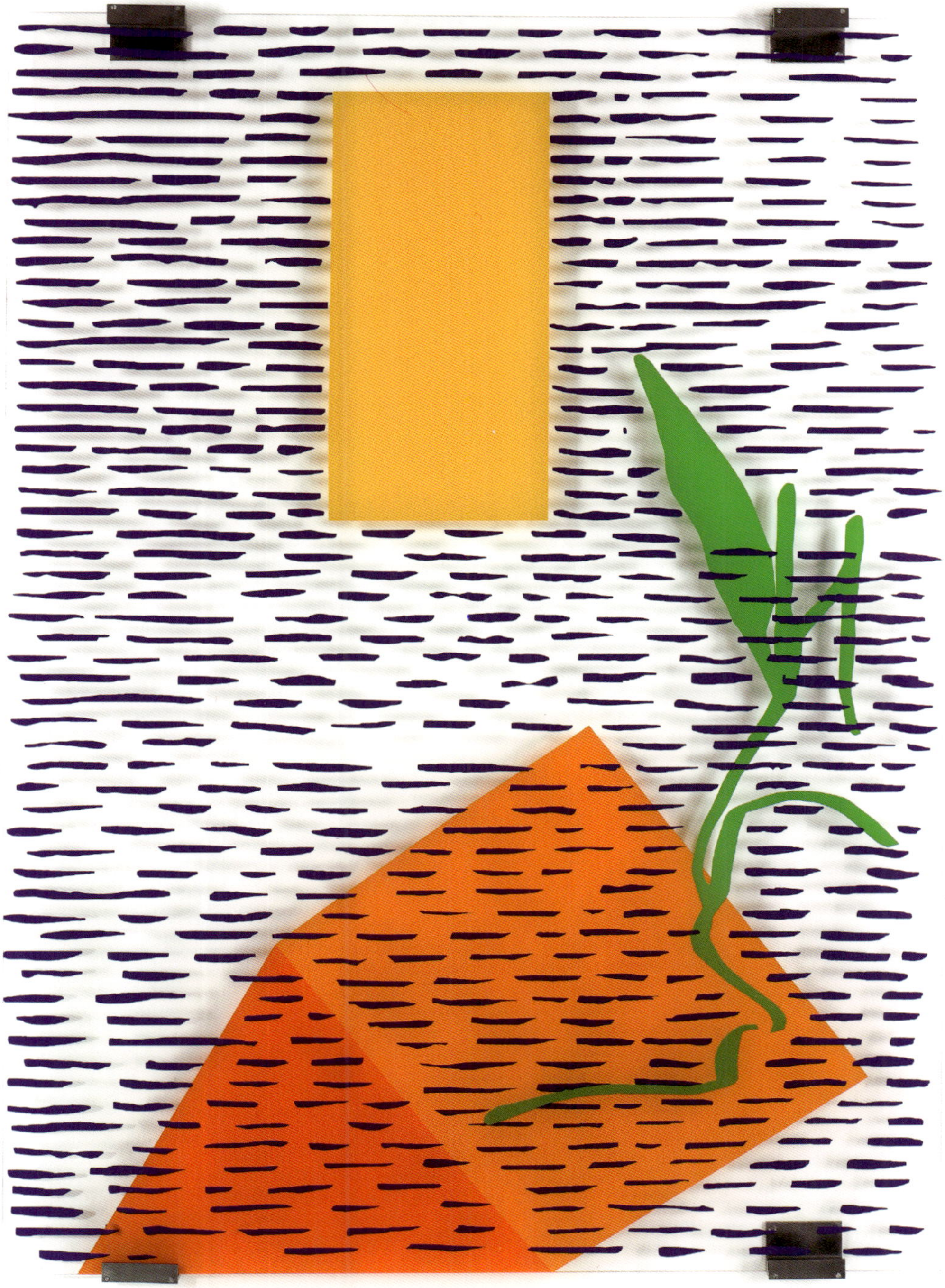

L' Ordre Ancien, 2007
Ink on Plexiglas, 195 x 305 x 4 cm

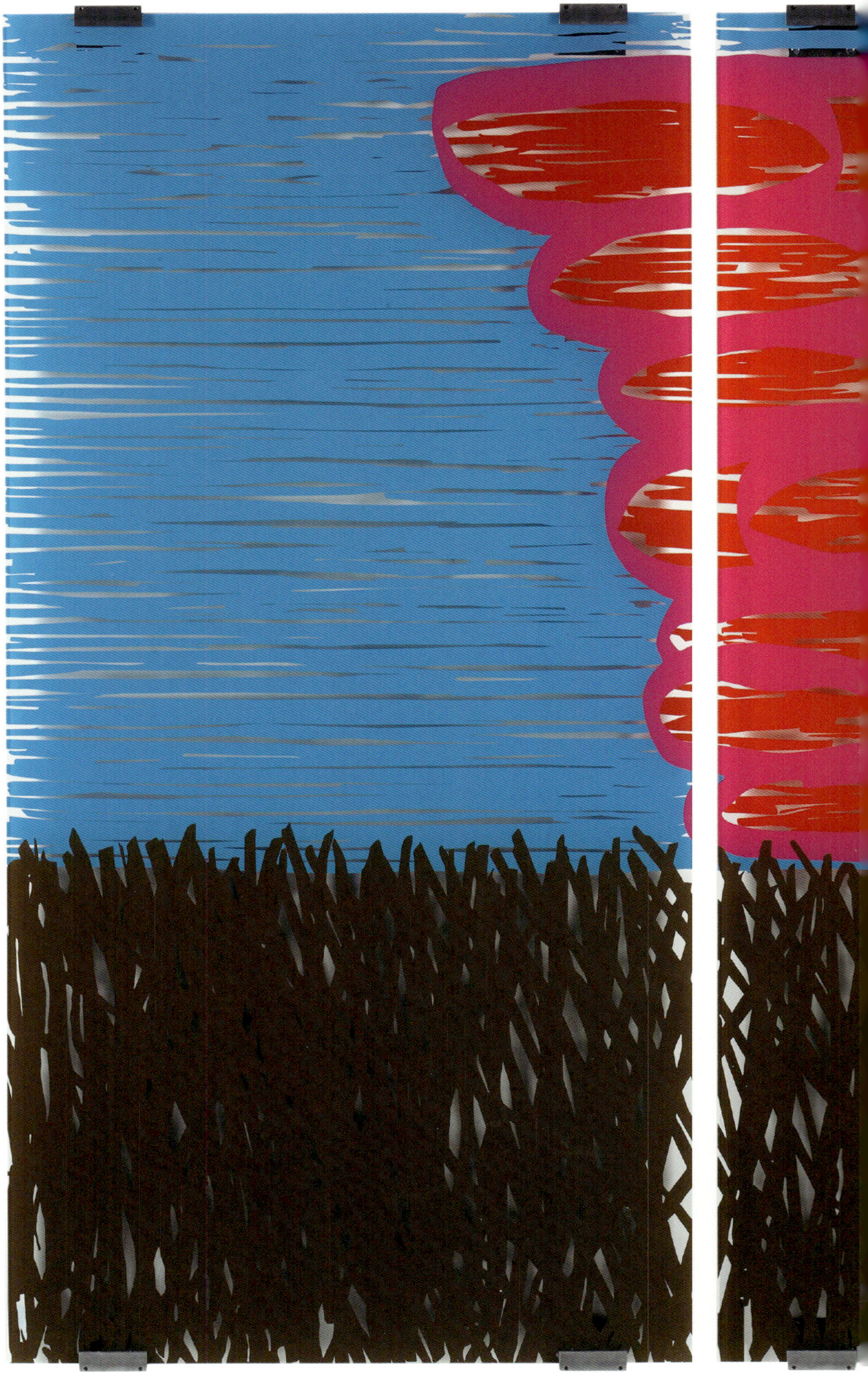

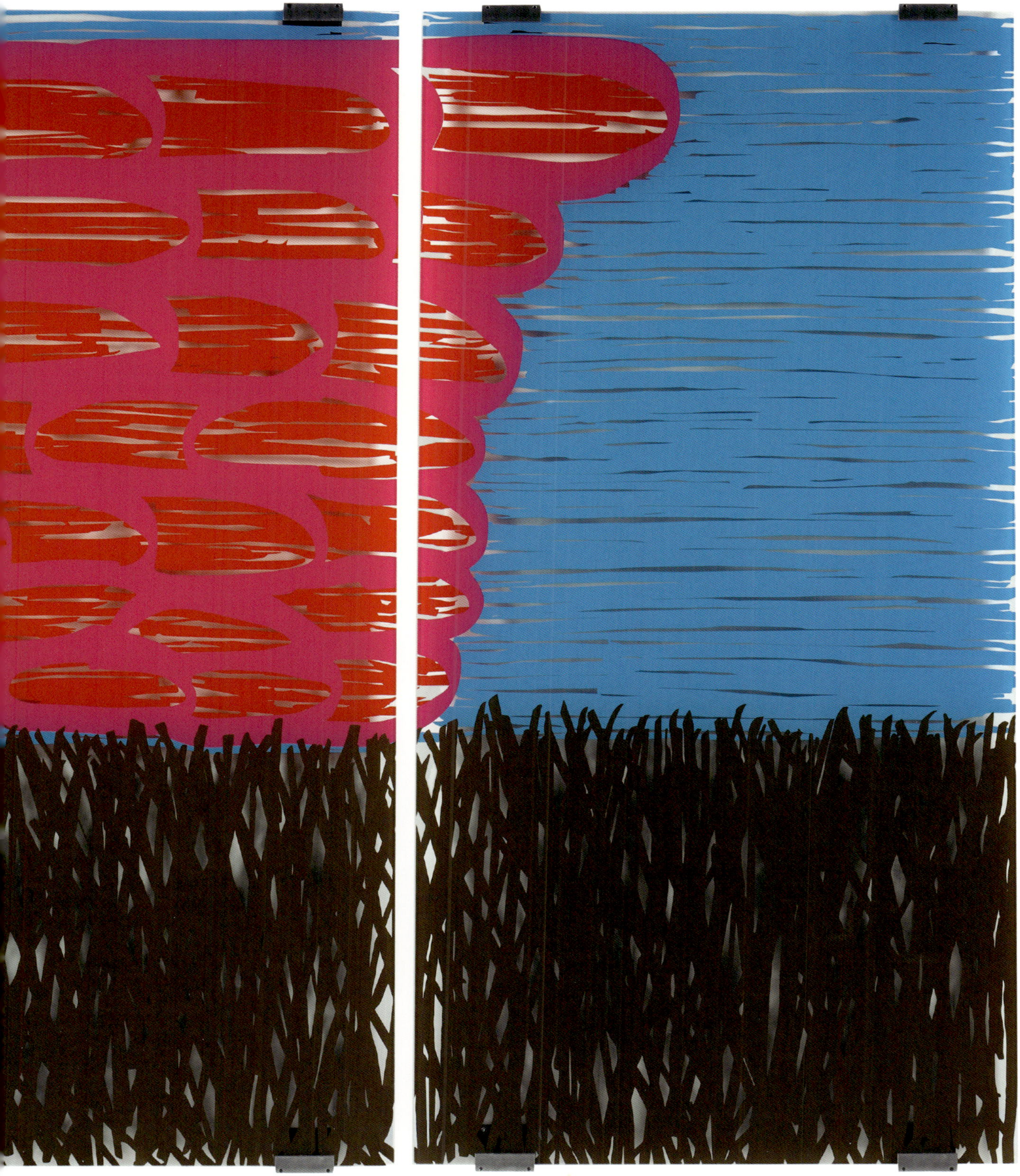

Calice, 2007
Ink on Plexiglas, 195 x 147 x 4 cm

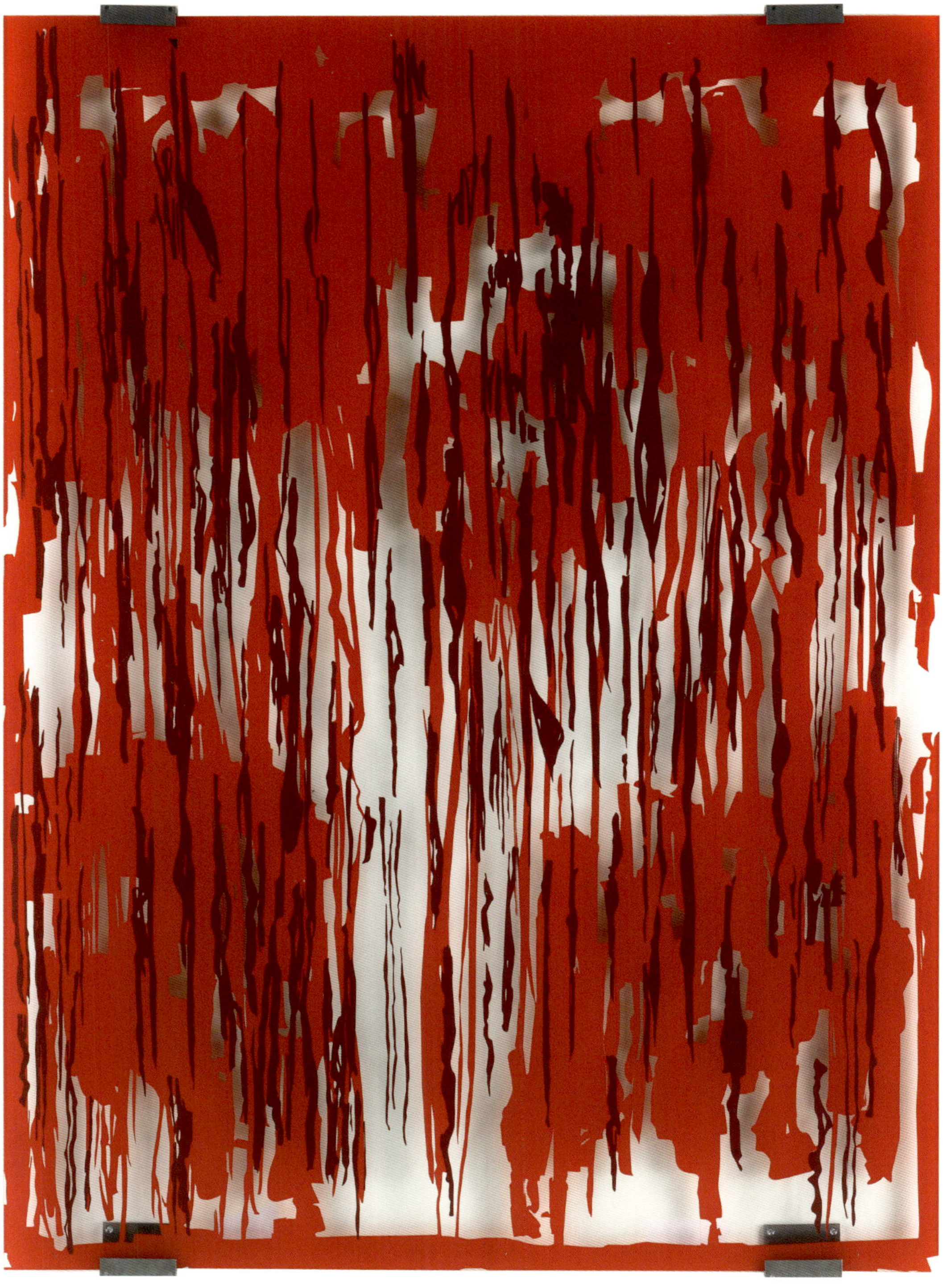

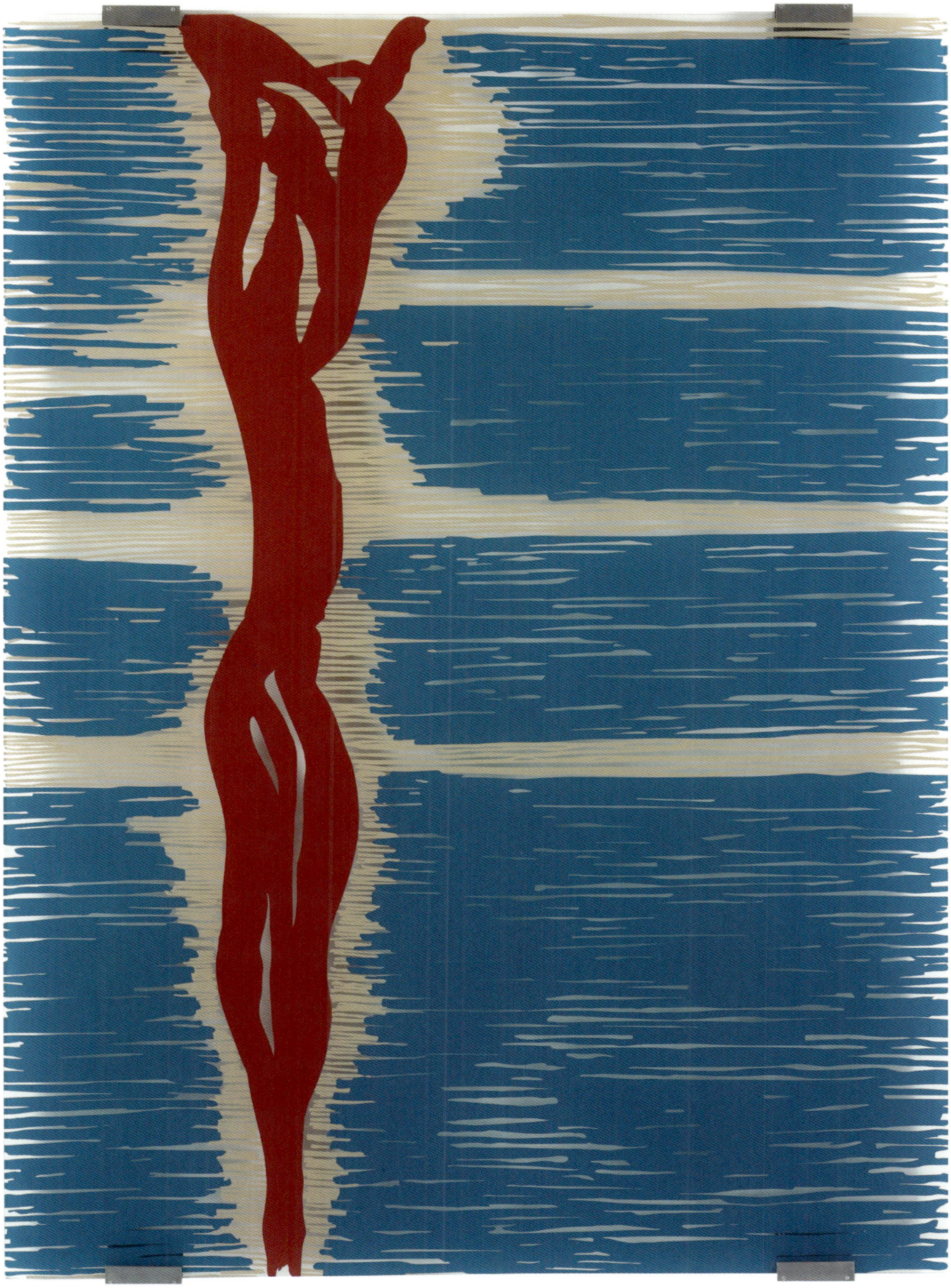

Nègre nu, 2007
Ink on Plexiglas, 195 x 147 x 4 cm

Acquaviva, 2006
Ink on Plexiglas, 195 x 147 x 4 cm

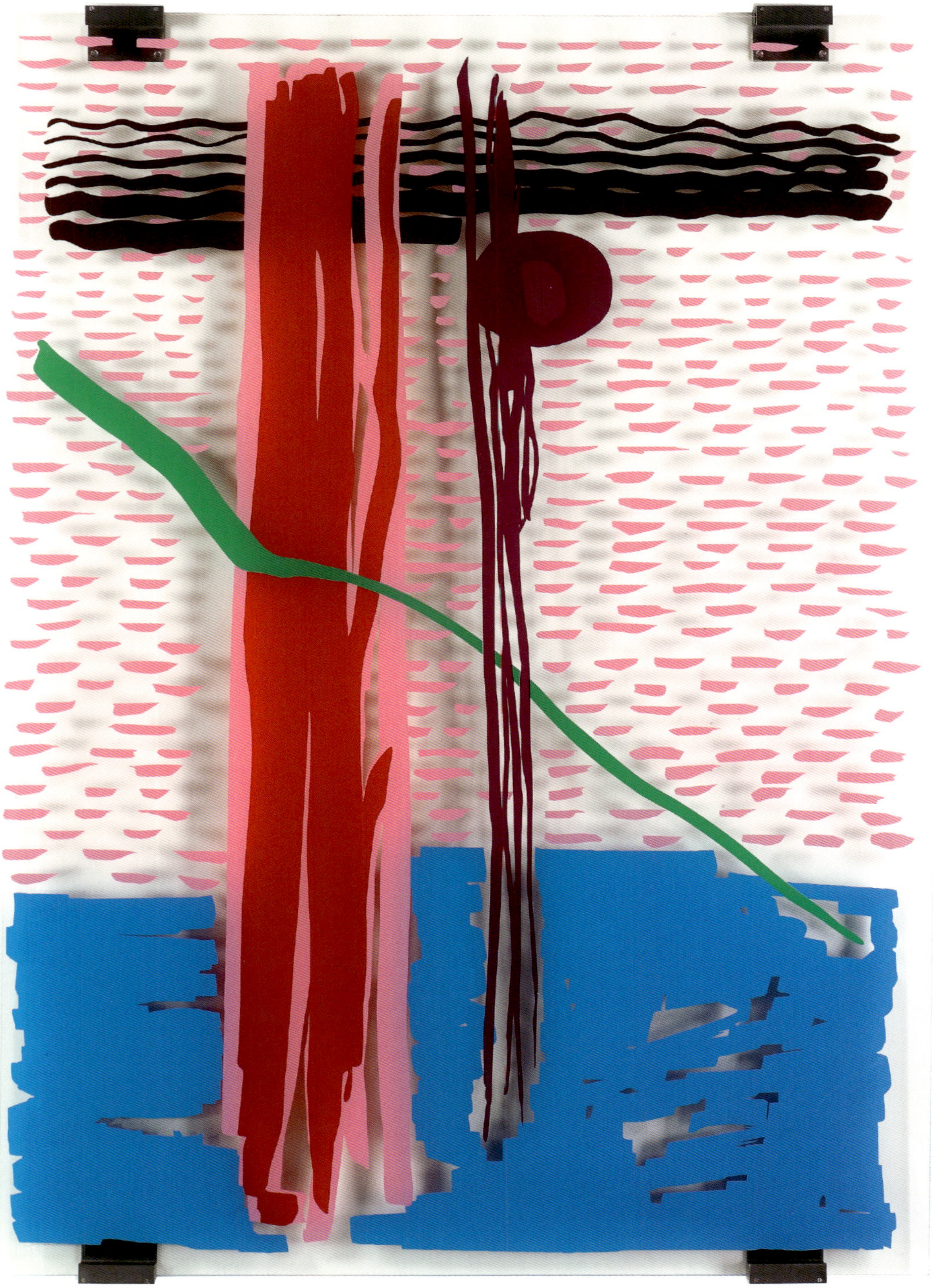

Lady H, 2006
Ink on Plexiglas, 195 x 147 x 4 cm

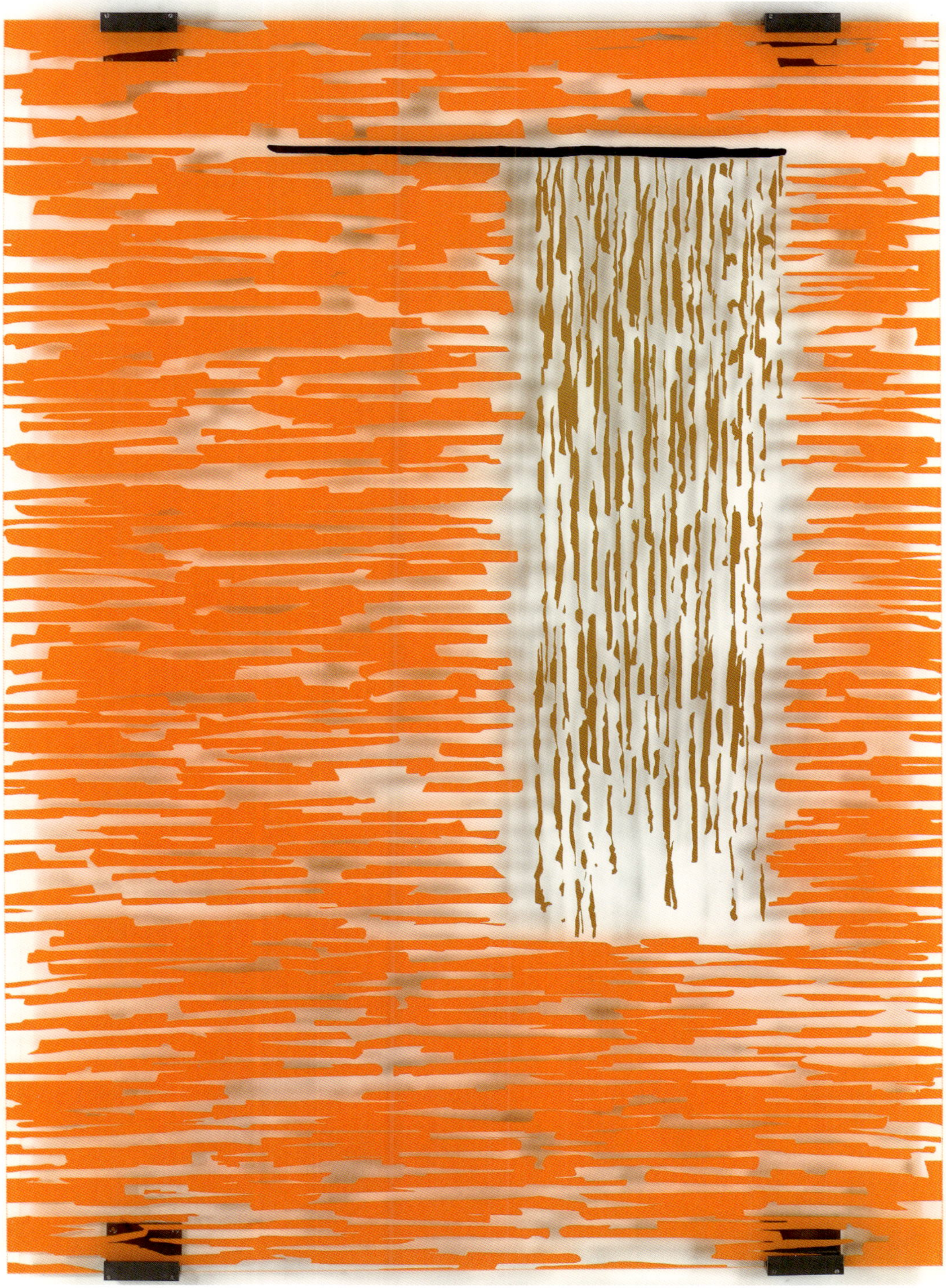

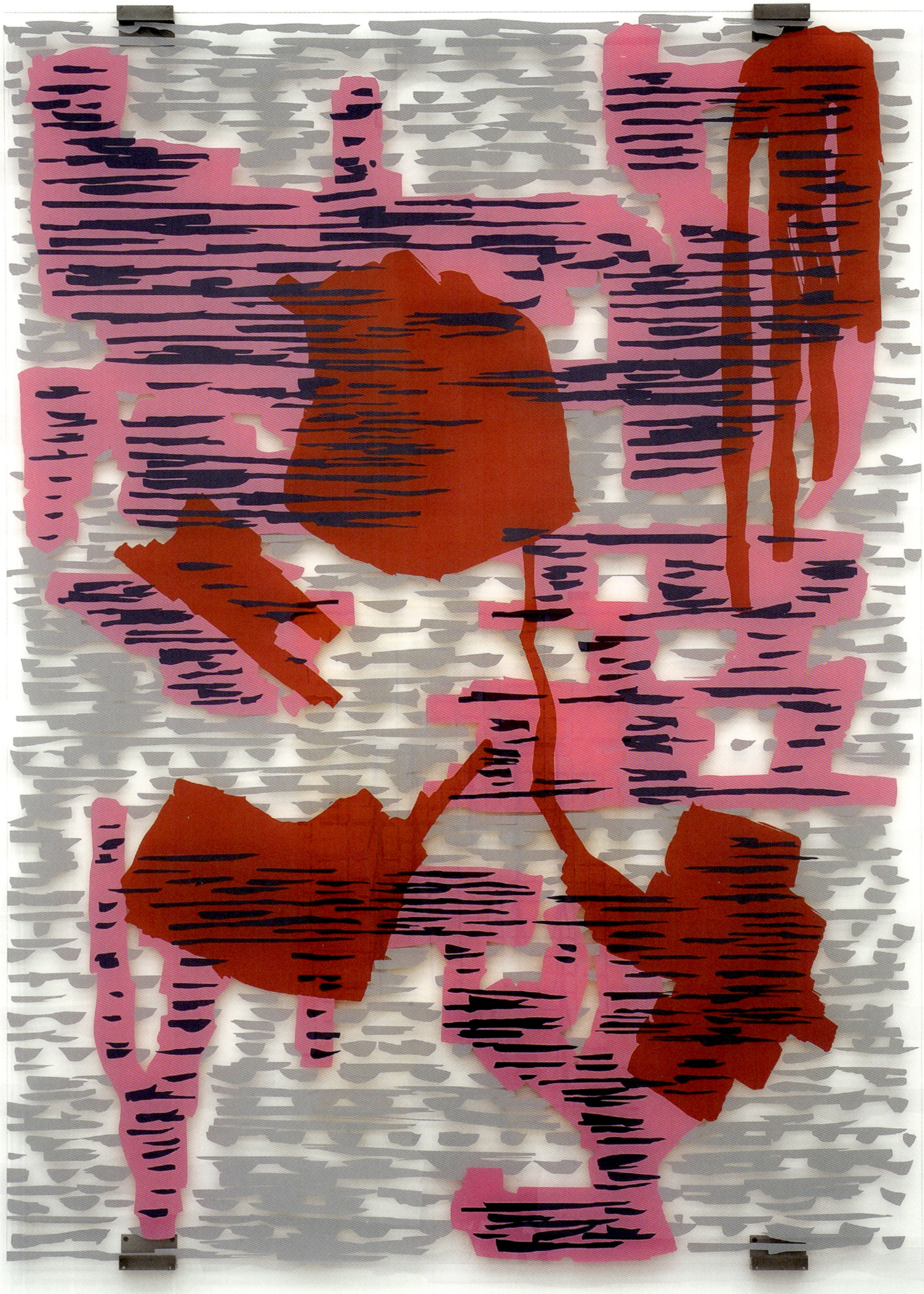

Ossian, 2008
Ink on Plexiglas, 265 x 205 x 4 cm

in some senses as a ground, but in others it acts as an anti-ground, or pre-ground to the ground of the wall behind; it functions as the means by which the work becomes simultaneously sculpture as well as painting and drawing. It is the means by which the wall behind the work becomes activated, and in this sense Bustamante's paintings start to locate themselves both as sculpture and within the wider field of installation, having a relationship to their surroundings, reflecting local conditions such as lighting, shadows and imperfections. Thus the traditional visible ground of a drawing, or the invisible ground of a painting, are both overturned: for Bustamante creates two interconnecting grounds – the first shining, reflective, transparent; the second an element of the existing building, co-opted by the artist into the work. This is a non-autonomous form of painting, attaching the history or nature of the built environment to itself. The visible nature of the wall behind is an aspect Bustamante has quite specifically played with, sometimes colouring the walls or creating special wallpapers against which the paintings hang, providing further visual disruption and interplay.[16] Chassey comments that 'it is as if Bustamante had found the way to conjure up the richness of colour and complexity of form (linked to an elevated genre of painting) with the provisionality of drawing',[17] to which we could add the three-dimensionality of sculpture and installation. Indeed this three-dimensionality is reinforced by the reflectiveness of the Plexiglas which permits not only the connection with the wall behind, but also incorporates into itself the reflection of the space the work inhabits, as well as the body of the viewer. The most recent paintings from 2010 differ in format from earlier manifestations: now square, the heavy industrial brackets have been replaced by crude steel frames, making a reference to Minimalist painting explicit.

Further conundrums emerge from Bustamante's use of brushes for his drawings, which suggest the drawings are closer to watercolours than anything else – that hybrid medium that Benjamin correctly classified as standing squarely between painting and drawing. In a fascinating essay, 'Painting and the Graphic Arts' of 1917, Benjamin intriguingly identifies a far-reaching difference between painting and drawing, based upon differences in how they function physically within the world and how we experience them. Benjamin says that paintings are viewed vertically, but that drawings should be viewed flat. He even suggests that viewing children's drawings vertically will conflict with their inner meaning.[18]

Benjamin goes on to suggest a profound difference between the representational order of painting and the symbolic order of drawing: 'We see here a profound problem of art and its mythic roots. We might say that there are two sections through the substance of the world: the longitudinal section of painting, and the cross-section of certain pieces of graphic art. The longitudinal section seems representational; it somehow contains the objects. The cross-section seems symbolic; it contains signs.'[19] Bustamante's paintings, which start as horizontal drawings done on his studio table, are later translated into the longitudinal form as completed paintings. In fact, the process preserves the mode of the sign in the guise of the object – this is precisely what Bustamante achieves in his painting, thereby unifying these two modes.

Bustamante's paintings are a complex enmeshing of media and a blurring of the inherent qualities of each. They combine aspects of the photographic, the computer-manipulated, the sculptural, as well as drawing and painting within one object. As he himself puts it, 'you take something hot (the drawing) and cool it down ...',[20] creating a profoundly enigmatic object, that is in some senses present and absent at the same time, its nature strangely unstable and mutable. They seem to propose the possibility of a new kind of painting, a painting that has freed itself from many of its historical and material trappings. These paintings confront certain aspects of contemporary desire combining drawing – the mythic root of art, the source of authenticity and uniqueness – with computer manipulation, the

Untitled, 2010
Ink on Plexiglas, 150 x 150 x 5 cm

screen-like qualities of Plexiglas, and industrial production. In fact, these works, precisely because of the mundanity of their content, act as perfect signs for our contemporaneity, existing both within and outside a continuum of the history of painting.

NOTES

1. Eric de Chassey, '12 Peintures', *Jean-Marc Bustamante*, Xavier Hufkens, Brussels, 2007, p. 3.
2. Caroline A. Jones, *Machine in the Studio: Constructing the Postwar American Artist*, University of Chicago Press, Chicago, 1996, p. 345.
3. Chassey, '12 Peintures', op. cit., p. 17.
4. Ibid. In this exhibition catalogue, Bustamante has illustrated for the first time some of the preparatory drawings for the paintings, making the sense of a translation from one form to another more evident.
5. From a conversation with the artist in Paris in September 2010.
6. Chassey, '12 Peintures', op. cit., p. 3.
7. Michel Gauthier, 'Constructing Aura', *Jean-Marc Bustamante*, Gallimard, Paris, 2003, p. 65.
8. Ibid.
9. Gauthier, 'Constructing Aura', op. cit., p. 68.
10. Gauthier, 'Constructing Aura', op. cit., p. 65.
11. Ibid.
12. From a conversation with the artist in Paris in September 2010.
13. Michael Newman, 'The Marks, Traces, and Gestures of Drawing', in Catherine de Zegher (ed.), *The Stage of Drawing: Gesture and Act*, Tate and The Drawing Center, London and New York, 2003, p. 95.
14. Norman Bryson, 'A Walk for a Walk's Sake', in *The Stage of Drawing*, op. cit., p. 151.
15. Walter Benjamin, *Selected Writings*, vol. I, Harvard University Press, Cambridge, Massachusettes, 1996, p. 84.
16. See, for example, the yellow walls in the exhibition *L'horizon chimérique: Ed Ruscha and Jean-Marc Bustamante,* Musée d'Art Moderne et Contemporain, 2007, and the wallpapers in *Le Grand Tour* (Musée des Arts Contemporains, Site du Grand-Hornu, 2008 and *A wall with a view,* Matthew Marks Gallery, New York, 1999.
17. Chassey, '12 Peintures', op. cit., p. 3.
18. Benjamin, *Selected Writings*, op. cit., p. 82.
19. Ibid.
20. From a conversation with the artist in Paris in September 2010.

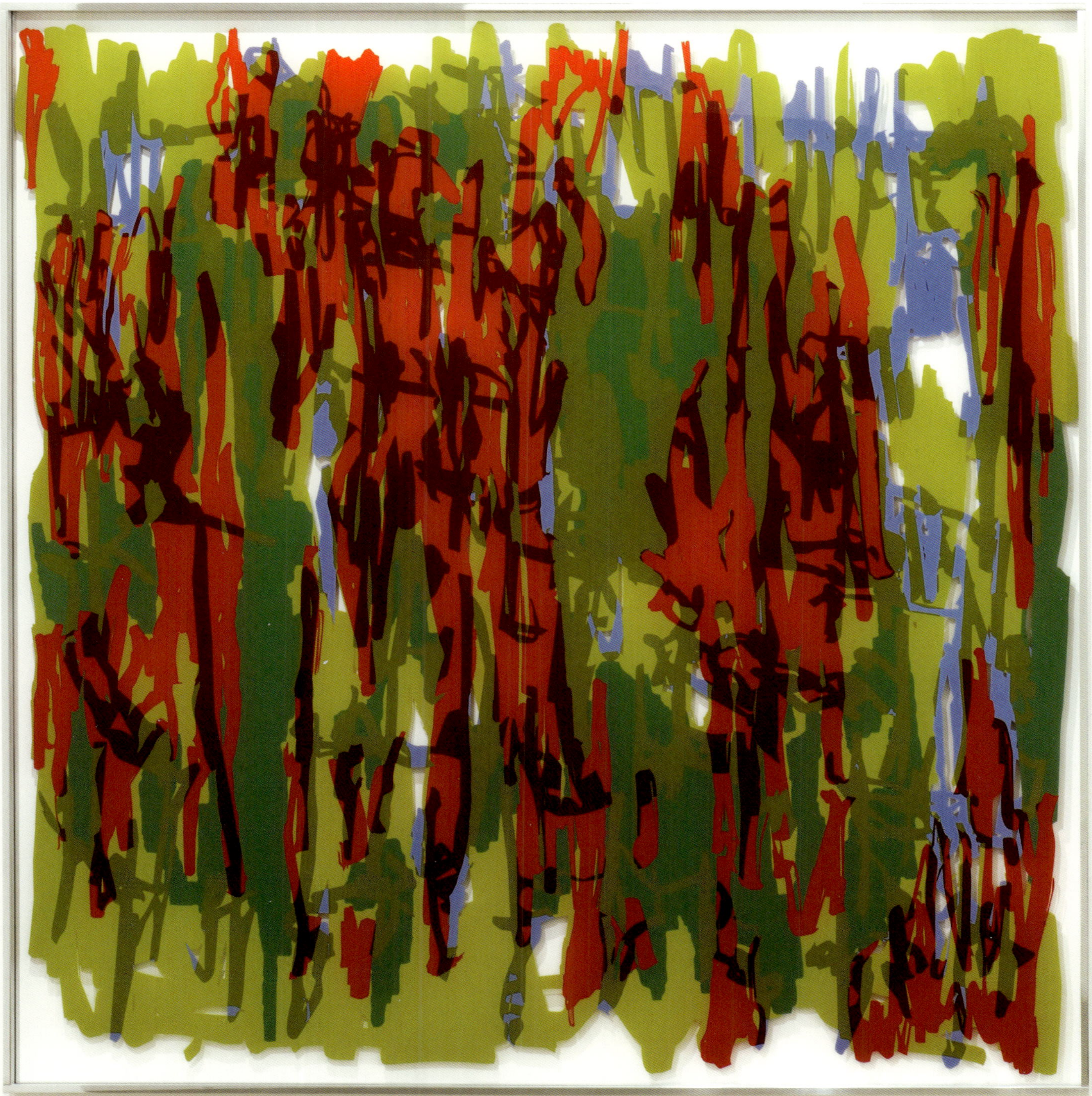

Preparatory drawings, 2010

opposite: *Landau*, 2010
Ink on Plexiglas, 150 x 150 x 5 cm

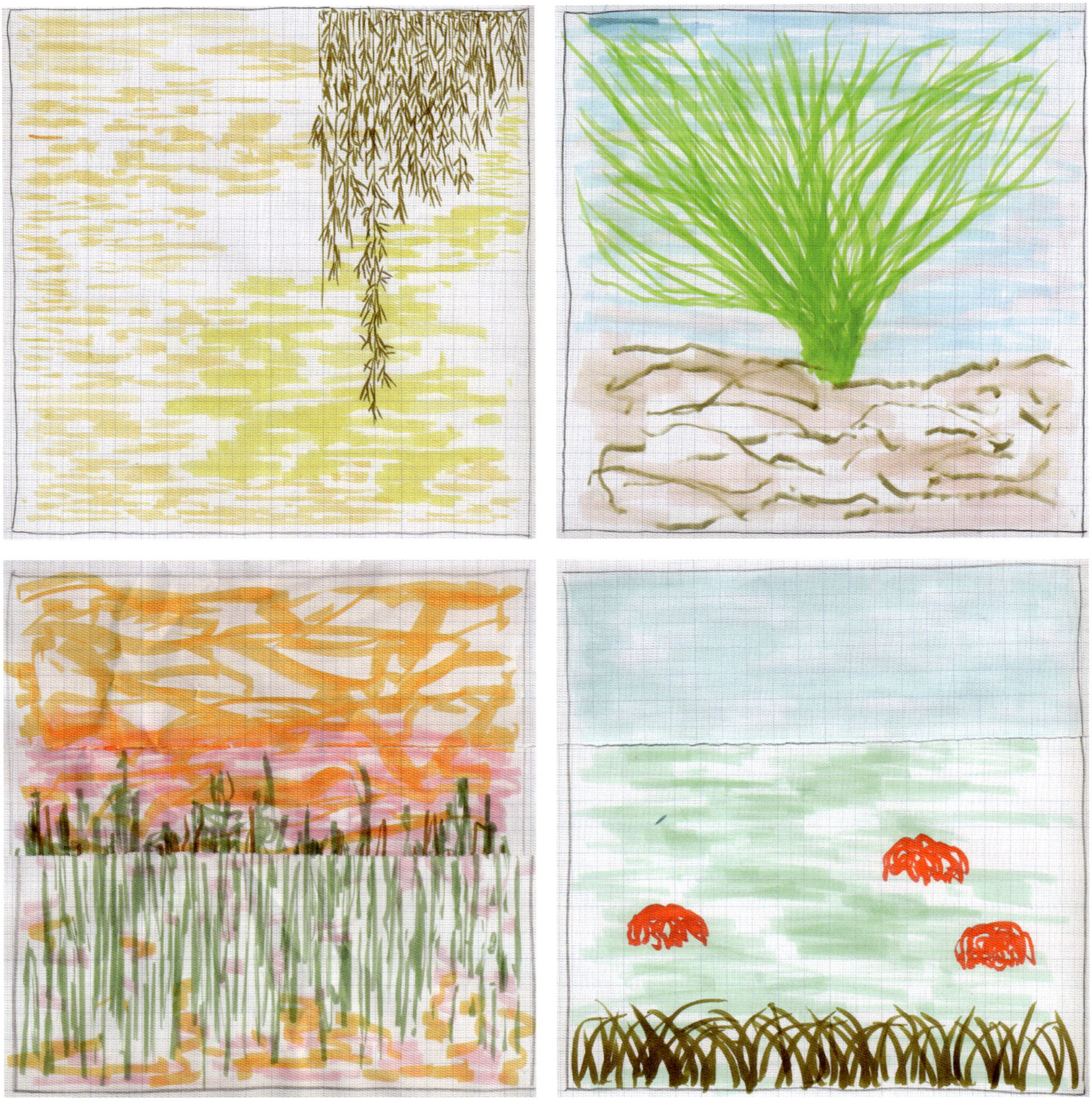

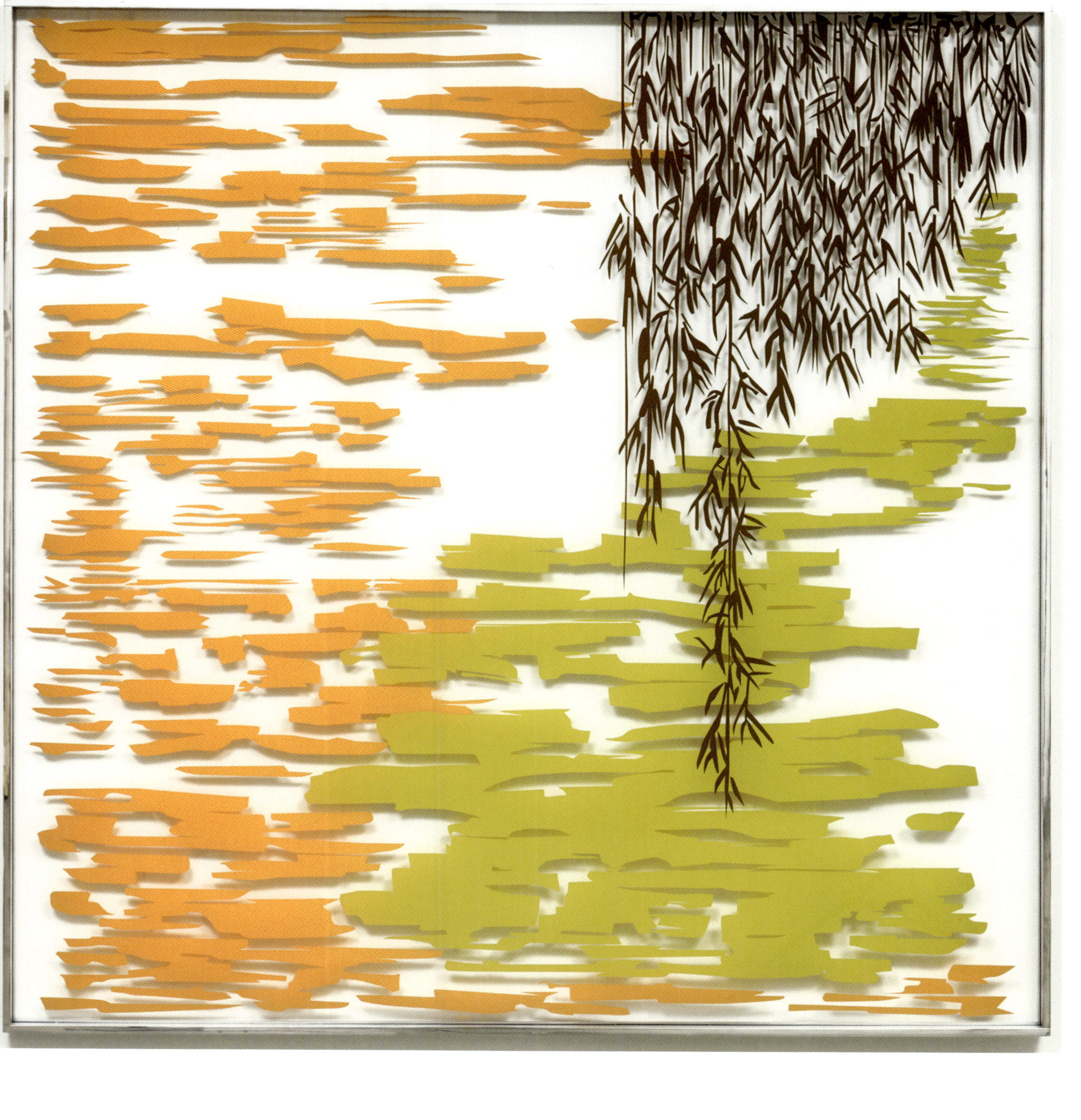

BACKMATTER

/

LIST OF WORKS

/

All dimensions are given in centimetres, height x width x depth.

Works shown only at The Fruitmarket Gallery

Balbec, 2010
Ink on Plexiglas with crude steel frame
150 x 150 cm
Courtesy the artist and
Timothy Taylor Gallery

Cardinal, 2010
Ink on Plexiglas with crude steel frame
150 x 150 cm
Courtesy the artist and
Timothy Taylor Gallery

Landau, 2010
Ink on Plexiglas with crude steel frame
150 x 150 cm
Courtesy the artist and
Timothy Taylor Gallery

Landscape Table, 2008
Steel, painted glass, candles
76 x 250 x 110 cm
Courtesy the artist

La porte, 2010
Ink on Plexiglas with 4 steel brackets
305 x 244 cm

Les lacs des saintes, 2008
Diptych: ink on Plexiglas
2 panels: 249 x 191 x 4 cm (each)
Courtesy the artist

Lumière 6.91, 1991
Ink on Plexiglas
145 x 185 cm
Galerie Thaddaeus Ropac, Paris

Manège III, 2008
Zinc-coated steel, painted steel, glass
350 x 310 x 260 cm
Courtesy the artist

Mercator, 2010
Ink on Plexiglas with crude steel frame
150 x 150 cm
Courtesy the artist and
Timothy Taylor Gallery

Ozelot, 2010
Ink on Plexiglas with crude steel frame
150 x 150 cm
Courtesy the artist and
Timothy Taylor Gallery

Untitled, 1993
Painted steel
206 x 134 cm
Collection of Van Abbemuseum,
Eindhoven

Untitled, 2010
Ink on Plexiglas, zinc-coated steel,
painted steel
20 x 195 x 116 cm
Courtesy the artist

Works shown at The Fruitmarket Gallery and Henry Moore Institute

Bac à sable I, 1990
Cement, wood, sand
28 x 231 x 182 cm
Collection of Van Abbemuseum,
Eindhoven

Bac à sable II, 1990
Cement, steel, anti-rust paint, wax
28 x 231 x 182 cm
Musée d'Art moderne
de la ville de Paris

Double miroir, 1991
Painted steel
174 x 160 x 15 cm
Collection Gilles Peyroulet & Cie, Paris

Intérieur I, 1988
Wood, steel, lacquer
3 parts: 96 x 13 x 196 cm;
96 x 13 x 196 cm; 100 x 35 x 202 cm
Collection of Marc Van de Velde,
Lovendegem

S.i.M.13B.97, 1997
C-print
60 x 40 cm
Courtesy the artist

Stationnaire II, 1991
C-print, resin, epoxy
12 boxes, 66 x 56 x 8 cm (each)
Musée d'Art moderne
de la ville de Paris

T.11.78, 1978
C-print
103 x 130 cm
Musée d'Art moderne
de la ville de Paris

T.17.79, 1979
C-print
103 x 130 cm
Courtesy the artist

T.25.79, 1979
C-print
103 x 130 cm
Courtesy the artist

T.50.82, 1982
C-print
103 x 130 cm
Courtesy the artist

T.104.91, 1991
C-print
150 x 120 cm
Collection of Van Abbemuseum,
Eindhoven

T.105.91, 1991
C-print
150 x 120 cm
Courtesy the artist

T.106.91, 1991
C-print
150 x 120 cm
Courtesy the artist

T.111.91, 1991
C-print
150 x 120 cm
Collection of Van Abbemuseum,
Eindhoven

T.112.91, 1991
C-print
150 x 120 cm
Collection of Van Abbemuseum,
Eindhoven

Works shown only at the Henry Moore Institute

Ouverture I, 1993
C-print, wood
43 x 210 x 120 cm
Centre national des arts plastiques, Puteaux

Jean-Marc Bustamante's studio, Paris, 2010

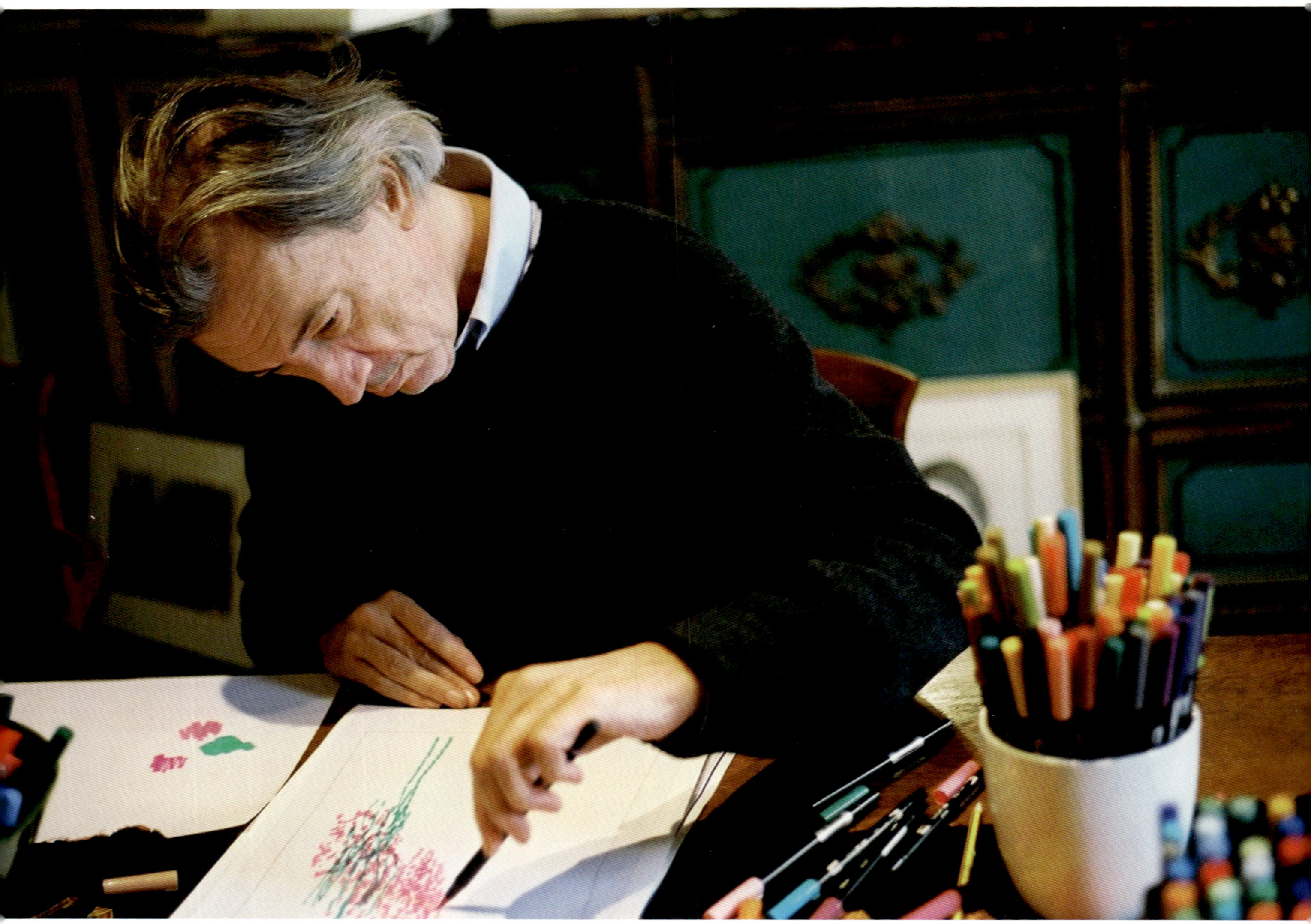

JEAN-MARC BUSTAMANTE

/

Born in Toulouse, 1952
Lives and works in Paris

SELECTED SOLO EXHIBITIONS

/ 2011
Take something hot and cool it down, Timothy Taylor Gallery, London*
Dead Calm, The Fruitmarket Gallery, Edinburgh*
Dead Calm, Henry Moore Institute, Leeds*
Villa Medici, Rome
Galerie Vera Munro, Hamburg

/ 2010
Jean-Marc Bustamante, The Cultural Foundation Ekaterina, Moscow*

/ 2009
Jean-Marc Bustamante: *Pedigree*, Galeria Filomena Soares, Lisbon*
Éditions et Multiples, Galerie Sollertis, Toulouse*

/ 2008
Jean-Marc Bustamante: *Le Grand Tour*, Musée des Arts Contemporains, Site du Grand–Hornu*
Jean-Marc Bustamante: *Le Grand Tour*, Palais des Beaux-Arts, Brussels
Jean-Marc Bustamante: *La Chambre des Saintes*, Galerie Thaddaeus Ropac, Paris

/ 2007
L'horizon chimérique: Ed Ruscha and Jean-Marc Bustamante, Musée d'Art Moderne et Contemporain, Strasbourg*
Jean-Marc Bustamante: *Fuentes & Recoursos/Sources & Resources*, Instituto Cervantes, Paris
Jean-Marc Bustamante: New Works, Galerie Vera Munro, Hamburg
Jean-Marc Bustamante: Obra Reciente, Galeria Helga de Alvéar, Madrid
12 Peintures, Galerie Xavier Hufkens, Brussels*

/ 2006
Jean–Marc Bustamante, Timothy Taylor Gallery, London
Beau fixe, Musée d'Art Moderne, Saint Etienne Métropole*
Perfect Dreams, Galerie Thaddaeus Ropac, Paris
beautifuldays, Kunsthaus Bregenz, Bregenz*

/2004
Jean-Marc Bustamante, Galerie Vera Munro, Hamburg

/ 2003
Nouvelles Scènes, Timothy Taylor Gallery, London*
Recent Works, Galerie Thaddaeus Ropac, Salzburg
Jean-Marc Bustamante, French Pavilion, 50th Venice Biennale, Venice*
Private Crossing, Yokohama Museum of Art; Yamaguchi Prefectural Museum of Art, Tokyo; Centro de Arte de Salamanca, Salamanca*

* denotes exhibition catalogue

/ 2002
Jean-Marc Bustamante: New Works, Galerie Paul Andriesse, Amsterdam
Jean-Marc Bustamante, Galeria Helga de Alvéar, Madrid
Jean-Marc Bustamante, Matthew Marks Gallery, New York

/ 2001
Jean-Marc Bustamante, Donald Young Gallery, Chicago
Long Playing, Deichtorhallen Hamburg, Hamburg
Jean-Marc Bustamante, Timothy Taylor Gallery, London
Jean-Marc Bustamante, Galerie Max Hetzler, Berlin
Jean-Marc Bustamante, Galeria Estrany de la Mota, Barcelona
Jean-Marc Bustamante, Galerie Daniel Templon, Paris
Jean-Marc Bustamante, Galerie Nathalie Obadia, Paris

/ 2000
Jean-Marc Bustamante: Inédits, Tableaux 1978–1982, Galerie Xavier Hufkens, Brussels
Jean-Marc Bustamante, Galerie Bob van Orsouw, Zurich
New Works, Galerie Vera Munro, Hamburg

/ 1999
Jean-Marc Bustamante, La Galerie, École d'Art, Quimper
A wall with a view, Matthew Marks Gallery, New York
Jean-Marc Bustamante, Galerie Daniel Templon, Paris; Galerie Nathalie Obadia, Paris
Jean-Marc Bustamante, Raum Aktueller Kunst, Vienna
Jean-Marc Bustamante, Galerie Karlheinz Meyer, Karlsruhe
Rétrospective de l 'oeuvre photographique, Centre national de la Photographie, Paris*

/ 1998
Jean-Marc Bustamante, Galerie Xavier Hufkens, Brussels
Jean-Marc Bustamante, Centre Culturel Français, Turin
Jean-Marc Bustamante, Gallery Shimada, Tokyo
Something is Missing, Tate Gallery, London

/ 1997
Something is Missing, Anadiel Gallery, Jerusalem
Jean-Marc Bustamante, Matthew Marks Gallery, New York
Jean-Marc Bustamante, Villa Arson, Nice
Suspension, Galerie Bob van Orsouw, Zurich
Jean-Marc Bustamante, Galerie Max Hetzler, Berlin
Jean-Marc Bustamante, Gallery Shimada, Tokyo
Jean-Marc Bustamante, Seomi Gallery, Seoul
Jean-Marc Bustamante, Galerie Vera Munro, Hamburg

/ 1996
Jean-Marc Bustamante, Galeria Antoni Estrany, Barcelona
Jean-Marc Bustamante, Galerie Max Hetzler, Berlin
Lent Retour, Jeu de Paume, Paris*

/ 1995
Serena (permanent public commission), Kröller-Müller Museum, Otterlo*
Jean-Marc Bustamante, Moderna Galerija, Ljubljana

/ 1994
Jean-Marc Bustamante, Gallery Shimada, Tokyo
Des Arbes de Noël, Galerie Ghislaine Hussenot, Paris
Un monde à la fois, Kunstmuseum Wolfsburg, Wolfsburg*
Tableaux 1978–1982, Kunstalle Bern, Bern*
Jean-Marc Bustamante, L' Aquarium, École des Beaux Arts de Valenciennes, Valencia
Un monde à la fois, Synagogue de Delme, Delme

/ 1993
Jean-Marc Bustamante, Donald Young Gallery, Seattle
Jean-Marc Bustamante, Renaissance Society at the University of Chicago, Chicago; Art Gallery of York University, Toronto*
Jean-Marc Bustamante, Galerie Karlheinz Meyer, Karlsruhe
Jean-Marc Bustamante, Musée départemental d'art contemporain de Rochechouart, Rochechouart
Jean-Marc Bustamante, FRAC Languedoc Roussillon, Montpellier
Jean-Marc Bustamante, CRG Art Incorporated, New York

/ 1992
Jean-Marc Bustamante, Van Abbemuseum, Eindhoven; Galerie Vera Munro, Hamburg

/ 1991
Jean-Marc Bustamante, Galería Marga Paz, Madrid
Oeuvres récentes/Stationnaire II, Galerie Ghislaine Hussenot, Paris
Jean-Marc Bustamante, Galerie Samia Saouma, Paris

/ 1990
Jean-Marc Bustamante, Museum Haus Lange, Krefeld*
Jean-Marc Bustamante, De Appel Foundation, Amsterdam*
Landschappen 1978–1982, Galerie Paul Andriesse, Amsterdam
Paysages, Intérieurs, Musée d'Art moderne de la Ville de Paris, Paris*
Jean-Marc Bustamante, Galerie Locus Solus, Genova

/ 1989
Jean-Marc Bustamante, Galerie Joost Declercq, Ghent

/ 1988
Jean-Marc Bustamante, Galerie Ghislaine Hussenot, Paris

/ 1987
Jean-Marc Bustamante, Galerie Micheline Szwajcer, Antwerp

/ 1986
Jean-Marc Bustamante, Galerie Bärbel Grässlin, Frankfurt
Jean-Marc Bustamante, Galerie Philippe Nelson, Villeurbanne
Jean-Marc Bustamante, Musée d'art Contemporain de Lyon, Lyon

/ 1984
Jean-Marc Bustamante, Galerie Crousel-Hussenot, Paris

/ 1982
Jean-Marc Bustamante, Galerie Baudoin Lebon, Paris

SELECTED GROUP EXHIBITIONS

/ 2010
Le Mont Analogue, Centro Cultural Metropolitano de Quito; MNAV, Montevideo

/ 2009
Sculptural – Collection, Stedelijk Museum Voor Actuele Kunst (S.M.A.K.), Ghent

/ 2008
Summer Exhibition, Timothy Taylor Gallery, London

/ 2007
The Hamster Wheel, Tesa Della Nuovissima 105, Arsenale di Venezia, Venice Biennale
Festival Printemps de Septembre, Toulouse
Hidden in Plain Sight: Contemporary Photographs from the Collection, Metropolitan Museum of Art, New York
Anos 80: Uma Topologia, Fundação Serralves, Museu de Arte Contemporánea, Porto

/ 2006
Portrait d'une collection: IDEA, Musée de la Photographie, Charleroi
UBS Openings: Photography From The UBS Art Collection, Tate Modern, London

/ 2005
Nature Cultivée, Centre Photographique d'Ile de-France, Pontault-Combault
Perspective contemporaine, Galerie Vedovi, Brussels

/ 2004
Somewhere Everywhere Nowhere, The Fruitmarket Gallery, Edinburgh/ Dundee Contemporary Arts, Dundee
In Focus: Themes in Photography, Albright-Knox Art Gallery, Buffalo
Take Five! Huis Marseille Turns Five, Huis Marseille Foundation for Photography, Amsterdam
The 9th International Architecture Exhibition: Photographic Section, Venice Biennale
Vague II, Hommages et digressions, Musée Malraux, Le Havre
Glare éblouissement, Jeu de Paume, Paris
Portraits d'arbres: Henri Gadeau de Kerville au regard de la photographie contemporaine, Musée D'Evreux, Evreux
Love Me or Leave Me, Museum of Contemporary Art Kiasma, Helsinki

/ 2003
Jean-Marc Bustamante, Candida Höfer, Galerie Karlheinz Meyer, Karlsruhe
Colocatairs, Centre d'art contemporain de Castres, Castres
Regarde, il neige (schizogeographie de la vie quotidienne), Centre international d'art et du paysage, Vassiviére
La Collection Ordóñez Falcón, Une passion partagée, Le Botanique, Centre Culturel de la Communauté Wallonie-Bruxelles, Brussels
Realidad y Representación. Coleccionar Paisaje Hoy, Fundació Foto Colectania, Barcelona
Pictures of You, Galeria Estrany-de la Mota, Barcelona

/ 2002
Regarding Landscape, Museum of Contemporary Canadian Art, Toronto
Wallflowers, Kunsthaus Zurich, Zurich
Límites de la percepión, Fundació Joan Miró, Barcelona

/ 2001
Places in the Mind: Modern Photographs from the Collection, Metropolitan Museum of Art, New York
Eine Wanderung zwischen Landschaft und Kunst, Spiral Jetty und Potsdamer Schrebergärten, Kunstmuseum Basel, Basel
Oublier l'exposition: Contemporary Photography from France, Huis Marseille, Amsterdam

/ 2000
L'invitation á la ville, Brussels
Dépaysement, Museum Dhondt-Dhaenens, Deurle
Enclosed and Enchanted, Museum of Modern Art, Oxford*
Abstrakte Fotografie, Kunsthalle Bielefeld, Bielefeld
Finale de partita, Istituto Francese di Firenze, Florence*

/ 1999
TRAFIC, FRAC Haute–Normandie, Sotteville-lés-Rouens
Abstraction, Galerie Daniel Templon, Paris
Ruines, FRAC PACA, Marseille

/ 1998
Maverick, Matthew Marks Gallery, New York

Wounds: Between Democracy and Redemption in Contemporary Art, Moderna Museet, Stockholm
Premises: Invested Spaces in Visual Arts, Architecture and Design from France 1958–98, Guggenheim Museum SoHo, New York
Minimal Maximal, Neues Museum, Weserburg, Bremen
Home Sweet Home, Gilles Peyroulet & Cie, Paris

/ 1997
Documenta X, Kassel*
Absolute Landscape: Between Illusion and Reality, Yokohama Museum of Art, Yokohama
From here to there, Fundação Calouste Gulbenkian, Lisbon

/ 1996
Paysages, Gilles Peyroulet & Cie, Paris
Le lieu de combat, Centre d'art contemporain, Domaine de Kerguéhennec

/ 1995
Jean-Marc Bustamante, Rodney Graham, Jan Vecruysse, Thomas Schütte, Centre Genevois de Gravure Contemporaine, Geneva
Architecture Plurals, Centre Cultural de Palma, Mallorca
Autour du paysage, Galerie Ghislaine Hussenot, Paris
Du Paysage Incertain, Fragments, Centre International d'art et du Paysage de l'île de Vassivére
Des limites du tableau: Les possibles de la peinture, Musée départemental d'art contemporain de Rochechouart, Rochechouart
Morceaux choisis, Le magasin, Centre National d'Art Contemporain, Grenoble

/ 1994
Espaces révélés, Galerie Bob van Orsouw, Zurich
Collection de la Fédération des Coopératives de Migros, Museo Cantonale d'Arte, Lugano*
Places, Moderna Galerija, Ljubljana
Même si c'est la nuit, CAPC, Musée d'Art Contemporain, Bordeaux
The Epic and the Everyday: Contemporary Photographic Art, Hayward Gallery, London*
Jean-Marc Bustamante, Stan Douglas, Mario Martone, Cesare Accetta, Thomas Struth, Hiroshi Sugimoto, Gillian Wearing, James Welling, Galeria Theoretical Events, Naples
Los generos de la pintura: Una vision actual, Centro Atlàntico de Arte Moderno, Las Palmas; Museo Español de Arte Contemporàneo, Madrid
XXIIé Biennale Internationale de Sao Paulo*
L 'arca de Noé, Fundaçao de Serralves, Porto

/ 1993
Kunstbücher I, Museum Haus Esters, Krefeld
Jean-Marc Bustamante, Rosemarie Trockel, James Welling: Pièces récentes, Galerie Samia Saouma, Paris
A propos des paysages, Institut Néerlandais, Paris
Azur, Foundation Cartier pour l'art Contemporain, Jouy-en-Josas*
L'image dans le tapis, Cercle de l'Arsenal, 45th Venice Biennale, Venice*
Accrochage, Galerie Xavier Hufkens, Brussels
The Sublime Void: On the memory of the imagination, Koninklijk Museum voor Schone Kunsten, Antwerp
Jean-Marc Bustamante and Franz West, Galerie Bruges la Morte, Bruges
Allégorie de la richesse: Barock und Kunst der Gegenwart, Humboldt Universität, Parochialkirche, Berlin

/ 1992
Ashley Bickerton, Chris Burden, Jean-Marc Bustamante, Sophie Calle, Tony Cragg, Gary Hill, Cristina Iglesias, Jeff Koons, Sherrie Levine, Hirsch Perlman, Martin Puryear, Charles Ray, Susana Solano, Jana Sterbak, Rosemarie Trockel, Didier Vermeiren, Bill Viola, James Welling, Donald Young Gallery, Seattle
Ce n'est pas la fin du monde, Galerie Art & Essai, Universite de Rennes II; Galerie du Théâtre National de Bretagne; La Criée, Halle d'Art Contemporain*
Documenta IX, Kassel*
Schwerpunkt Skulptur: Hundertvierzig Werke von achtzig Künstlern: 1950–1990, Kaiser Wilhelm Museum, Krefeld*
Une seconde pensée du paysage, Centre d'Art Contemporain, Domaine de Kerguéhennec
Wasteland: Landscape from now on/Het Landschap Vanaf Nu, Third Photography Biennal, Rotterdam
350. Place d'Youville, cinq créateurs français à Montréal (Bustamante, Hondelatte, Perrault, Roche & Stark), Centre de Design de l'Université du Québec, Montréal; Institut Français d'Architecture, Paris*
Paysage intérieur, Kröller-Müller Museum, Otterlo

/ 1991
Vanitas, Galerie Crousel Robelin/BAMA, Paris
Metropolis, Martin-Gropius-Bau, Berlin*
Paysage: Vision contemporaine, Galerie du Crédit Commercial, Brussels
L 'invention du paysage, FRAC Corse, Corte*
Sguardo di Medusa, Castello di Rivoli, Turin *Exhibitions of acquisitions*, Van Abbemuseum, Eindhoven
Jean-Marc Bustamante, Richard Deacon, Katarina Fritsch, Ettore Spalletti, Jan Vercruysse, Galleria Locus, Solus, Genoa
Lieux communs, figures singuliéres, Musée d 'Art moderne de la Ville de Paris, Paris*
...In anderen Raümen, Museum Haus Lange and Haus Esters, Krefeld

/ 1990
French Spring: From the Collection of the FRAC Nord Pas-de-Calais, Scottish National Gallery of Modern Art, Edinburgh

Un art de la distinction?, Abbaye Saint André, Centre d'art contemporain, Meymac*
De Afstand, Witte de With, Rotterdam*
Camera Works, Galerie Samia Saouma, Paris
Possible Worlds: Sculpture from Europe, Institute of Contemporary Art/Serpentine Gallery, London*
Weitersehen, Museum Haus Lange and Haus Esters, Krefeld
Le diaphane, Musée municipal des Beaux Arts, Tourcoing

/ 1987
Kunst Mit Fotografie, Galerie Ralph Wernicke, Stuttgart
BAZILEBUSTAMANTE, Jean-Luc Vilmouth, Beelben,
Van Krimpen Gallery, Amsterdam
L 'époque, la mode, la morale, la passion, Centre Georges Pompidou, Paris*
Documenta VIII, Kassel*
BAZILEBUSTAMANTE, Musée Saint-Pierre art contemporain, Lyon; Frankfurter Kunstverein, Frankfurt*

/ 1986
Art Français: Position, B.I.G. Berlin
Een Keuze, Kunst R.A.I, Amsterdam
Sonsbeek '86, Park Sonsbeek, Arnhem
Aperto 86, Venice Biennale, Venice
A Distance View, The New Museum of Contemporary Art, New York
BAZILEBUSTAMANTE, Centre d'art contemporain, Geneva*
6th Sydney Biennale, Art Gallery of New South Wales, Sydney

/ 1985
Alles und noch viel mehr. Das poetische ABC, Kunsthalle Bern, Bern
Rendez-vous, Lothringerstrasse, Munich
12 Artists in the Space, Seibu Museum of Art, Tokyo*
Graz Biennal, Graz
Seconds 'Ateliers Internationaux des Pays de la Loire', Abbaye de Fontevraud,

/ 1984
Lumières et sons 84, FRAC Aquitaine, Château de Biron, Dordogne
BAZILEBUSTAMANTE, Galerie Crousel-Hussenot, Paris

/ 1983
1ère Biennale d'Art contemporain de Tours Adamah. La Terre, ELAC, Lyon

/ 1982
Marseille Art Présent, Musée Cantini de Marseille

/ 1980
Biennale de Paris*
43 Rue La Bruyère, 43 Rue La Bruyère, Paris
Portrait d'artiste, Galerie NRA, Paris

SELECTED BIBLIOGRAPHY

/ 2010
Jean-Marc Bustamante (texts: Alfred Pacquement, Christian Bernard and Pauline de Laboulaye), The Cultural Foundation, Ekaterina, Moscow

/ 2009
Pedigree (text: David Rosenberg), Galerie Filomena Soares, Lisbon
Éditions et Multiples, Galerie Sollertis, Toulouse

/ 2008
Jean-Marc Bustamante: Le Grand Tour (texts: Laurent Busine, Denis Gielen), Musée des Arts Contemporains, Site du Grand-Hornu
L'horizon chimérique: Ed Ruscha and Jean-Marc Bustamante (texts: Jean-Pierre Criqui, Céline Flécheux), Musée d'Art Moderne et Contemporain, Strasbourg

/ 2007
Sources & Resources (text José Jiménez), Instituto Cervantes, Paris
12 Peintures (text: Eric de Chassey), Galerie Xavier Hufkens, Brussels

/ 2006
Beau fixe (text: Pierre Tillet), Musée d'Art Moderne, Saint-Étienne Métropole
Jean-Marc Bustamante: beautifuldays (Eckhard Schneider (ed.), texts: Christine Montalbetti, Eckhard Schneider), Kunsthaus Bregenz, Bregenz

/ 2005
Jean-Marc Bustamante (texts: Jacinto Lageira, Ulrich Loock, Christine Macel, Xavier Veilhan), Flammarion, Paris

/ 2003
Jean-Marc Bustamante: Nouvelles Scènes (text: Matthew Arnatt), Timothy Taylor Gallery, London
Jean-Marc Bustamante (texts: Jean-Pierre Criqui, Michel Gauthier, Alfred Pacquement, Michel Poivert, Katy Siegel), Gallimard, Paris
Jean-Marc Bustamante: Private Crossing (texts: Doris von Drathen, Jean-Pierre Criqui), Yokohama Museum of Art/ Yamaguchi Prefectural Museum of Art, Tokyo/Centro de Arte de Salamanca, Salamanca

/ 2001
L'Art Dans le Paysage du Tramway d'Orléans (Serge Lemoine (ed.) texts: Serge Lemoine, Thierry Dufrêne, Marianne Le Pommeré, Guitemie Maldonado, Christine Poullain, Pascal Rousseau), Réunion des Musées Nationaux, Paris
Jean-Marc Bustamante: L.P. (Long Playing) (texts: Zdenek Felix, Sophie Berrebi), Deichtorhallen Hamburg, Hamburg

/ 1999
Jean-Marc Bustamante: Something is Missing (texts: Jean-Marc Bustamante, Manel Clot), Universidad de Salamanca, Salamanca
Jean-Marc Bustamante: Oeuvres Photographiques 1978–1999 (text: Jean-Pierre Criqui), Centre National de la Photographie, Paris

/ 1997
Jean-Marc Bustamante: Amandes amères Bitter Almonds Bittere Mandeln, Phaidon Press, London

/ 1996
Jean-Marc Bustamante: Lent Retour, Jeu de Paume, Paris

/ 1995
Jean-Marc Bustamante (texts: Jacinto Lageira, Christine Macel, Perelman Marc), Éditions Dis Voir, Paris
Jean-Marc Bustamante: Serena (text: Denys Zacharopoulos), Kröller-Müller Museum, Otterlo

/ 1994
Lumières 1987–1993 (text: Catherine de Smet), Centre national de l'Estampe et de l'Art imprimé, Chatou
A World at a Time, (texts: Uta Grosenick, Catherine Franeblin), Hatje Cantz Verlag, Ostfildern
Jean-Marc Bustamante: Tableaux 1978–1982 (text: Jacinto Lageira), Musée départemental d'art contemporain de Rochechouart, Rochechouart, FRAC Languedoc Roussillon and Kunsthalle Bern, Bern

/ 1993
Jean-Marc Bustamante (texts: Jan Debbaut, Danielle Cohen-Levinas), Van Abbemuseum, Eindhoven
Jean-Marc Bustamante, (ed. Jean-François Chevrier), The Renaissance Society at the University of Chicago, Chicago

/ 1992
Jean-Marc Bustamante (text: Julian Heynen), Museum Haus Lange, Krefeld
Jean-Marc Bustamante (text: Saskia Bos), De Appel Foundation, Amsterdam
Jean-Marc Bustamante (texts: Alain Cueff, Suzanne Pagé), ARC, Musée d' Art Moderne de la Ville de Paris, Paris

/ 1989
Jean-Marc Bustamante (texts: Alain Cueff and Ulrich Loock), Kunsthalle Bern, Bern

/ 1985
BAZILEBUSTAMANTE (text: Bernard Blisténe), Galerie Crousel-Hussenot, Paris

Preparatory drawing for *La Porte*, 2010

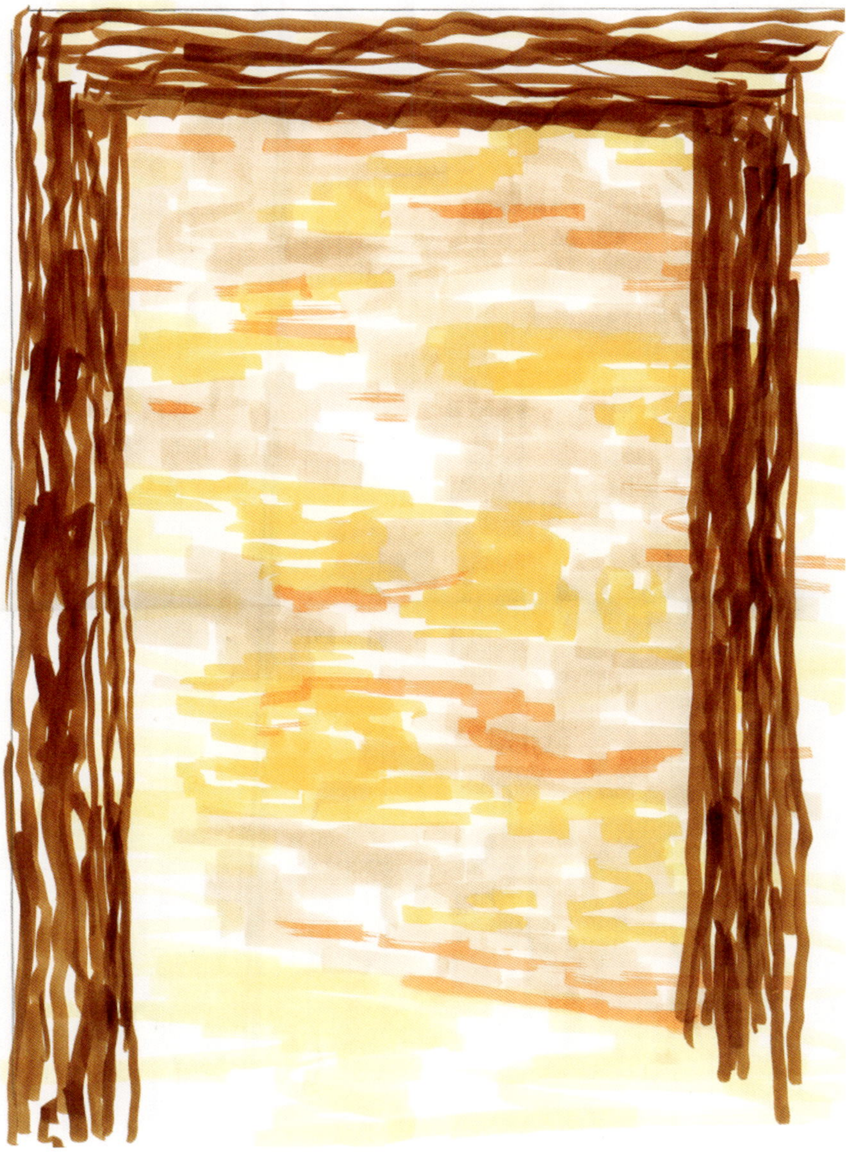

ACKNOWLEDGEMENTS

/

JEAN-MARC BUSTAMANTE
DEAD CALM

Published by

The Fruitmarket Gallery
45 Market Street, Edinburgh, EH1 1DF
Tel: + 44 (0)131 225 2383
www.fruitmarket.co.uk

and

Henry Moore Institute
The Headrow, Leeds, LS1 3AH
Tel: + 44 (0)113 246 7467
www.henry-moore.org

Exhibition supported by
The Henry Moore Foundation
Cultures France
The French Embassy in the UK

Publication supported by
Timothy Taylor Gallery
15 Carlos Place, London, W1K 2EX
Tel: + 44 (0)20 7409 3344
www.timothytaylorgallery.com

Distributed by
Art Data, 12 Bell Industrial Estate,
50 Cunnington Street, London, W4 5HB
Tel: +44 (0)20 8747 1061
www.artdata.co.uk

Edited by Fiona Bradley
Designed and typeset by Elizabeth McLean
Assisted by Samantha Woods and Susan Gladwin
and Studio Bustamante: Thierry Leviez, Luc Chopplet

Printed by Stewarts of Edinburgh. Printed in the UK.

The Fruitmarket Gallery

Director Fiona Bradley
Deputy Director Elizabeth McLean
Development Manager Armida Taylor

Administrator Amelia Smith; Bookshop Manager Matthew Williams; Children and Young People's Programme Manager Johnny Gailey; Commercial Opportunities Manager Iain Morrison; Exhibitions and Publications Organiser Samantha Woods; Finance Manager Celeste Stamenkovic; Gallery Manager Jamie Mitchell; Installation Technician Simon Shaw; Press and Marketing Manager Louise Warmington; Research and Interpretation Manager Stacy Boldrick; Senior Installation Technician Colin MacFarlane

The Fruitmarket Gallery is a company limited by guarantee, registered in Scotland No. 87888 and registered as a Scottish Charity No. SC 005576. VAT No. 398 2504 21. Registered Office: 45 Market St., Edinburgh, EH1 1DF

Henry Moore Institute

Head of Sculpture Studies Lisa Le Feuvre

Administrator Catherine Aldred; Archivist Claire Sawyer; Assistant Administrator Sharon Sawyer; Assistant Curator (Collections) Sophie Raikes; Assistant Librarian Karen Atkinson; Communications Manager Adelle Stripe; Curatorial Assistant (Collections) Jackie Howson; Exhibitions Organiser/ Registrar Michelle Allen; Librarian Ann Sproat; Library Assistant Nathan Richards; Library Trainee Catherine Spinks; PA to Head of Sculpture Studies Gill Armstrong; Press Cuttings Assistant Paul Stirk; Research Coordinator Jon Wood; Research Programme Assistant Kirstie Gregory; Senior Receptionist Bruce Davies; Senior Technician Matthew Crawley; Web Editor David Cotton; Weekend Receptionist Emma Fitzjohn

The Henry Moore Foundation is a company limited by guarantee, registered in England No. 1255762 and registered as a charity No. 271370. Registered Office: Mitre House, 160 Aldersgate Street, London, EC1 4DD

The Fruitmarket Gallery — Creative Scotland

Henry Moore Institute — The Henry Moore Foundation

Timothy Taylor Gallery

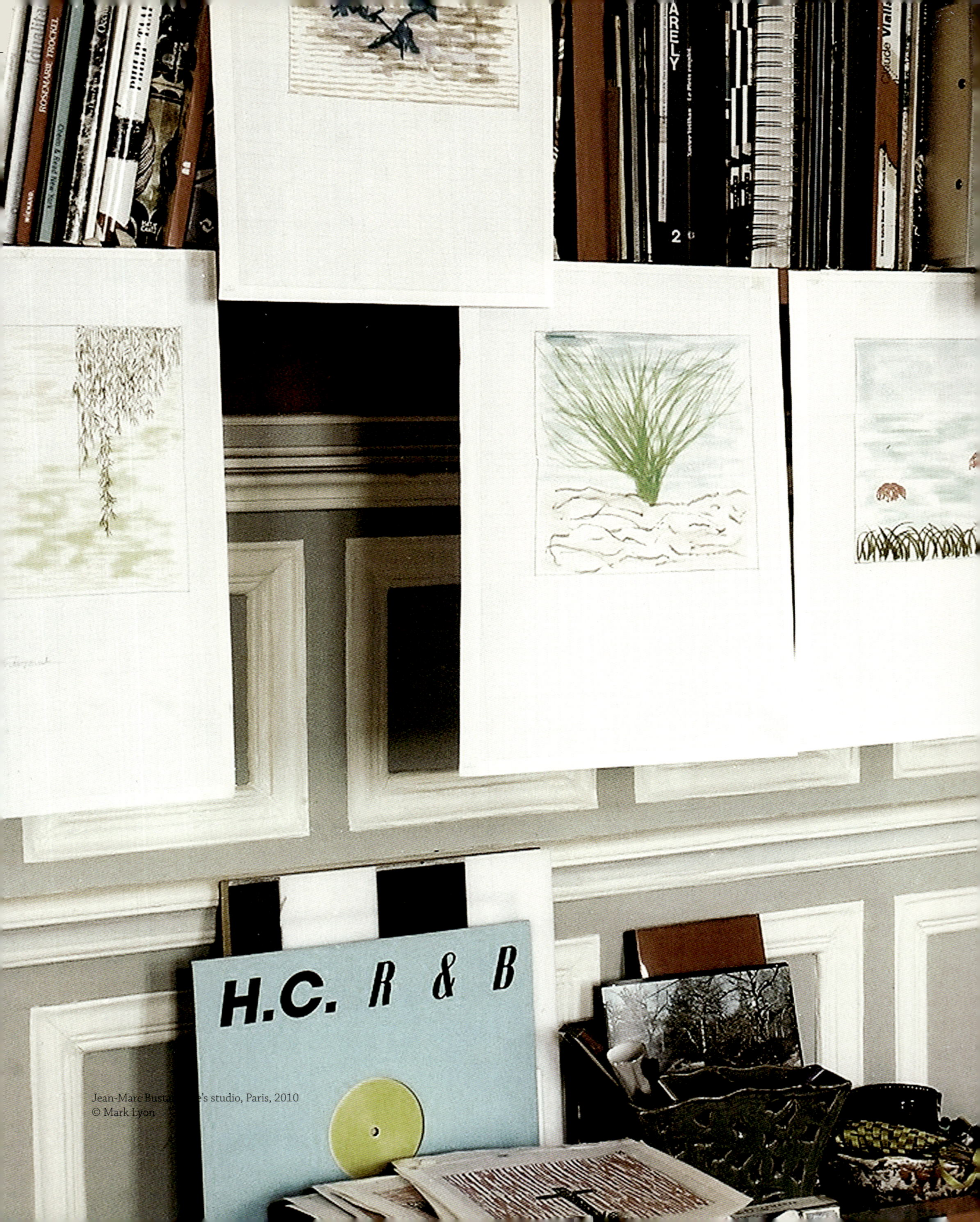

Jean-Marc Bustamante's studio, Paris, 2010

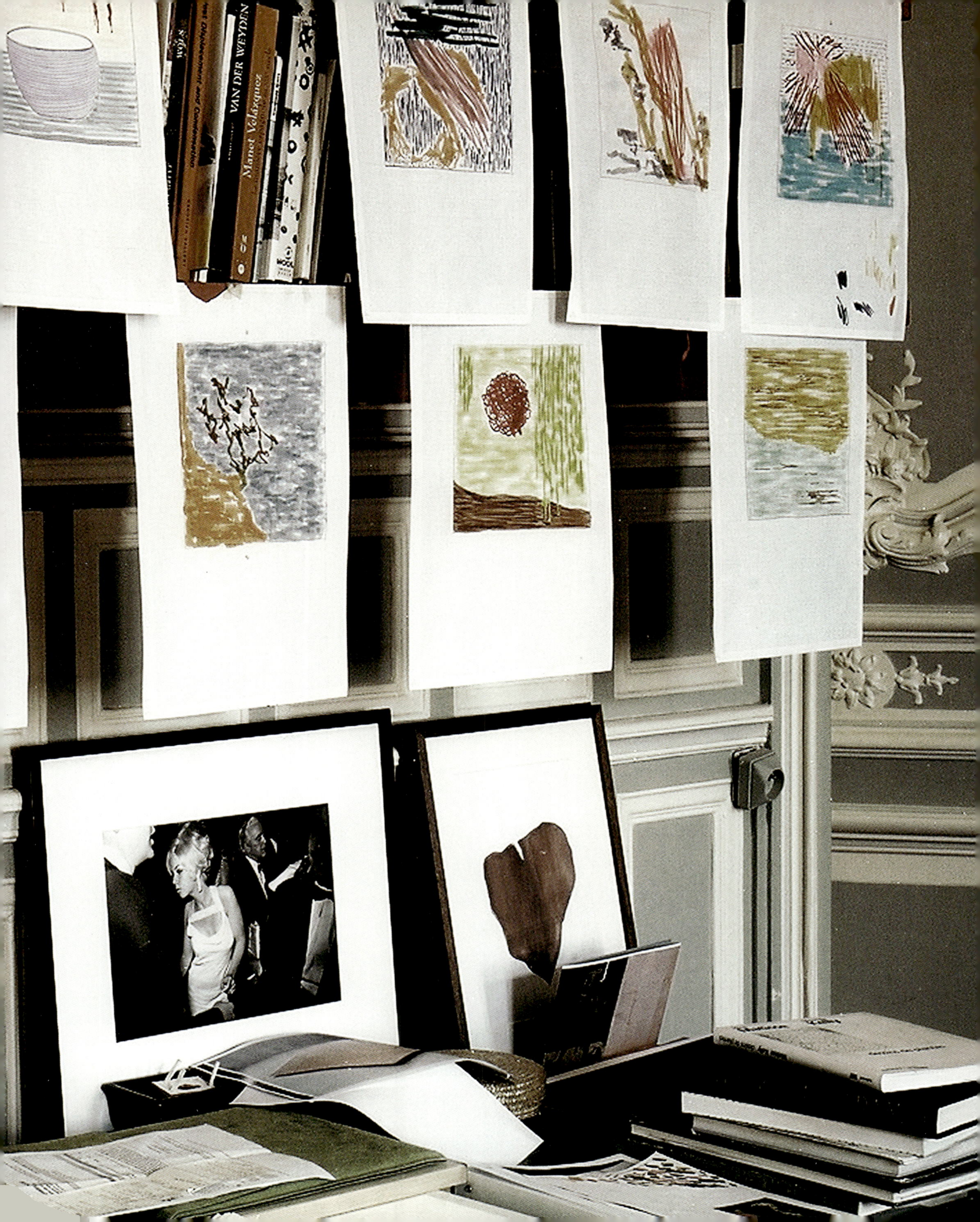
VAN DER WEYDEN
Manet Velázquez